THE RISE AND FALL OF

HOMO ECONOMICUS

THE MYTH OF THE RATIONAL HUMAN
AND THE CHAOTIC REALITY

YANNIS PAPADOGIANNIS

Translated into English by Nick Roussos

Editing by Elise J. Marton

ISBN: 1499646674
ISBN 13: 9781499646672

Library of Congress Control Number: 2014909791
CreateSpace Independent Publishing Platform
North Charleston, South Carolina

CONTENTS

INTRODUCTION

Close to the ruins of corporate titans such as Lehman Brothers, AIG, Merrill Lynch, and General Motors, which sustained severe blows or even perished in the whirlwind of the 2007 crisis,* lies economic science, heavily wounded.

The 2007 crisis caused shock and awe among economists. The magnitude, fierceness, and intensity of it came as a surprise to both the scientific community and the institutional authorities, who had been for many years immersed in nonchalance and certainty about the strength and the potential of the global economy. According to economic theory, such a crisis could not occur. It was an inexplicable anomaly, something unimaginable and completely unexpected.

It not only underlined the failure of economics to anticipate the impending disaster in due time, but also emphatically raised a new, inexorable question: Was it economic science—with its optimistic and dogmatic certainties regarding the efficiency of markets, its belief in the substantial reduction of macroeconomic instability, its blind faith in the supremacy of mathematical tools and financial innovations, and its reassurances that all risks had been put under control—the cause of the financial crisis of 2007? Did economics nurture the crisis monster, giving legitimacy to the implementation of policies that turned out to be catastrophic, bringing the global economy face-to-face with the pale specter of the Great Crash of 1929?

Going back in economic history, we can see that reality never ceases to discredit the mainstream theories of each time, as well as the experts' certainties regarding the economy's prospects. Sooner or later, societies get trapped in painful crises. Who is to blame? Why are economies being systematically hit by crises? What are the roots and causes of instability? What gives rise to the tides of optimism and pessimism that drive societies to extremes? And why does economic science fail to set economies on a smooth and controlled course using the sophisticated navigation instruments it has developed?

The purpose of this book is to bring attention to economic science's ineffectiveness in following the chaotic reality of our world, as it is shaped by the complex psyches and behaviors of human beings, the intricacy of social relations, chance, and a stream of many other, quite often indiscernible, factors. This book is mainly meant not for experts but for laypeople: inquisitive readers who, above all, want to understand as many of the things that happen around them as possible, even if they lie far beyond their area of expertise or profession.

This text is an update to the Greek edition, which was published in the summer of 2012. I have enriched this new volume with lots of new facts and information and have also made major changes to the structure of the text.

At the center of this book is the argument that the inability of economic science to stay clear of failure is the inescapable result of the first academic economists' highly unwise choice to establish their field as a "hard"** science whose accuracy and objectivity cannot be doubted. In order to achieve this ambitious goal, the theorists made extensive use of mathematics to reformulate economics along the lines of Newtonian physics. However, a mathematical representation of human behavior, society, and economy could be achieved only through extensive simplification and generalization. All the things that couldn't "fit" into mathematical equations (emotions, passions, social and political relations, etc.) were weeded out. Thus, economics created a parallel universe that is nothing more than a dim reflection of reality. In the end, economics managed to establish itself as a hard science, on a par with physics and biology, albeit by paying an unbearable price: being cut off from reality and the world of action.

THE STRUCTURE OF THE BOOK

Part One presents the dawn of the Industrial Revolution, which led to the modern economic era and the creation of the field of economics. It examines the pioneers of economics, their work, and how the first academic economists, under the huge intellectual influence of Newtonian achievements, embarked in the late nineteenth century on a radical reconstruction of the field along the lines of classical physics. It also shows how neoclassical theory gradually became the absolute economic orthodoxy, which prevailed for more than forty years as the main economic model.

Part Two focuses on financial crises. Economic theory does not have much to say about them: It assumes that each one is unique and independent, and therefore that crises cannot be studied as a single phenomenon. According to the theory, economies generally run like clockwork; given the rationality of economic agents, crises are nothing more than small-scale episodes –arrhythmias- that are soon overcome. But if everything works like clockwork and people learn from their mistakes, why do crises occur with such frequency and intensity? Part Two presents the shared characteristics, the common denominators, that -contrary to what theory says- more or less recur in every crisis, irrespective of era or ideology. Experience shows that crises, from 1600 to today, follow an astonishingly similar pattern. The culmination of this repeated pattern was the crisis of 2007: Its birth, evolution, and resolution were very similar to those of previous ones. The familiar pattern emerged once again: People followed the same path and repeated the same mistakes, totally certain that "this time is different."

Part Three focuses on human beings, social relations, and the unpredictability of the complex evolutionary world we live in. It presents certain findings from disciplines such as neuroscience, psychology, anthropology, sociology, biology, and physics that overturn our idealized view of the skills, abilities, and knowledge we possess both as individuals and as societies. *Homo sapiens* -that is, all of us- remains an enigmatic creature: Our senses, our language, the way memory and perception operate, our thinking process, the way we make decisions, our intelligence, and our emotional world are complex functional structures that we comprehend only to a limited degree. As shown by hundreds of experiments, our daily behavior is a far cry from the standards of rationality. In fact, there is no aspect of human life that remains untouched by illusions, fallacies, biases, and other tricks of the mind, the senses, and chance. Economic science chooses to ignore these significant findings and considers them irrelevant, insisting on an exaggerated, simplified approach of human nature and a belief in the absolute superiority of free markets.

Part Four compares the firm beliefs of modern economics with complex, dynamic, and chaotic reality. It illustrates the departure of economics from the world of action and its self-entrapment in a futile preoccupation with a parallel, imaginary economic universe that has very little to do with reality. It highlights the role of economic theory in creating the great crisis of 2007 and stresses the need to set economics on a new foundation, incorporating the knowledge accumulated by other disciplines, in order to help it get back in touch with a dynamically changing reality and become useful to society.

Yannis Papadogiannis, Athens, June 2014

*Some firms went bankrupt (Lehman Brothers), some were taken over (Merrill Lynch), and still others were bailed out by the U.S. government (AIG, General Motors).

** The term *hard science* is used to describe natural sciences (physics, chemistry, biology, etc.) that are based on experimental and quantitative data, and that have developed scientific methods providing objective and accurate descriptions of the phenomena under examination. In contrast, the term *soft science* is applied to social sciences (history, sociology, psychology, etc.) that cannot develop scientific methodologies of similar effectiveness.

PART ONE

THE BIRTH OF ECONOMICS

1

A WORLD WITHOUT ECONOMISTS

Given today's apotheosis of economic and individual freedom, conceiving of models of economic organization and operation that lie outside the free market is not an easy thing to do. It is difficult to conceive of a world without banks, corporations, stocks, free markets—a world without economists.

That said, it was not so long ago that the world scraped along without economists and without the ministrations of economic science. Economics, nowadays an integral part of quotidian life, has not been around for very long. It was founded by Scottish philosopher Adam Smith in his monumental work *The Wealth of Nations*, which was published in 1776. Nonetheless, more than one hundred years had to pass before universities started granting degrees in economics, at the end of the nineteenth century.

Why such a long delay? Simply put, it was because economics had no reason to exist. Before the advent of free-market capitalism,* modern economic theory was as irrelevant as an electric lamp back in the days when electricity had not been yet invented.

---

* The term *capitalism* is used to describe the economic and social system in which private capital and free enterprise are the key factors of economic life.

For many centuries, society was organized along the lines of tradition, rigid social structures, and the brute force of the aristocracy's authoritarian rule. In medieval Europe, social authority stemmed from networks of interaction between the nobility and the Christian Church. "The priest prays, the knight defends, the peasant works"[1]—this was the orthodoxy of medieval times.

Whether one would be a clergyman, a king, a prince, a prince-bishop, a count, an abbot, a craftsman, a freeman, or a serf was neither the result of free choice nor the outcome of each individual's specific skills. Everything was hereditary. Most serfs had almost no hope of escaping serfdom. Even the freemen were bound by legal and customary ties to a specific lord and his land, and upsetting this relation was forbidden. If a "free" peasant decided to leave and seek his fortune elsewhere, the lord had the right to drag him back to his land by force. Prospects were also limited for the lesser nobility, since there was no way of breaking the stranglehold of the establishment. Society resembled a well-built, solid pyramid where any movement, whether from bottom to top or top to bottom, was extremely rare, if not impossible.

The church, and Christianity in general, constituted a mighty force that dominated not only the social life but also the economic life of the Middle Ages. By condemning all worldly pleasures, Christianity did not encourage progress and economic growth. Quite the contrary. According to its teachings, life was nothing more than a preparatory stage for the eternal kingdom of heaven. The desire for profit or for accumulating wealth was considered to be a mortal sin. As the Bible notes, "It is easier for a camel to go through the eye of a needle than for a rich man to enter the Kingdom of God." In contrast, poverty was considered a virtue. Merchants and profiteers were castigated as immoral, second-rate individuals and were the objects of derision and disdain. The church forbade laymen from lending money for interest; those accused of usury were tried by ecclesiastical courts, and avaricious sinners risked even excommunication. The word *usurer* continues to bear its medieval stigma today.

The medieval world was radically different from ours. In preindustrial Europe there were no nation-states, but a mosaic of huge tracts belonging to local noblemen, who pledged allegiance to a king. Communities formed around the lands of the aristocracy, and each community had political autonomy as well as its own currency, rules, and regulations. As described by the historian Robert Heilbroner, in the spring of 1550 Andreas Ryff, a German merchant, headed back to his home in Banden after visiting almost thirty markets. On the way he was stopped approximately every ten miles to pay a customs toll. On the route from Basel to Cologne he had to pay thirty-one levies! In the area around Banden alone there were 112 different measures of length, sixty-five different dry measures, 163 different measures for cereals, and 123 for liquids.[2]

Moreover, in medieval times, the concept of a labor market, where workers freely choose which profession to follow and which employer to work for, was nonexistent. A person's occupation was determined by unwritten, customary rules that ensured continuity from one generation to the next. A son had to walk in his father's steps. He spent his life in the place he was born, doing the same work his father and his grandfather had done. In the country, peasants lived their life tied to their master's estate, while in the towns apprentices were under the complete control of a master. The rate of pay, the hours of work, the number of each apprentice's colleagues, and the methods he used were determined in detail by the appropriate guild. Even privileged (and greatly prized) skilled workers were at the mercy of the authorities. They couldn't even move to another city. In 1575, the Grand Duke of Florence authorized the killing of any craftsman who left the city without permission, offering impunity for the murder and a reward of 200 scudi for each expatriate craftsman brought back dead or alive.[3] Whenever the lords needed craftsmen, they did not hesitate to kidnap them from competing towns in order to satisfy their needs.

Also nonexistent was the concept of competition and the conscious effort to produce better and cheaper goods. Technological progress during the

Middle Ages was like a forbidden fruit, and every effort of a craftsman to produce products of better quality than those of his colleagues was regarded as an act of treason. Stability was the ideal of this era. One of the major goals of the guilds, which spread out in Europe in the late twelfth century, was to control the market and debilitate any attempt of their members to compete with each other. In 1666, French society was dogged by an unprecedented question: whether a guild master of the weaving industry should be allowed to try an innovation in his product. The case was brought to court, and the verdict was the following: "If a cloth weaver intends to process a piece according to his own invention, he must not set it on the loom, but should obtain permission from the judges of the town to employ the number and length of threads that he desires, after the question has been considered by four of the oldest merchants and four of the oldest weavers of the guild."[4] Shortly after the cloth weaver incident, it was the turn of the button makers' guild to raise a cry of outrage. Tailors started making buttons out of cloth, an unheard-of thing. The government, offended by this innovation's threat to an established industry, imposed a fine on cloth-button makers. But this was not enough to satisfy the button makers' guild. They demanded the right to search people's homes, impose fines, and even arrest on the street any person "wearing these subversive goods."[5]

Moreover, in feudal Europe there was no such thing as "land" in the sense of freely tradable real estate. Although there were huge tracts of land owned by the aristocracy and the church, these could not be sold at will. It was unthinkable that a self-respecting nobleman would sell his estates. There were some sales from time to time, but these were exceptions to the rule.

Thus, European societies plodded along for centuries, guided by tradition, prayer, and coercion. When the nobles wished to build majestic cathedrals and luxurious palaces, they did not seek bank financing; they just made their serfs work more, and if the money in their treasuries was not enough, they might invade some neighboring kingdom. When they wanted more land, they did not approach real estate agents; they just formed an army out of their subjects and started a war in order to win the lands they coveted.[6] Finding solutions to the economic problems of that time did not require economists, with their theories and complex equations.

Obviously, economic relations, markets, transactions, commercial activity, economic challenges, and people in pursuit of profit existed both then and in much earlier times. But nothing compared to what would come in the aftermath of the Industrial Revolution. The works of Plato and Aristotle contain many profound analyses of various economic problems; however, their economic thinking mainly reflected the slave-owning structure of ancient society.

This suffocating context did not leave much room for change. The economic reality of medieval Europe was, as pointed out by the Hungarian philosopher and economist Karl Polanyi (1896–1964), more or less the same as that of ancient Persia, India, and China. Medieval economies "certainly could not rival in riches and culture the New Kingdom of Egypt, two thousand years before."[7] The typical local market, where housewives procured some of their daily needs and growers and craftsmen offered their wares for sale, remained unchanged until the middle of the eighteenth century, even in the most advanced societies of that time. They were "an adjunct of local existence." Polanyi wrote, and differed but little, whether they formed part of "Central African tribal life, or a *cite* of Merovingian France, or a Scottish village of Adam Smith's time."[8]

Although markets did exist, there was no such thing as a market economy. In such a world of immobility and inertia, any scientific theory that would explain economic phenomena had no reason to exist.

2

THE INVISIBLE REVOLUTION

Our era is identified with rapid, incessant technological progress. Everything changes swiftly, and we change along. Take the car, the means of transportation that revolutionized human life: Consider how unsophisticated and primitive was the Ford Model T, the vehicle Henry Ford created in 1908, and how spectacularly different automobiles were less than thirty years later, in 1936, when the Volkswagen Beetle came into our lives, as if from another world altogether.

Or consider the airplane. Today, the Wright brothers' flying machine, which in 1903 made the first controlled flight, resembles more a kite than an aircraft. It took only a few years to construct fully controlled and operational airplanes, and the first jet aircraft was created shortly before the end of World War II. The use of airplanes in transportation eliminated travel distances for both people and merchandise, turning our once vast planet into a global village.

Finally, consider the computer. The first computer—the famous ENIAC, which was introduced in late 1945—contained 18,000 vacuum tubes, weighted almost thirty tons, and took up 1.800 feet: an building's entire floor! In 1975, an IBM computer that could perform ten million operations per second cost almost $10 million. Twenty years later, in 1995, a simple game console could perform 500 million operations per second and cost only $500. Today, we use computers that are thousands of times faster and much cheaper than the first personal computer, introduced by IBM in 1981.

Still, the speed, intensity, and impetus of incessant change and innovation are phenomena as recent as economics. For many centuries, humanity moved forward at a human pace, not at the supersonic speeds of our times. "If an Ancient Greek," writes the economist and historian Douglass North, "had been miraculously transported through time to the England of 1750, he or she would have found much that was familiar. The Greek alighting two centuries later, however, would discover what would appear to be an 'unreal' world in which little would be recognizable or even understandable."[9] It would be like landing on another planet.

This dramatic change in the global scenery in such a short time was the result of the Industrial Revolution, the greatest revolution humanity has ever seen. The Industrial Revolution produced what we perceive of as the modern world. It was a radical, many-sided, spontaneous revolution, lacking any organizational and ideological leadership, incomprehensible to the people of that age. It was a revolution bitterly opposed by both the ruling class and the simple folk. The transition to the industrial era generated great discontent and caused misery in a large part of the population.[10] But it was also a process that, to paraphrase Karl Marx, paid no attention to likes and dislikes and could not be stopped.

The Industrial Revolution crushed the old regime, the unshakable and absolute power of the aristocracy, and dissolved all social bonds except "the implacable gold and paper ones of the cash nexus."[11] The established stability, the peculiar harmony and stillness of medieval times, were gone for good. "The gods and kings of the past were powerless before the businessmen and steam-engines of the present."[12]

The Industrial Revolution began around the end of the eighteenth century. Sometime during the 1780s, in England, there was an invisible, indefinable "click" that woke the productive forces out of their prolonged hibernation. And in this quiet, unconscious manner, human societies taxied and took off to a radically new world: the world of economic freedom. Freeing the factors of production—labor, capital, and land—enabled industrial societies to achieve unprecedented, explosive growth. Since then, people, goods, and services have been incessantly multiplying at stunning rates.

Nonetheless, this great transformation went unnoticed in its time. It took many decades for people to grasp the profound and multifaceted change that was taking place. It was only in the 1830s that "literature and the arts began to be overtly haunted by that rise of the capitalist society."[13] and the word *capitalism* didn't enter the economic and political vocabulary of the world until the 1860s.[14]

The Industrial Revolution was not an episode with a beginning and an end.[15] It is impossible to pinpoint its starting point, let alone the events or factors that caused it. To reduce reality to a finite number of causes—something that we systematically do—is to simplify a highly complex chain of events.

The Industrial Revolution did not begin some sunny morning in England because a marvelous new machine was invented or because someone came up with a brilliant idea or because the noblemen decided to enclose their vast landholdings (turning them into pastures) and throw their serfs out on the street. It was the outcome of a long preparatory process, which started hesitantly in the tenth century and picked up speed with the demise of the feudal world around the end of the fourteenth century. For all those centuries, the old and the new had been walking hand-in-hand. A huge number of human decisions, actions, and behaviors brewed together

---

* In England, the enclosure movement reached its peak during the eighteenth century. Landowners erected fences around their estates, which for centuries had been common lands housing thousands of serfs. The enclosed lands were turned into sheep-grazing pastures, and the serfs were expelled.

in the cauldron of history and, through complex interactions both voluntary and involuntary, created a unique and unpredictable mix, which some time in the late eighteenth century led to the outbreak of the Industrial Revolution.

Out of this colossal jumble, historians have singled out certain events as chief catalysts for the birth of this new world.

THE ADEPTS OF TRADE

In the Middle Ages, commercial activity was initially left to adventurers. Roving merchants wandered all over Europe, selling goods in order to secure a livelihood. These wandering merchants were usually fugitive serfs or sons of serfs and stood on the lowest step of the social ladder.

Starting around the year 1000, developments in Europe gathered speed as population growth put pressure on feudal societies. Feudalism's limited productive capacity was not enough to feed the new mouths, and as a result more and more people were forced to seek their fortune in new, unknown places.

The "first adepts of trade" could be found "among this crowd of foot-loose adventurers."[16] These people sought their livelihood in places such as markets, harbors, trade fairs, and towns, where they had a greater chance of actually succeeding. The most active, competent, and venturesome among them quickly managed to create fortunes, literally out of nothing.

Gradually, merchant groups started to emerge, comprising traders who ventured on increasingly long and dangerous—but also profitable—voyages. Merchants traveled to the ends of the then known world in pursuit of local "products which were there found in abundance, in order to be able to resell them later at a profit" in Europe.[17] Those who managed to survive these dangerous voyages reaped huge profits, amassing funds that would enable them to invest in other sectors.

And while bold merchants swiftly accumulated wealth and power, the aristocracy everywhere—with the exception of Italy—watched passively, considering commercial activity and, in general, all kinds of work to be a disgrace. Such base activities were unthinkable for the aristocracy.

This new reality, the merchants' financial strength, gradually led to their social emancipation. According to the law, "one who could not be ascribed to a master" was "necessarily treated as a free man."[18] Gradually, thanks to the power of wealth, their humble origins were forgotten and merchants became free citizens, placed under the protection of public authority and enjoying privileges that were hitherto reserved solely for the nobility and the clergy. This led to the emergence of a new, dynamic, economically powerful social class that would soon become a key factor of major social and political change.

"TOWN AIR MAKES ONE FREE"

The growth of European cities after the tenth century represented a turning point for Western societies. Although the city, as an administrative entity, had been born thousands of years earlier, in Mesopotamia and on the banks of the Nile, it took a long journey through time before it became the great melting pot that dissolved traditional and ancient social bonds. In the towns of the classical world, as in the towns of China and the Byzantine Empire, merchants, professionals, and craftsmen had never achieved a socially prominent position.[19]

The major shift took place during the Middle Ages. The growth of cities also provided less privileged individuals with a golden opportunity to escape serfdom. Migration to the city became an escape route toward a promising new world, where people could hope that their industriousness and mettle would be rewarded with social attainment and a better life. Serfs, free peasants, even the lesser nobility, who had no hope of breaking the stranglehold of the feudal establishment, grabbed at the opportunity: "Town air makes one free." it was said in medieval times.[20] During this period more than 1,000 towns were formed throughout Europe, becoming incubators for the emergence, growth, and final triumph of the bourgeoisie, whose actions were instrumental in the ascendancy of capitalism.

Cities turned into a symbol of social revolution, terrifying the feudal establishment. "In the Italian communes they do not disdain to grant the girdle of knighthood or honorable positions to young people of inferior station, and even to workers of the vile mechanical arts, whom other peoples bar like the plague from the more respectable and honorable circles."[21]

Today it is in vogue, especially in the wake of the 2007 financial crisis, to believe that markets oppose and constrain democracy. But in reality, the ascendancy of liberalism and the development of market economies were among the major forces that led to Europe's liberation from aristocratic absolutism and to the prevalence of bourgeois democracy.

PROFIT: FROM ANATHEMA TO VIRTUE

As indicated above, in the pre-capitalist world the church believed that commerce was incompatible with the effort of saving man's soul and treated merchants as parasites. It absolutely condemned usury and profit and equated the accumulation of wealth with the deadly sin of avarice.

The church's aversion to worldly affairs did not keep it from turning into a major economic force, however. Availing itself of taxes such as the tithe, donations, and various dealings with the feudal lords, the church amassed enormous wealth. By 1430, almost 15 percent of English land was owned by English monasteries.[22] Moreover, in between praying and fasting, the church also developed banking operations, becoming the precursor of financial institutions. It lent to monarchs in need of cash, was responsible for the safekeeping of the nobility's wealth, organized the safe transport of gold, and so on. Though these activities were obviously at odds with the church's own teachings, the church maintained its firm theological belief in the futility of earthly existence.

This unyielding attitude toward worldly matters would gradually change after 1500, spurred by the radical ideas of the Protestant reformer John Calvin (1509–1564). Calvinism recognized work as a sign of spiritual worth. Contrary to Catholic theologians, who unequivocally rejected all worldly activities, Calvinists praised work, encouraged people to be industrious, and emphasized the virtue of self-restraint. This new theological philosophy lifted the stigma from wealth and encouraged its accumulation, as long as this wealth would be put to good use. This cleared the way for the utilization of savings through investments that were useful to society at large. Bit by bit, profit, the pursuit of personal interest, and the effort to improve one's material reality ceased to be anathemas.

THE BIRTH OF THE NATION-STATE

The compartmentalization of authority during the Middle Ages was one of the most important impediments to economic development. There was no single, centralized authority, but hundreds of local nobles who occasionally banded together in support of this or that monarch, acting as a peculiar loose confederation, a miniature of the early European Community. There were roughly 1,000 polities in fourteenth-century Europe, and around 500 independent units 200 years later.[23] Each local nobleman and each town had total control over their respective areas; they had their own currencies, rules and regulations, and even their own weights and measures.

At the end of the fifteenth century there were so many toll stations along the Seine in France that the cost of shipping grain over a distance of 200 miles accounted for half its final selling price.[24] The story of Andreas Ryff, mentioned above, was not the exception but the rule of that time. The fragmentation of France was so deeply rooted and so extensive that complete unification was possible only after the French Revolution of 1789.[25]

The centralization of government authority and the creation of nation-states as we know them today were facilitated by a series of political, religious, social, economic, and purely practical reasons. The emergence of an increasingly strong merchant class had a major influence on this process. Merchant princes suffocated within the narrow confines of local trade. The feudal economy depended on local commerce, and any effort of foreign merchants to penetrate local markets constituted a cause for war. Feudal lords imposed strict controls on trading activity, protecting local commercial interests by every means possible.

Nevertheless, the balance was gradually tipped in favor of the new economy, and the relationship between the trading and the feudal worlds was inverted. The growth of the economy and commerce was accompanied by the loss of power of the nobility and the old establishment. In 1530 in the Gevaudan district of France, 121 lords had an aggregate income of 21,400 *livres*. However, "one of these seigneurs accounted for 5,000 livres of the sum, another for 2,000—and the rest averaged but a mean 121 livres apiece." At the same time, "the richest town merchants had annual incomes up to 65,000 livres."[26]

Recognizing the great opportunities and the huge potential created by the amalgamation of local markets, the merchant class turned to the monarchs, supplying them with a powerful weapon: cash. Thus, the relatively shaky monarchs gathered military and political power, outflanking the local feudal lords, whom they finally subjugated. The consolidation of national authority had multiple effects on economic life. It led to a single currency, common rules and regulations, universal laws, better policing, and the creation of a large, single market. Subsequently, the combination of a single currency and a large market led to the complete ascendancy of money as a means of transaction, a development that, in turn, further boosted commerce and economic life.

Moreover, in many countries, the new monarchies took certain industries under their wing in order to ensure their further growth and the smooth flow of revenues into the royal coffers.

The creation of nation-states had an exponential effect on the speed of the economic machine. These new, territorially expanded entities had to maintain large armies and strong bureaucracies in order to survive and prosper. Thus, in order to secure the necessary surpluses, states had no option other than expanding and exploiting, in a more intensive and efficient manner, the resources that were available to them.

"FOR GOD, GOLD, AND GLORY"

The Crusades, which began in 1096 with the (soon to go amiss) aim of liberating the Holy Lands, brought into contact, for the very first time, the still-slumbering society of European feudalism with the wealth and urban vitality of Byzantium and the East. The noble knights and the barefoot pilgrims who followed them found a sophisticated, cultured, and rich world, which upset their deeply rooted belief that they would be met by "untutored heathen savages."[27]

14

In one of the most woeful and dramatic episodes of these supposedly divine expeditions, Constantinople (Istanbul) was sacked in 1204, and the Crusader hordes returned to their homes with countless spoils and endless stories about the brilliant world of Byzantium. The Venetians, for instance, shipped to Venice the famous gold-plated horses that adorned the Hippodrome in Constantinople; they can be seen today at St. Mark's Basilica. The riches of the Orient spawned great expectations.

However, no one stirred the people's imagination more than the legendary Marco Polo (1254–1324), who created an inexhaustible mythology of distant, mysterious, exotic worlds full of immense riches that awaited daring explorers. Following in the footsteps of his father and his uncle, young Marco arrived in China in 1275 and lived there for twenty years. Upon his return to Europe, in 1295, he was imprisoned by the Genoese. While in captivity he met Rustichello, a well-known author of fantastic tales, who was carried away by Polo's narrations and persuaded him to co-write a book. The book, titled *The Travels of Marco Polo*, was published in 1298, containing the memories and adventures of Polo in China and elsewhere (such as the Middle East, Japan, India, Southeast Asia, the eastern coastline of Africa, and Russia). The book became a huge success, and many writers rushed to imitate him, writing similar books about faraway worlds despite having never set foot outside their own villages.

The stories of Marco Polo—not to mention the fabrications of his imitators—were so bizarre and exotic that they were considered by many to be the product of pure imagination. Still, they became a powerful source of inspiration, instilling courage and hope into the hearts of bold explorers. One of these explorers was Christopher Columbus (1451–1506), who was said to always carry with him a copy of Marco Polo's book.

Thus, since the thirteenth century, more and more adventurers started setting sail to the unknown, roaming the vast Atlantic Ocean "for God, gold, and glory." The years from 1450 to 1650 saw extensive exploration by those seeking foreign lands that could be financially exploited. Searching for gold, spices, and, sadly, slaves, the Portuguese, Spaniards, Dutch, English, and French sailed around the Cape of Good Hope (1487), discovered the Americas (1492), conquered and plundered the Inca, Aztec, and Maya civilizations, and engaged in many more adventures and wars.

The profits were indeed fabulous, beyond all expectations. It is said that the golden coins offered by the Incas to Pizarro as ransom for the release of their emperor could fill a room with a floor area of 17 x 23 feet.[28] Eventually these explorations and the bold adventurers who had initiated them came under the protection of the royal authority. Nations embarked on a race to secure as many lands as possible, financing the daring explorers' fleets and expeditions with royal money.

If you find yourself in central London, it is worth looking, on the banks of the river Thames, for the replica of the Golden Hind, the famous galleon with which, in 1577, Sir Francis Drake led an expedition to South America.* Queen Elizabeth I of England was one of the main backers of the trip. When Drake returned to London, the share of the profits that the Queen received as an investor was so large that it enabled her to pay off the kingdom's entire foreign debt, with enough money left over to invest in a new trading company. The journey of the Golden Hind offered investors a return of 47 pounds for every pound invested—a total return of 4,700 percent.[29]

The explorations paved the way for the settlement of the New World (Africa, North America, etc.) and the establishment of colonies, as well as new commercial networks. Access to precious metals and natural resources, combined with the creation of a far-reaching "global" commercial network, provided a huge boost to commerce and the world economy

---

* The greatest success of Drake's exploratory mission was the capturing of the Spanish galleon *Nuestra Señora de la Concepción*, a Spanish vessel laden with treasure.

in general. According to historians' estimates, between 1500 and 1800, precious metals worth $175 billion at today's prices was shipped from the New World to Europe or Asia.[30]

A SPLENDID ENCOUNTER

During the Middle Ages, science and technology moved in parallel universes. They were marching on slowly, independent of each other, and interaction between them was limited. Technological progress was slow and irregular, while scientific curiosity, as we think of it today, was nonexistent. It may seem unbelievable by today's standards, but "it is a question whether Europe in the year 1200 was significantly more technologically advanced than it had been in the year 200 BC."[31]

However, despite the slow pace, things were changing. The sixth century saw the dissemination of the water mill, the seventh century saw the invention of the mouldboard plough, and iron horseshoes were introduced in the eighth century. In the eleventh century, the development of business methods picked up pace: Trade fairs were organized, and trading manuals made their appearance, along with new accounting methods, checks and their endorsement, and insurance. In the twelfth century the first windmill was invented, in the thirteenth century Europeans learned about gunpowder and the compass (from the Chinese), and the fourteenth century saw the discovery of mechanical clocks and cannons.

The year 1454 was a landmark year for humanity. In that year, the great German inventor Johannes Gutenberg (1398–1468) succeeded, after many years of research and experimentation, in printing the Bible with the use of movable type, a method that employs components that can be rearranged and reused many times. Up to that point, books had been handwritten and were expensive, unaffordable even among the affluent. The easy recording and dissemination of knowledge through typography had multiplying effects, paving the way for the emergence of mass media.

Back then, science was considered to be a lesser source of knowledge, since all questions about the world and its workings had definitively and categorically been answered by the great authorities. The writings of the church fathers and the works of certain great philosophers, such as Aristotle and Plato, which the Church had incorporated in its teachings, constituted the great axiomatic truths. There was no room for doubt. Those arrogant enough to question the authorities not only faced excommunication but, in certain cases, risked being condemned to the stake.

This would change, thanks to the liberating, creative tide of the Renaissance and the steady weakening of the church's influence—which was, as discussed above, accelerated by the growth of the cities and the strengthening of the merchant class. The ascent of critical thinking and inquisitiveness, which aimed at answering the whys and hows of how the world works, finally led to mankind's domination of the natural environment. Nothing escaped scientific curiosity, and nothing was considered taboo to scientists. So, little by little, the authorities were undermined and science emerged as the only method for acquiring knowledge.

Galileo (1564–1642), Newton (1642–1727), Huygens (1629–1695), Van Leeuwenhoek (1632–1723), Descartes (1596–1650), Harvey (1578–1657), Copernicus (1473–1543), Leibniz (1646–1716), and many more sealed the victory of the experimental method and the use of mathematics in explaining reality.

Despite this impressive scientific awakening and the great discoveries it produced, science and technology made little difference in regard to social progress and people's lives before the end of the eighteenth century. Even so, this long process laid deep and solid foundations for the emergence of a new world: the industrial world.

3

THE ADVENT OF THE ECONOMISTS

From the sixteenth century to the eighteenth, there were two main schools of thought when it came to addressing economic concerns and problems: mercantilism and physiocracy. From time to time, great thinker-philosophers, such as William Petty (1623–1687) and David Hume (1711–1776), dealt with more sophisticated economic problems, such as how prices are determined in the market (value theory) and the effect of "a protracted rise in the overall volume of money" on a nation's wealth.[32] However, all these efforts fell far short of forming the basis of an economic theory, let alone establishing an independent discipline.

Mercantilism was not a theory but a web of practical ideas regarding the role of the state in economic life, ideas that coalesced in the wake of the rapid growth of commerce. Mercantilists argued that the state should play an active role in economic life, with the aim of attaining commercial goals and increasing the nation's wealth. They stressed that a state's prosperity depended on the acquisition of precious metals, most notably gold, and emphasized the importance of export trade as a means of augmenting the stock of precious metals.

The physiocratic school was developed as a response to mercantilism and opposed any state intervention in the economy. "Do not interfere—such must be the motto of every public authority."[33] the physiocrats said, advocating a laissez-faire approach. They believed that the economic development and prosperity of a nation depends on agriculture and "considered it essential to replace the small-scale peasant holding with large-scale farming."[34] For the physiocrats, agriculture was the heart, the lifeblood of the economy, and agricultural production was the key element of the economic process. *Tableau Economique* by François Quesnay (1694–1774) is considered to be the physiocrats' paramount legacy. In a few lines, Quesnay managed to sketch out the entire flow of an economy, including the production, circulation, distribution, and consumption of goods within a society.

However, the gradual transformation of society through the Industrial Revolution rendered both the mercantilist and physiocratic ideas insufficient to describe and explain the increasingly complex operation of the economic world. The ascendancy of merchant and industrial capital and theories of individualism and economic freedom overturned traditional structures, releasing powerful forces of change.

Everything seemed to be confusing and inexplicable. Where was society going? How could we prevent the breakdown of social cohesion if all people were pursuing their own interests? How could society be protected from the risk that most people might shift toward certain occupations and activities and abandon others? Who would do all the hard and undesirable jobs (coal mining, leather tanning, etc.) that were absolutely essential to the smooth operation of society as a whole? What would happen if not enough meat or bread were produced, or if there were an excess supply of shoes or glasses? And without any central planning and political control, how would we deal with the risk of a rapid increase in poverty and distress, which would finally lead to social unrest and revolution?

The economists came forth to answer all these questions, concerns, and problems. Economic science gained flesh and blood, found its role in society, and soon became indispensable—not only for shedding light on all aspects of the new industrial world, but also for suggesting solutions and policies aimed at dealing with economic problems more efficiently, advancing growth, and boosting social well-being.

The father of this new science was Adam Smith, a renowned Scottish philosopher who laid the ideological foundations of modern economics. Many of his ideas regarding the importance of economic freedom and competition still prevail in most parts of the globe.

However, free-market capitalism was not hailed by everyone as the inescapable, natural course of mankind. At the dawn of the new industrial age, the harsh, inhuman face of capitalism intrigued many great thinkers, who soon brought attention to its shortcomings and proposed alternative systems of economic organization.

THE INVISIBLE HAND OF ADAM SMITH

Adam Smith (1723–1790) taught moral philosophy at the University of Glasgow and was considered one of the most important philosophers of his age. He was eccentric, well-meaning, comically absentminded, and "a beau in nothing but my books." [35] as he described himself.

He loved talking walks, during which he often talked to himself, a habit of his since childhood. He would be so carried away by the world of ideas that he'd lose touch with reality. It is said that one time, walking along in earnest disquisition with a friend, he fell into a tanning pit. Another time, absorbed in conversation, he tried to brew tea by using bread and butter. Yet another time, lost in his thoughts, he came out of his house clad only in a dressing gown and walked 16 miles before the tolling of a bell brought him back to reality.[36]

In his time, society was in a state of great unrest. Economic freedom and the doctrine of laissez-faire were sweeping everything away. For most people, the daily routine was an incessant struggle for survival. Hordes of hungry ex-serfs wandered the country in search of casual work, while young children labored under terrible conditions, seventy to eighty hours a week, for a pittance. They occupied wretched hovels, living in misery and squalor. The concept of the welfare state was totally nonexistent.

Stupefied, the aristocracy watched these rapid changes as the first industrialists and merchant princes stopped at nothing in order to increase their profits. Adam Smith gazed at this jumbled, unpleasant picture and, sensing a hidden harmony, noticed that the new system possessed an amazing internal beauty and order that was not easily visible. In 1776 he published his monumental work, *The Wealth of Nations*." which gave new meaning to many things that hitherto had seemed incomprehensible. The book became the ideological beacon of capitalism and the new industrial era, as Smith's argumentation laid the foundations of the individualist and rationalist approach.[37]

The new system of natural liberty, as Adam Smith called it, was the most efficient in organizing economic life and automatically led, he claimed, to long-term growth and the multiplication of social well-being. His main idea was that when economic life unfolds "naturally." without any government restrictions, benefits are maximized, not only for the individual but for society as a whole.

In response to the question of how cohesion and smooth operation would be maintained in a society where everyone pursued his or her own self-interest, Smith described an automatic mechanism, an "invisible hand," that harnessed opposing individual interests and put them to the service of society as a whole. In his own words: "It is not from the benevolence of the butcher, the brewer, or the baker that we expect our dinner, but from their regard to their own interest."[38] But if everyone is free to pursue and maximize profit, what would protect us from greedy profiteers who, in order to gain more, have no qualms about exploiting society? Competition, of course, replied Smith. If someone tried to sell his wares at a higher price, he would soon find himself out of the market, as some other competitor would be content with a smaller profit. And even if a group of greedy merchants colluded on a policy of selling at higher prices, some other, equally greedy merchants would see the opportunity and rush to take advantage of it, crushing the conspiracy. This clash of individual interests—that is, competition—was the steadfast and vigilant guardian of society's interests.

At the same time, competition regulated not only the price of a good but also the quantity produced to meet society's needs. If a good were in excess supply, prices would inevitably fall, rendering its production unprofitable. As a result, certain producers would shift toward the production of other, more profitable, and more socially useful goods, thus restoring equilibrium. For the first time, everyone and everything worked to the benefit of the individual, the consumer. For the first time ever, the consumer was the center of the world.

Specialization, the division of labor, and the accumulation of wealth were instrumental to the system of natural liberty. "The greatest improvements in the productive powers of labour." Smith wrote, "and the greater part of the skill, dexterity, and judgment, with which it is anywhere directed, or applied, seem to have been the effects of the division of labour."[39] His reference to a pin factory is very well known:

> One man draws out the wire; another straights it; a third cuts it; a fourth points it; a fifth grinds it at the top for receiving the head. it is even a trade by itself to put them into the paper...I have seen a small manufactory of this kind, where ten men only were employed, and where some of them consequently performed two or three distinct

operations. But though they were very poor, and therefore but indifferently accommodated with the necessary machinery, they could...make among them about twelve pounds of pins in a day. There are in a pound upwards of four thousand pins...Those ten persons, therefore, could make among them upwards of forty-eight thousand pins in a day. But if they had all wrought separately and independently, and without any of them having been educated to this peculiar business, they certainly could not each of them have made twenty, perhaps not one pin in a day.[40]

According to Smith, the industrialists' selfish tendency to accumulate wealth not only was permissible and necessary for the economy, but was eventually transformed, through the mechanism of the market, into a wonderful altruistic offer to society. How was this achieved? By accumulating capital, capitalists created new factories and acquired new machines, multiplying productive capacity. This enhanced the specialization of labor, created new jobs and additional income, and finally led to a higher level of social well-being. In other words, even the greediest, most avaricious financier inadvertently worked toward maximizing the prosperity of society as a whole. All of this outlined the dawn of an amazing era of ceaseless progress, an almost automatic process since no intervention or guidance was required.

The rising capitalists of that time rallied around the ideas of Adam Smith, stressing the importance of liberty and the necessity that the state not interfere in economic life. "Let the market alone" was the motto of that time. It is a fact that Adam Smith detested any state interference in the economy, firmly believing that the market and capitalism could maximize economic benefit only when operating freely. He maintained that government needed to do only three things for society: defend the country against invasion, promote justice, and provide certain public works (roads, bridges, harbors etc.) and public education.[41]

However, the great philosopher was in no way the champion of capitalists or an advocate of unaccountable liberty. He did not hesitate to stress the cruel rapacity of the capitalist class, also pointing out that "the scanty maintenance of the labouring poor…is the natural symptom that things… are going fast backwards."[42]

THE GLOOMY VIEW OF THE REVEREND THOMAS MALTHUS

The great expectations for self-propelling, long-term progress were violently interrupted by the pessimistic findings of the Reverend Thomas Robert Malthus (1766–1834). In 1798, his treatise *An Essay on the Principle of Population* sounded like a cacophony in the midst of a splendid melody.

He wrote the treatise in order to counter the optimism of his father, Daniel Malthus, which echoed that era's overall faith in humanity's potential for unlimited improvement and progress. The reverend rejected all such expectations, pointing out that there is a tendency in nature for human population "to outstrip all possible means of subsistence."[43] In other words, the number of mouths would always be greater than the stocks of food, condemning a large part of the population to hunger and misery. Malthus pointed out that while humans multiply rapidly by breeding, land does not breed. The number of people, he said, grows exponentially (1, 2, 4, 8, 16, and so forth), while the area of cultivable land is finite and the quantity of the food that can be produced grows only arithmetically (1, 2, 3, 4, 5, and so forth). Thus, there would always be a gap between the number of people and the capacity to produce enough food to sustain them. The balance, emphasized Malthus, abruptly bringing optimists back to harsh reality, would be violently struck through famine, disease, and war. Humanity had a way out only if we could control our reproductive urges, something the reverend considered to be impossible.

Malthus viewed competition as the mechanism through which nature distinguishes the weak from diligent and productive individuals. In referring to the threat of "general gluts," he was the first economist to approach the concept of business cycles and depressions, though he did not manage to bring the idea to completion.

DAVID RICARDO'S INSURMOUNTABLE OBSTACLE

Further obstacles to society's progress were identified by David Ricardo (1772–1823). Ricardo was a charismatic trader, businessman, and landowner. By the age of twenty-five he was "already enjoying a reputation in London as a millionaire and a prominent banker."[44] Despite being a man of affairs—he had never studied at a university—he felt irresistibly attracted to the world of theory and ideas and devoted most of his time to the pursuit of the invisible laws that governed the economic universe. His contribution to the theoretical evolution of economics is substantial.

Despite being himself an owner of large tracts of arable land, in his work *On the Principles of Political Economy*, published in 1817, he branded landowners as mortal enemies of society and progress. He said that in the mechanisms of production, workers offered their labor while capitalists and industrialists coordinated the process. The workers' wages depended on their population, while the capitalists' profits depended on competition and their ability to be efficient. However, the landowners' rents were, to a great extent, independent, since the amount of land is finite. Those who happened to acquire or inherit large tracts simply lay back and enjoyed the flow of income, without any particular toil. Given that the most productive areas are limited, Ricardo claimed that the competition among those wishing to use them would lead to a significant increase in rent. This, in turn, would lead to an increase in the cost of producing food and in the

26

price of food as well, which determined the basic wage.* In other words, industrialists would be forced to pay increasing wages, while landowners would earn more and more. Thus, Ricardo identified a structural flaw in the system: Most of the profits went not to those who set the economic machine in motion, namely the capitalists, but to those who happened to own arable land. As he wrote, "The interest of the landlords is always opposed to the interest of every other class in the community."[45] He stressed that "the landlord is doubly benefited by difficulty of production," since "first, he obtains a greater share, and secondly the commodity in which he is paid is of greater value."[46]

Ricardo, like Adam Smith, was opposed to state intervention and the imposition of protective measures. As he wrote, paraphrasing Adam Smith's famous "invisible hand," the "pursuit of individual advantage is admirably connected with the universal good of the whole."[47]

His ideas were very influential, and his theory of comparative advantage is considered to be his greatest contribution to economics. According to this theory, even if a country can produce all goods more efficiently than other countries, it will maximize its profits if it specializes in those goods in which it enjoys the greatest advantage. Ricardo also made a decisive contribution to the methodology of economics, being the first to employ deduction to create models for better understanding, analysis, and interpretation of economic phenomena.

JOHN STUART MILL: THE LAST OF THE CLASSICS

As a rule, the classical school of economics is taken to have begun with the publication of Adam Smith's *Wealth of Nations* and to have ended with

---

* In those harsh, inhuman years at the dawn of the industrial era, a worker's wages were equivalent to the amount of money that prevented starvation.

the appearance, in 1848, of *Principles of Political Economy* by John Stuart Mill (1806–1873).[48]

Mill was a prodigy. Under the strict guidance of his father, James, young Mill began to learn Greek at the age of three and had digested Plato, Herodotus, Xenophon, and others before turning eight. Next came the great Latin philosophers, and at the age of twelve he started studying the work of the philosopher Thomas Hobbes (1588–1679). "There were no holidays, "lest the habit of work should be broken, and a taste for idleness acquired."[49] Given all that, it is no surprise that he suffered a nervous breakdown in his twenties.

In his work, Mill, influenced by the utopian socialists, underlined the shortcomings in the thinking of the economists of the old school. "I confess," he wrote in his *Principles*, "I am not charmed with the ideal of life held out by those who think that the normal state of human beings is that of struggling to get on; that the trampling, crushing, elbowing, and treading on each other's heels, which form the existing type of social life, are the most desirable lot of human kind, or anything but the disagreeable symptoms of one of the phases of industrial progress."[50] Mill claimed that a way out of this situation must be sought through a "general reconsideration of all first principles" on which the economy was founded.[51] Although he began his career as "a staunch defender of laissez-faire capitalism, toward the end of his life…he called himself a socialist."[52]

KARL MARX: THE PROPHET OF DESTRUCTION

Soon, Malthus's and Ricardo's pessimistic ideas regarding the future of the free-market society would seem harmless in comparison with the prophecy of Karl Marx (1818–1883) about the inescapable and complete collapse of capitalism. Marx studied philosophy and was decisively influenced by the philosophy of Hegel (1770–1831). According to Hegel, the driving force of historical change was the dialectic, "a process of development in which interaction between two opposing forces leads to a further or higher stage."[53] Marx, with his collaborator Friedrich Engels (1820–1895), developed the concepts of dialectical materialism and historical materialism. Marx and Engels were connected by a deep, sincere, and lifelong friendship. "Each was strong where the other was weak," Engels was the one who turned Marxist philosophical thought into a method and did much to simplify and popularize Marx's ideas.[54]

According to their philosophy, the ultimate causes of all social and political change should not be sought in people's ideas, but in the methods of producing and exchanging goods, the material forces of production. Marx's materialism does not reject the importance and dynamism of ideas; nonetheless, it maintains that ideas are a product of the environment, even ideas that aim to change the very environment that brought them into being.

According to Marx's philosophy, "'Before men do anything else they must first produce the means for their subsistence,' namely the food they eat, the clothing they wear, the houses they live in. Everything else follows from the necessity to produce the material means of our subsistence."[55]

These material forces of production vary from society to society. The way an economy is organized in an agricultural society is radically different from how it is organized in an industrial society. According to Marx's thinking, equally important are the social relations of production that are formed within a society, i.e., each individual's place in production, the division of labor. These social relations of production give rise to the social classes, which also differ across societies and eras.

Apart from the way the economy is organized—the economic base that will be chosen—societies must also create an ideological superstructure: They must have laws, select a method of government, and be inspired by a certain religion and philosophy. This ideological superstructure is not selected at random but is an extension of society's economic organization. "No hunting community would evolve...the legal framework of an industrial society, and similarly no industrial community could use the conception of law, order, and government of a primitive village."[56] Whatever the superstructure of thought may be, its main function is "to explain, justify, and legitimize the division of labour, class differences, and vast disparities of wealth."[57]

Marx's dialectic did not depend only on the interaction among social structures and ideas, but also on another, much more powerful, factor: The economic base on which society rests, and out of which the ideological superstructure arises, undergoes constant change. "The hand-mill gives you society with the feudal lord; the steam-mill, society with the industrial capitalist."[58] As the situation changes, the classes fight each other in order to preserve or improve their positions. "The feudal lord fights the rising merchant, and the guild master opposes the young capitalist." This historical process, Marx pointed out, pays no attention to likes and dislikes and cannot be averted: "Gradually conditions change, and gradually, but surely, the classes of society are rearranged."[59] For Marx and Marxists, analyzing the class system is the key to understanding history. As Marx wrote in *The Communist Manifesto*, "The history of all hitherto existing society is the history of class struggles."[60]

Although Marx admitted that, in the course of history, capitalism had been a progressive, radical force (hastening the demise of feudalism and so forth), he maintained not only that it should be overthrown, but that its downfall was inevitable.

Capitalism, he claimed, was an outdated system that leads to the alienation of both the workers and the capitalists themselves. The former cannot find any satisfaction in their labor, lose any creative spirit, are alienated from each other, and become an appendage of the machine. Similarly, capitalists unknowingly lose their freedom and become slaves of the market.[61] Moreover, Marx believed, capitalism is self-subverting. The economic base of capitalism was industrial production, and its superstructure was the system of private property. According to Marx's analysis, the downfall of capitalism was unavoidable because the base and the superstructure were incompatible: "Factories necessitated social planning while private property abhorred it." According to the Marxist view, "Capitalism had become so complex that it needed direction, but capitalists insisted on a ruinous freedom."[62]

The result of this clash would be twofold. First, capitalism would destroy itself, as the planless nature of production would lead to increasingly harsh crises and recessions. Second, capitalism would inadvertently create its successor. Within its great factories it would create the technical base for socialism: rationally planned production and, at the same time, a trained and disciplined class, the proletariat, "which would be the agent of socialism."[63]

In their monumental, voluminous work *Das Kapital*, Marx and Engels embarked on completely taking capitalism's structure apart. To achieve this they did not attempt an easy attack on the manifest shortcomings and flaws of the system. Instead they employed cold logic to analyze the best and most efficient form of capitalism. Their aim was to prove that even this ideal, perfect capitalism was headed for disaster. And if this ideal capitalism could not escape disaster, then actual capitalism, with all this problems, will, by all means, "follow the same path, only quicker."[64]

Das Kapital describes the generation of profit through the surplus value inherent in labor; the importance of capital accumulation; and the fierce competition that leads to shrinking profit margins and crises (which lead to the formation of increasingly large business enterprises), which are themselves followed by bigger and more violent crises. Finally, the end comes: "The integument is burst asunder. The knell of capitalist private property sounds. The expropriators are expropriated."[65]

4

THE DEPARTURE

MODELED ON NEWTON

At the dawn of the new era, economics barely resembled the strictly defined, austere, and heavily mathematized discipline that currently passes
for economic science. During its early period of development, the new
science was known as political economy.

The pioneers of economics aspired to provide answers to the great questions and problems, to identify the basic forces that drive capitalism, and
to shed light on the dynamic interaction among political, social, and economic factors. In order to study economic phenomena they combined
knowledge derived from a wide range of disciplines, including philosophy, history, mathematics, logic, and ethics.

Grand ideas and ideology were the predominant elements. The mercantilists focused on defending merchant capital, while the physiocrats,
who were opposed to mercantilism, attacked government intervention.
Observing the mechanisms of the market, Adam Smith saw an invisible
hand that led individual interest in a direction that was most suited to
the interests of society as a whole. In contrast, Karl Marx, looking at
the laws of the market and the economic base of capitalism, identified

structural failures that, in his opinion, would sooner or later lead to its destruction. According to Thomas Malthus, societies were doomed because, owing to man's uncontrollable reproductive instincts, population would grow much faster than production. In a nutshell, different economists looked at the same things and perceived totally different realities.

In addition to being brilliant intellectual accomplishments, the works of these thinkers were brimming with passion and emotion. They were heavily imbued with personal views as well as ideological and political elements, and it was difficult to distinguish scientific reasoning from plain speculation. Could this unbelievable jumble be regarded as real science? The answer is no. Early economists seemed more like passionate visionaries, whose beliefs were based on insight and instinct, than like scientists.

The vague formulation of this new field was an embarrassment to the newly established academic order, which aspired to establish economics as a proper discipline, equal to the other sciences. The nineteenth century saw the triumph of science. The scientists of that time, wielding the power of Newtonian laws and Descartes's coordinates, which created an image of the universe as a vast grid, believed that everything could be understood and described on the basis of mathematics and mechanics. The conventional wisdom of that time was that soon nothing would be uncertain: Everything would be understandable and predictable. The French physicist Pierre Laplace (1749–1827) was convinced that one day scientists would create a mathematical equation, a universal formula, powerful enough to explain everything.[66] The famous "demon" posited by Laplace was an intellect that, at any given moment, had knowledge of all the forces that animate nature and all the positions of all the items of which nature is composed. Nothing could be uncertain for such an intellect, and the future would always be present before its eyes, just as the past was.

The scientists of that time firmly believed that every particle in the universe followed strict and rational laws and that everything was part of a grand scheme, which could be understood only through scientific knowledge.[67]

As John Briggs and David Peat write in their book *Turbulent Mirror: An Illustrated Guide to Chaos Theory and the Science of Wholeness*, at the end of the nineteenth century humanity dethroned the gods and reenthroned science and the possession of knowledge. It now "saw itself as the product of an improbable collision of particles following…universal laws." Scientists believed that, by knowing the laws, they would be able to predict with increasing deftness and control the entropy that afflicts complicated systems.[68]

Philosophers like Bacon and Descartes entirely agreed with physical scientists that the ideal of science should be to establish mathematically formulated theories that could be tested by proof and offered the possibility of exact prediction.[69]

Newton introduced differential calculus to describe his laws of motion, which correlated the pace of change with various forces. Soon, linear differential equations became the basis of the scientific process: Phenomena as diverse as the trajectory of an artillery shell, the growth of a plant, the combustion of carbon, and the operation of a machine could be described by such equations. Differential equations were an amazingly powerful and universally applicable tool. So, at a time when the laws of Newtonian physics were seen as the expression of ideal, objective, and complete knowledge,[70] economists embarked on a wide-ranging effort to purge economics of all inconvenient, unscientific, and controversial elements.

Since the late nineteenth century, a group of academics, led by Alfred Marshall (1842–1924), Leon Walras (1834–1910), Francis Ysidro Edgeworth (1845–1926), William Stanley Jevons (1835–1882), Vilfredo

Pareto (1848–1923) and others, worked methodically toward restructuring economics along the lines of classical physics. To achieve this, they freely borrowed concepts from Newtonian mechanics and made extensive use of deduction mathematics as a key tool for the presentation and analysis of economic phenomena. The economists' goal was to identify universally applicable laws.

They constructed economic models along the lines of Newtonian laws, which made it possible to study economic problems with a high degree of scientific accuracy. The work of Marshall and his fellow travelers led to the creation of economic science as we currently perceive it. In reorienting economics, they shied away from the ambitious pursuit of theories that would provide answers to the great questions and problems, focusing instead on models and methodology. Ideology was replaced by sophisticated mathematical techniques. Marshall believed that the purpose of economics was to answer questions such as how equilibrium prices are reached, and not to seek answers to "dark" issues like how economic relations and structures are formed within a society.

Remaking economics in the mold of physics had a crucial result: Economics was equated with Newtonian determinism—that is, with the notion that every event, phenomenon, or action is fully determined by its causes. According to this notion, the laws of nature, as formulated by Newtonian physics, are rooted in an ideal knowledge that is tantamount to certainty, and since initial conditions are given, everything is determined. Similarly, the neoclassical school claimed that economic phenomena are objective, are completely independent from human will and social action, and operate just like natural phenomena. Neoclassical economists stripped all the inconvenient angles of the human psyche away from political economy, uprooted ideological elements, burned all bridges with philosophy, and reformulated economics in a purely scientific language based on differential calculus. The new economic science focused on the pursuit of equilibrium and maximization. The main goal of neoclassical economists was to demonstrate how free-market forces ensure the optimum distribution of scarce economic resources.

This bizarre grafting of physics onto economics was seemingly successful. Academic economists managed to construct a solid scientific structure and establish economics as a hard science whose scientific method, accuracy, and objectivity were beyond any doubt. As smugly stated in modern economics textbooks, "Economists, like astronomers and evolutionary biologists, usually have to make do with whatever data the world happens to give them."[71]

This effort culminated in 1968, when—following a proposal from the Bank of Sweden—a new Nobel Prize in Economics was created. No other social science has ever been given such an honor.* However, the price of this success was dear. In order to wear the cloak of hard science, economics had become estranged from reality, society, and the world of action. The mathematical presentation of the economic world and human economic behavior was made possible only through drastic simplifications and generalizations.

Unable to mathematize the complexity of human behavior, the dynamics of interaction among societies, and the unpredictability of historical process and technological development, economists created a parallel universe. This universe contains assumptions and axioms that have nothing to do with reality, and it is inhabited by a rather peculiar being: *Homo economicus.*

---

* Unlike the other Nobel Prizes (in Chemistry, Physics, Medicine, Literature, and Peace), the creation of a Nobel Prize in Economics was never requested by Alfred Nobel in his will. The prize was established in 1968, seventy years after Nobel's death, by the central bank of Sweden on the occasion of the bank's 300th anniversary. It is awarded by the Royal Swedish Academy of Sciences on the basis of the same criteria used to determine the other prizes. In the mid-1990s the definition of the Nobel Prize in Economics was revised in order to include all the social sciences (political science, psychology, and sociology).

HOMO ECONOMICUS

Out there, in the streets and the town squares, lives a very strange human being. This creature does not feel any love, affection, hate, anger, remorse, fear, embarrassment, or jealousy; is not affected by those around him or her; is not riddled by moral dilemmas and does not know what corruption is; is not greedy, nor arrogant; has no sexual urges; does not (systematically) make any mistakes; and is devoid of passion.

This creature is you, me, all of us, as economists understand us. This is *Homo economicus*, an intelligent, single-minded, and automated creature who, being fully aware of economic conditions, acts rationally solely on the basis of his or her personal interest. The choices of this weird individual are consistent and independent from his or her social environment. There is no society, there are no social groups, there are no interest groups.

This *Homo economicus*—who does not sleep because he feels sleepy, but because the satisfaction he will derive from sleeping exceeds the satisfaction he will derive by staying awake for another hour—is the centerpiece of the neoclassical economic universe.

The English philosopher Jeremy Bentham (1748–1832), who, among others, developed the theory of utilitarianism, was the first to approach the concept of the economic man. In his book *An Introduction to Principles of Morals and Legislation* (1789), he claims that "nature has placed mankind under the governance of two sovereign masters, pain and pleasure," and that "it is for them alone to point out what we ought to do, as well as to determine what we shall do."[72] Bentham compared humanity to a mass of living, calculating machines that incessantly computed profits and losses and aimed solely at maximizing their pleasure. He created an algorithm, which he called the Hedonistic or Felicific Calculus, and used it to calculate the degree or amount of pleasure that a specific action was likely to cause.

Francis Edgeworth took Bentham's assumption that every man is a plea-sure machine, dressed it up in pretty mathematical garments, and, un-der the incontestable authority of differential calculus, showed that in a world of perfect competition every pleasure machine would achieve the maximum amount of pleasure society could offer. Although the concept of *Homo economicus* was nonexistent in reality, it enjoyed an unequaled ad-vantage: It could be perfectly aligned with the economists' sophisticated mathematical models leading to clean solutions and equilibrium.

5

CHALLENGING HOMO ECONOMICUS

Do these things, the concept of the economic man and this imaginary unchangeable world, have anything to do with the dynamic and complex real world we live in? Obviously not. Despite their evident departure from reality, neoclassical economists succeeded—by building strong and high walls around them—in establishing economics as a hard science.

However, their effort did not go uncontested. Since the beginning, the academics' effort to purge and reconstruct economics met strong resistance. As early as the late nineteenth century, many economists emphatically stressed that the economic man, equilibrium, and other lofty concepts were mere fantasies, totally disconnected from reality. In the twentieth century, anthropologists, sociologists, psychologists, biologists, neuroscientists, and others succeeded, through lots of experimental research, in dealing fatal blows to the concept of the economic man. However, this had only a limited impact on economic theory.

THORSTEIN VEBLEN: THE PSYCHOPATHOLOGY OF DAILY LIFE

In 1899, the great Norwegian-American economist Thorstein Veblen (1857–1929) rocked the boat of academia with his startling work *The Theory of the Leisure Class*. Veblen was an odd character. Highly intelligent, eccentric, detached from his environment, he seemingly read every book that fell into his hands. His immense learning was legendary.

Veblen viewed references to man's rational behavior as unsophisticated approaches that had nothing to do with reality, and in his work he dived deep into the waters of the psychopathology of daily life, shattering the anthropomorphic construct of *Homo economicus*.

Having studied, among many other things, anthropology and sociology, he knew that many societies—from Polynesia to feudal Japan to feudal Europe—had leisure classes, which did not contribute to society through work, instead seizing resources by force from the community and amassing riches. These upper classes were exempt from work—apart from waging war, in the case of noblemen, and executing religious duties, in the case of the clergy. Strangely enough, these societies not only did not react to this situation, but admired this predatory spirit and all those who managed to rise to the ranks of this aggressive ruling class. Little by little, the activities of the leisure class came to be regarded as highly enviable, and its members were considered to be the most able and intelligent members of society.[73] In contrast, labor, especially manual labor, came to be considered inferior and was branded as an occupation for the less gifted.

Veblen ridiculed the arrogance and certainty of his contemporaries regarding the superiority of "civilized man." With amazing insight he stressed that man did not appear on the planet just yesterday. He pointed out that humankind has a long history that is lost in the depths of time, most of it taking place under savage and primitive conditions. Therefore, by heredity, human nature has many deeply rooted, primitive characteristics that strongly affect behavior.[74] Modern, civilized man, he argued, is not so different from his primitive ancestors.

He wrote about the display of material wealth, which people use as a means of showing off and exhibiting their strength. According to Veblen's thinking, in more primitive times the leisure class exhibited its strength by seeking women or booty, or through "scalps hanging on one's tepee." Now, in the civilized world, men have replaced these barbaric habits with "the accumulation of money and its lavish...display."[75] Man exhibits his power and superiority by wearing expensive clothes, buying expensive things, eating at expensive restaurants, and so on. Consumption equals power—and more consumption equals more power.

Veblen also addressed social cohesion and the fear that inequality might lead to social conflict. There is no class struggle, he stated, because workers do not seek to displace their managers, but to emulate them. They hope they (or their children) will climb up to the superior—predatory—class and enjoy its privileges, including being able to consume lavishly without working.

Robert Heilbroner perfectly sums up Veblen's economic thinking in *The Worldly Philosophers—The Lives, Times and Ideas of the Great Economic Thinkers*. He writes:

> [J]ust as he ridiculed the classical attempt to resolve the primitive human struggle by fitting it into a fleshless and bloodless framework, so he highlighted the emptiness of trying to understand the actions of modern man in terms that derived from an incomplete and outmoded set of preconceptions. Man, said Veblen, is not to be comprehended in terms of sophisticated "economic laws" in which both his innate ferocity and creativity are smothered under a

cloak of rationalization. He is better dealt with in the less flattering but more fundamental vocabulary of the anthropologist or the psychologist: a creature of strong and irrational drives, credulous, untutored, ritualistic. Leave aside flattering fictions, he asked of the economists, and find out why man actually behaves as he does.[76]

THE ANIMAL SPIRITS OF JOHN MAYNARD KEYNES

John Maynard Keynes (1883–1946) is considered to be the greatest economist of the twentieth century. He was an extremely gifted man, with many talents and skills, and his many-sided personality made him stand out. A member of the famous Bloomsbury Group, a lover of art, and a keen trader in currency markets, Keynes was one of those people who cannot do only one thing. In addition to being a professor of economics at Cambridge University, he also was chairman of a life insurance company and a director of the Bank of England. He also took part in the diplomatic negotiations regarding the reconstruction of Europe after both the First and Second World Wars. Harry Hopkins, one of Franklin D. Roosevelt's advisers, called Keynes "one of those fellows that just knows all the answers."[77]

Keynes rejected *Homo economicus*, saying that it was frustrating to reduce economic science to a mere mathematical application of Bentham's Hedonistic Calculus. He formulated a theoretical construct to explain why the general equilibrium of the neoclassical theory does not guarantee, and is not tantamount to, maximum efficiency.[78] In 1936, Keynes's historic work, *The General Theory of Employment, Interest and Money*, left an indelible mark on the development of economic thought and highlighted the key role of psychological factors in determining economic behavior.

Keynes believed that economic life is based on rational decisions and actions, but stressed that a large part of the economy is under the control of "animal spirits." He argued that people, despite seeking to maximize their economic interests, do not function rationally when under the influence of psychopathological factors. Animal spirits, he argued, affect business cycles and cause crises. "Uncertainty, not assurance, lay at the very core of capitalism," he wrote.[79]

His work demonstrated how psychological factors affect markets, liquidity, interest rates, and, in general, the economy. He is well known for comparing the operation of stock markets with a famous beauty contest that was organized at that time by a newspaper in England. He wrote:

> [P]rofessional investment may be likened to those newspaper competitions in which the competitors have to pick out the six prettiest faces from a hundred photographs, the prize being awarded to the competitor whose choice most nearly corresponds to the average preferences of the competitors as a whole; so that each competitor has to pick, not those faces which he himself finds prettiest, but those which he thinks likeliest to catch the fancy of the other competitors, all of whom are looking at the problem from the same point of view. It is not a case of choosing those which, to the best of one's judgment, are really the prettiest, nor even those which average opinion genuinely thinks the prettiest. We have reached the third degree where we devote our intelligences to anticipating what average opinion expects the average opinion to be. And there are some, I believe, who practise the fourth, fifth and higher degrees.[80]

Keynes spoke about uncertainty, the state of confidence in an economy and overturned the conventional wisdom of his time regarding the self-regulating properties of the economy. Classical economists believed that when unemployment rose, wages declined, giving businessmen a strong incentive to hire new workers. Moreover, they argued that during slumps the flood of savings would push down interest rates, encouraging businesses to draw cheap money for new investments. This way, the system would automatically correct anomalies.

Keynes questioned this logic, pointing out that the economy shrinks together with savings during crises (since people draw down their old savings in order to cover their obligations), and also that businesses cease investing and hiring when uncertainty and pessimism for the future prevail. He stressed that there is no automatic adjustment mechanism, arguing that an economy may reach equilibrium at a lower level, despite the existence of massive unemployment.

Whatever the financial figures may show, whatever rationality may dictate, is irrelevant, he said, unless confidence is restored and optimism about the future is boosted.

Keynes pointed to the need to "tame" our animal spirits in order to reverse an economy's decline. He introduced the concept of effective demand—the enhancement of demand through public expenditure and investment, designed to counter the private sector's unwillingness to take action. This, he maintained, can cover the deficit of confidence during crises and restore the smooth functioning of the economy. That said, Keynes was not an advocate of permanent government intervention in economic activity, nor did he encourage excessive public spending. He was in favor of moderately dynamic intervention, designed to help capitalism regain its footing during a difficult period.

The General Theory of Employment, Interest and Money was an instant success, securing Keynes a place in the pantheon of the great sages. Keynesian economic theory soon gained ideological preeminence, and after 1940 it prevailed in both Europe and America. However, after the 1960s, interest in Keynesian ideas started to wane.

THE BEHAVIORAL REVOLUTION

In the mid-1940s the concept of the economic-rational man and the entire structure founded on it came under heavy fire. Developments in psychology, biology, neurophysiology, neurochemistry, and other scientific fields opened new vistas regarding how we understand human beings.

The Nobel laureate and multi-scientist—economist, sociologist, psychologist, and social scientist—Herbert A. Simon (1916–2001), in his revolutionary work *Administrative Behavior: A Study of Decision-Making Processes in Administrative Organization* (1947), presented strong arguments that economic actors (individuals and organizations) have limited cognitive and computing capabilities and that therefore, their rationality is finite. In the real world, he stated, it is highly improbable that someone will be able to identify all available alternatives or determine all the consequences resulting from each of these alternatives, in order to reach a rational decision. Simon introduced the concept of uncertainty in decision making and questioned the neoclassical assertions that the free determination of prices, combined with perfect competition, led to optimization—in other words, the achievement of the best possible outcome. Simon maintained that the market mechanism may indeed lead to equilibrium, but this equilibrium may be far from optimum.

The development of cognitive psychology, after the 1960s, dealt a heavy blow to the neoclassical view. Cognitive psychologists study mental processes, focusing on perception, memory, language use, attention, problem solving, and so on. They examined how economic decisions are made under conditions of uncertainty, focusing on the behavior of consumers and investors, and tested in practice the hypothesis of the rationality of economic actors, which they disproved. They showed that traditional economic models are not adequate, since they do not take into account the cognitive, emotional, and social factors that determine, to a great extent, human behavior and, consequently, economic action.

In 1971, Amos Tversky (1937–1996) and Daniel Kahneman revolutionized social sciences, quashing many certainties, with the publication of their historic article "Judgment Under Uncertainty: Heuristics and Biases." In it they argued that, when making judgments or decisions, people do not behave in accordance with the model of expected utility, but employ a series of heuristic principles.[81] These are simple rules that individuals learn through experience and that lead to swift solutions and decisions. However, these decisions are not always correct, let alone rational. In the following years, many cognitive and empirical psychologists conducted impressive experiments showing that human behavior and decision making is much different from what we—until recently—believed with great certainty.

All these inquiries, and many more regarding the inconvenient angles of human behavior, will be examined in Part Three of this book.

6

THE NEOCLASSICAL EMPIRE

The nuclear bomb that was dropped by the behaviorists and the mounting criticism from other economists were met with Olympian calm by the neoclassical economists. They ignored them all. They did not concern themselves with their critics' findings, believing that they were irrelevant and did not affect their theoretical structure. Their response was to produce even more complex mathematics and equations. "Those who can, do science; those who can't, prattle about its methodology" was the derisive comment of Paul Samuelson (1915–2009), the first economist to apply, in economics, mathematical models that had been developed for the study of thermodynamics.

THE ORIGINS

Thorstein Veblen was the first person, in 1900, to use the term *neoclassical theory* to describe the efforts of Alfred Marshall and his fellow travelers to reposition economics on solid scientific foundations.[82]

The origins of neoclassical economics can be traced to the end of the nineteenth century. From 1871 to 1874, the economists Leon Warlas

(1834–1910), Carl Menger (1840–1921), and William Stanley Javons (1835–1882) published three landmark works in the development of economic science. Their work led to the so-called marginalist revolution and laid the foundations for neoclassical theory. The main aim of the new theory was to formulate general economic laws, having as a starting point the principle of methodological individualism, the idea that everything can be explained and interpreted on the basis of individual behavior.

After that, the torch was passed to great economists, such as F. Edgeworth, A. Pigou, J. Clark, and V. Pareto, whose work was instrumental to the theoretical founding, establishment, and dissemination of neoclassical economics. As discussed above, the most prominent among them was Alfred Marshall. Marshall minimized any differences with the classical school and systematized neoclassical theory. His successors followed on the path he had paved, making corrections in order to achieve a more rigorous scientific structure.

However, the man who elevated neoclassical theory to the highest pedestal was Lionel Robbins (1898–1984). At the age of thirty-one he became a professor at the London School of Economics, and he worked methodically to give neoclassical theory its final form, removing all traces of anything that might be ambiguous or abstruse. He gave the theory internal cohesion and armed it with a powerful mathematical arsenal, succeeding in establishing economics and neoclassical orthodoxy as a hard, pure science equal to physics, free of any value judgment[83] and able, using strictly scientific tools, to extract universally applicable economic conclusions.

THE NEOCLASSICAL VIEW

But what do neoclassical economists say? Neoclassical theory is founded on the exchange value of goods. According to price theory, the value of goods is determined by their exchange relationships, as formed by the mechanism of supply and demand. The neoclassical theoretical structure lacks the concept of money.

Browsing the introductory textbook to my undergraduate course in economics at the University of Piraeus, I read that price theory is a language-dialect that studies idealized problems and does not refer to specific cases.[84] It was as simple as that.

The goods and the preferences of individuals that participate in the market are taken for granted, and individuals, acting in a purely rational manner, make selections based only on maximizing their utility. As the economist Kenneth Arrow points out, "All social interactions are after all interactions among individuals."[85] Consequently, in the world of business, individuals—*Homo economicus*—rather than firms make all the critical decisions that direct economic activity.[86]

Neoclassical economists claim that the individual is to economy and society exactly what the atom is to chemistry. All economic phenomena can be reduced to the actions of individuals, and whatever happens in the economy can be explained on the basis of individual behavior. There are no social classes, only individuals—pleasure-seeking machines that, either as consumers or as producers, live and breathe to maximize their utility (or their profits, in the case of producers). Neoclassical theorists introduced rational and selfish human behavior into their models as a permanent and irremovable fact. According to their logic, rational persons think marginally; that is, they are always able to estimate the additional benefit gained from an action and the additional cost this action incurs. In other words, they compare marginal benefits to marginal costs and decide whether to act or not. A rational individual will act only if the benefit derived from an action is larger than its cost. Moreover, in order to buttress their model, neoclassical theorists made another important assumption: All the rational choices of individuals are consistent. Thus, if an individual chooses action A instead of action B and action B instead of action C, then it understood that he or she will also choose A instead of C.

Perfect competition was another founding assumption of the neoclassical universe. This is a purely intellectual creation. In perfectly competitive markets, there is such a large number of buyers and sellers that influencing the price of a good (or a factor of production) is impossible. All products are totally homogeneous, buyers and sellers are fully aware of market conditions and the alternatives available to them, there is complete freedom of entry and exit for both buyers and sellers, and everyone behaves rationally in order to maximize the satisfaction of self-interest.

In the neoclassical model, the free market economy was a perfect, self-regulating entity that would generate the maximum economic result, provided that market forces were unfettered, free of any intervention or regulations.

Acknowledging that perfect competition is an ideal concept, neoclassical economists dedicated great time and effort to study imperfect markets. Nonetheless, their entire intellectual effort is based on the orthodox view that even an approximation of the features of perfect competition will produce better economic results.

In the end, neoclassical, unlike classical, economists shifted their attention from the study of the long-term dynamics of the capitalist system to equilibrium in individual markets. The great questions that preoccupied the pioneers of economic science were cast aside, and the entire intellectual effort of orthodox economists was focused on the search for equilibrium and a "pursuit of ever increasing rigor."[87]

THE NEOCLASSICAL "EQUILIBRIUM"

Since the very beginning, theorists were concerned mainly with producing a rigorously structured system to prove that maximizing the efficiency of production was a natural consequence of the operation of a free competitive market.[88]

The Newtonian concept of equilibrium was introduced to economics by Alfred Marshall, who deeply believed in the self-regulating nature of the economic world. The neoclassical school believed that a free market always leads to equilibrium, which is the natural state of an economy. Gradually, the search for this "natural" equilibrium became an obsession.

When theoretical economists refer to the concept of equilibrium, they do not mean what most of us understand, namely a point where supply satisfies demand. Neoclassical equilibrium is a very abstract concept. In order to reach this ideal equilibrium, all data under consideration are assumed beforehand to be fixed, stable, and unchanged forever. The theoretical roots of the concept of general equilibrium transcend the concept of time: Equilibrium is achieved through time, until the end of time.[89] Yesterday, today, and tomorrow are merged into an eternal now. Just like conventional physics, neoclassical economics does not distinguish between the present and the future and claims that, if the initial conditions are known, then we can predict the future and reconstruct the past.

Based on its assumptions regarding perfect competition and *Homo economicus*, the neoclassical school showed that a form of stationary, motionless, and given capitalism reaches equilibrium and distributes resources in the best possible manner. Thus economics adopted a static approach, assuming that the influences of individual variables cancel each other out, leading to a stable and unchangeable world, a state of perfect equilibrium—a state that has never existed and can never exist in reality.

In 1954, Arrow and Gerard Debreu employed advanced mathematics to show that, under conditions of perfect competition, the actions of individual agents lead to general equilibrium, ensuring at the same time the optimum distribution of resources. This means that they lead the economy to the best point it can reach, the point of Pareto efficiency, or Pareto optimality. Beyond that point there can be no redistribution of resources that makes an individual better off without simultaneously making someone else worse off. In a nutshell, the free, unfettered operation of the market mechanism leads an economy to the optimum point it can possibly achieve.

Proving the theory of general equilibrium became the philosopher's stone, the hard core of neoclassical theory. Having proved that such general competitive equilibrium is possible, the neoclassical school asserted that market economy not only can be, but deserves to be, the center of economic theory.[90]

Nonetheless, general economic equilibrium can be proved mathematically only by making a series of unrealistic assumptions; even small deviations from the initial ideal conditions are enough to negate this proof. Without getting into much detail, I will stress only this: For the general equilibrium model to function, markets have to be not only competitive, but also complete. A market is considered to be complete when every future transaction, which depends on the future state of the economy, can be discounted today. In other words, individuals must be able not only to evaluate all available goods at the time equilibrium is reached, but also to compare them with tomorrow's goods!

All this happens without the existence of any money in the economy. Neoclassical economists believed that money is neutral, just a means of exchanging goods that does not affect the real economy. But reality forced them to acknowledge that monetary policy—the quantity of money circulating in a society—can affect the economy, albeit only in the short term. In the long term, monetary policy has no effect on the economy.

General equilibrium was such an unrealistic concept that soon neoclassical economists had to turn to the idea of partial equilibrium in order to analyze everyday, real-world economic problems.[91] Nonetheless, they did not yield an inch in their beliefs about the importance and accuracy of general equilibrium and the uncontested superiority of neoclassical theory.

The general equilibrium theory managed to establish a theoretical foundation but lost all contact with reality. Increasingly resembling mathematicians, neoclassical economists broke away from reality and everyday problems, developing theories applicable only to the imaginary economic universe of their own creation. It was theory for the sake of theory. As Maurice Allais wrote, a large part of modern economic literature gradually came under the control of pure mathematics, and economists became absorbed in the creation of theorems, forsaking the analysis of reality.[92] One winner of the Nobel Prize in Economics, Wassily Leontief, points out that "continued preoccupation with imaginary, hypothetical, rather than observable reality has...led to a distortion" of the purpose of economists.[93]

In this parallel universe, there were no limitations. Neoclassical economists, confident that they had mastered absolute knowledge, believed that their theory was universally applicable to all societies—not only those of the present, but also those of the past and the future. Given the rationality of individual agents, they asserted that they were able to provide answers for every aspect of social life where rationality was applicable.

THE RISE OF THE CHICAGO SCHOOL

In the 1960s, when Keynesian ideas still loomed large, the University of Chicago became the birthplace of a dissident core of economists who envisioned the rebirth of capitalism—to be precise, the rebirth of pure capitalism, free of any government intervention. This core, which evolved into the prominent Chicago school, became a bastion of neoliberalism and attracted some of the brightest minds of the twentieth century, including Frank Knight, Ronald Coase, Milton Friedman, George Stigler, Robert E.

Lucas, Richard Posner, Eugene Fama, Friedrich Hayek and others, many of whom received a Nobel Prize in Economics. The Chicago school is characterized by a deep belief in total economic freedom and the efficiency of free markets, and it rejects all efforts to intervene or regulate. It advocates extreme individualism and the need to limit as much as possible the state's involvement in economic activity. It advocates the privatization of all public services, including education, health, even parts of the armed forces.

"Less state is best government" is the neoliberal-neoconservative motto. In a few words, they deify complete economic freedom, market enterprise, and private enterprise and demonize government involvement with economic life as being wasteful and inefficient. According to the neoliberals, any redistributive intervention reduces not only freedom, but also the efficiency of the system. All government intervention, including any type of taxation, is called theft.[94]

The economists of the Chicago school developed many new theories of importance to the neoclassical structure. According to Milton Friedman's monetary theory, fluctuations in the supply of money (i.e., the printing of new money or the removal of liquidity whenever deemed necessary) have a decisive effect on the short-term course of the economy and the smoothing out of the business cycle. Another very important theoretical approach was the efficient market hypothesis (EMH), developed by Eugene Fama, which concerns the way information is incorporated by rational investors in the prices of the assets they invest in. According to this theory, all past information is useless in efficient markets, since it is immediately reflected in prices. Moreover, factors such as fear or optimism should not have any effect on financial markets. Fama demonstrated the efficiency of free money and capital markets and their ability to always determine the "right" prices.

Moreover, neoclassical economists absorbed certain Keynesian elements in an effort to unify economics, producing the so-called neoclassical synthesis. With great certainty, Paul Samuelson argued that economists had stopped being "Keynesian economists" or "anti-Keynesian economists." He stressed that 90 percent of American economists "worked toward a synthesis of whatever is valuable in older economics and in modern theories," thus creating neoclassical economics, which was "accepted," as he noted, "in its broad outlines by all but about 5 percent of extreme left wing and right wing writers."[95]

Thanks to its systematic work and unwavering belief in the power of neoclassical theory and the superiority of pure capitalism, the Chicago school gradually consolidated its presence and expanded its influence in the academic and political worlds. Milton Friedman's book *Capitalism and Freedom* (1962) became the ideological beacon of neoliberalism. Friedman argued that economic freedom is not only a crucial component of individual liberty, but also a necessary condition for political freedom. "Underlying most arguments against the free market is a lack of belief in freedom itself," he stressed.[96]

The 1970s saw the rapid rise of the Chicago school and the decline of Keynesianism. In 1971, President Richard Nixon echoed a famous statement first made in 1965 by Milton Friedman: "We are all Keynesians now." However, the countdown to Keynesianism's undoing had already begun. The collapse of the Bretton Woods system of fixed exchange rates, the oil shock of 1973, and the emergence of new economic problems, such as stagflation—sluggish economic growth combined with a high rate of inflation and unemployment—impaired the reliability of Keynesian prescriptions and faith in the efficiency of government intervention in the economy, paving the way for the advent of neoliberal ideas.

With economies on both sides of the Atlantic plagued by recession, Margaret Thatcher in the U.K. and Ronald Reagan in the U.S., deeply influenced by the work and ideas of Milton Friedman, launched a full-frontal attack on the government sector, which they viewed as inefficient and wasteful. Promising sweeping reforms aimed at drastically reducing the government's role in the economy, both rose to power* and dynamically and resolutely embarked on an effort to turn neoliberal teachings into action. The star of neoliberalism was starting to rise.

In the following years this star shone bright on the horizon, and after the sudden collapse of actually existing socialism in 1989, all dissenters were weakened and all advocates of the public sector lost their voice. No one could produce convincing arguments against the free economy and the absolute efficiency of markets.

"THERE IS NO OTHER ALTERNATIVE"

The universal ideological dominion of neoliberal-neoconservative views culminated in the famous Washington Consensus. In 1989, President Reagan commissioned the codification of neoliberal policies into ten key policy measures, which would become the ideological compass for all countries wishing to taste the fruit of the new economic era. These measures were the essence of the economic policies advocated by the U.S. Treasury, the International Monetary Fund (IMF), and the World Bank.

Originally this codification of policy measures was aimed at dealing with the economic crisis that had plagued Latin American countries since the 1980s. However, the Washington Consensus proposals soon were declared to be the economic orthodoxy that all countries wishing to become members of the new, global economy should adopt. The neoliberal "decalogue" called for fiscal austerity and balanced budgets, reduction of government expenditures, liberalization of international trade through the abolition of barriers, privatization of state enterprises, and the deregulation of markets.

---

* Margaret Thatcher became prime minister in 1979, and Ronald Reagan was elected president in 1980.

Any country that found itself in financial distress and sought the assistance of the IMF had to commit to implementing a set of reforms based on these ten neoliberal commandments.

The Washington Consensus did not aspire to be just another economic policy alternative. Neoclassical neoliberals saw themselves as the bearers of the absolute truth and their policy as the only solution. Margaret Thatcher's famous slogan, "There is no other alternative," perfectly summed up the neoliberal rationale.

PART TWO

ON CRISES

1

THE INCONVENIENT REALITY

Modern economic theory has little to say about economic crises. There is not much room in it for doubt and uncertainty. Given the rationality of individuals, crises are merely small-scale episodes—anomalies that are soon corrected.

The theorists claim that each crisis is unique and has its own special characteristics. There are no common features, they insist; therefore crises cannot be scientifically studied as a single phenomenon.

According to the theory, everything works like clockwork. If certain individuals (and, by extension, firms) make erroneous choices (rationality does not preclude errors), then other market participants will rush to take advantage of these errors, swiftly correcting the anomaly. Those who acted erroneously will soon realize their error and learn from it. Rational individuals may make mistakes from time to time, but they learn from these mistakes, never repeat them, and improve themselves.

Moreover, the theory says that despite its flaws (neoclassical economists acknowledge that conditions of perfect competition do not actually exist), the free-market mechanism functions in the best possible manner, efficiently determining prices. Prices, as set by the forces of supply and demand, are always fair reflections of real value. There are no "hidden" values or other anomalies. Firm belief in the rationality of individuals leaves no room for accepting concepts such as speculation or instability. At any given time, the market reflects reality and leads to optimality, provided that it operates freely, without any intervention or any meaningless, inefficient regulation. The closer we get to the conditions of perfect competition, the closer both the economy and society get to optimality.

Finally, markets and rational actors—firms and households—do not require any kind of guidance or protection. The system will balance itself in the best possible manner and will find its way. Any central intervention might offer some short-term relief, but it could also sow the seeds of even more serious anomalies and problems.

According to mainstream economic theory, free-market capitalism is more or less perfect and stable, provided that it can operate without any hindrance. But if everything works like clockwork, as the theory claims, then why is the economy frequently hit by violent crises? Why do we see extreme volatility and instability, even in foreign exchange and stock markets, which approximate the features of perfect competition like no other market?

Obviously, there are crises because there are no perfect and stable conditions in real life. Reality is infinitely more complex, multifarious, and chaotic to fit in any refined mathematical model. Unfortunately, reality is too inconvenient for elegant mathematical-economic theories.

2

STORIES ABOUT CRISES

Going back in economic history, we can see that all economic theories, no matter how convincing and irrefutable they seemed to be for a while, were finally swept away by a sudden, violent, and unexpected financial crisis that undermined the theoretical certainties.

The Great Depression of 1929 overturned the orthodoxy of classical liberal economics and led to the ascendancy of Keynesian ideas. The impasses of the 1970s led to the decline of Keynesianism and brought forth the neoliberals and neoclassical theory. The radically alternative proposal of communism, manifested in the experiment of the Soviet Union's centrally planned economy, ignominiously collapsed in 1989 under the weight of huge socioeconomic problems. The fall of the Soviet Union contributed to the reign of neoclassical beliefs and free markets; less than twenty years later, though, the financial crisis of 2007 almost confirmed Marx's prophecy regarding the collapse of capitalism, shattering neoliberal certainties and neoclassical teachings.

Obviously, financial crises are not a product of the industrial era. In the preindustrial world and in ancient times, societies were plagued by crises, but these were caused mainly by factors such as war, political instability, and epidemics, as well as natural phenomena including droughts, floods, earthquakes, and famines.

However, after the dawn of the new industrial era, instability took on a new form, fueled by purely economic causes. The periodic alternations of exuberance and panic, the business cycles that plague economies, are the only fixed variable of capitalism and are, quite possibly, the price we pay for our economic freedom. The existence of free people and free markets is coupled with excesses and instability that, sooner or later, lead to crises. These come in many forms: currency crises, banking crises, speculative stock market crises, fiscal crises, debt crises, and many more.

Professors Carmen Reinhart and Kenneth Rogoff have analyzed the "this time is different" syndrome that has been regularly appearing in societies over time. This peculiar syndrome is "rooted in the firmly held belief that financial crises are things that happen to other people in other countries at other times" and that "we are doing things better, we are smarter, we have learned from past mistakes."[1]

TULIP MANIA

The most incredible episode of financial speculation ever recorded was the tulip mania that took over the Dutch almost 400 years ago, demonstrating human irrationality in all its glory. Strange as it seems, the assets that led to this incredible speculative bubble were not stocks or real estate or some precious metal, but tulip bulbs!

These colorful, exotic flowers were introduced to the Netherlands around 1562, possibly from Constantinople, and were gradually turned into objects of adoration and ostentation, sparking a frenzy that swept the entire country. The phenomenon left an indelible mark on the history of speculation.

In the 1630s, following the end of Spanish rule, a wind of optimism blew in Holland. Economy and commerce were growing fast, and most people regarded the future with confidence. For some obscure reason, tulips came into fashion, and gradually their conspicuous display became a means of winning social recognition. Everybody wanted to show off their culture and good taste through these pretty blooms. Increased demand for tulip bulbs fueled a huge rise in their price, and soon they became objects of unbridled speculation. At a time when the average income was 150 florins, per year, the price of the rarest tulip bulbs was 1,000 florins in 1623, rose to 1,200 florins in 1624, climbed to 2,000 florins in 1625, and jumped to 5,500 florins in early 1637.[2] Shortly before the crash, a bulb weighing almost thirty-three grams, called the Viceroy, was auctioned for 4,200 florins.[3]

Dutch society was seized by a mania. Tulips were exchanged not only for money but also for land, property, even livestock. A tulip bulb could be traded for a house on Amsterdam's most beautiful canal. Investing in bulbs became—this is what most people believed, at least—a surefire method of getting rich. You just had to buy a bulb and wait for a few months!

In February 1637, though, the dream was over. Some foresighted, or just plain lucky, people decided, without any apparent reason, to sell their bulbs. The supply could not be absorbed by new investors, and soon many others followed the initial sellers' lead. Sales turned into mass disposals, which finally led to panic and financial meltdown.

Prices crashed, and those left holding tulip bulbs—many of whom had sold their houses or taken loans—went bankrupt. Overnight, respectable traders were turned to beggars, and many noblemen saw their wealth vanish into thin air. The decline in prices led to a decline in economic activity.[4]

THE WONDERFUL MR. LAW

John Law was born in Edinburgh in 1671 and was introduced to economics by his father, a goldsmith.[5] In 1715 Law found himself in France, which was then bankrupt as a result of wars and an overall chaotic economic situation. In France, Law became friends with the regent, Philippe II, Duke of Orléans, and offered him advice on how to fill the empty royal coffers. Law's main idea was to issue paper money instead of metal coins. He believed that boosting the money supply would boost economic activity and, consequently, the sovereign's revenues. It was a pioneering idea, and many years later, in the modern era, it would be widely applied.

In 1716 Law made use of his connections in high places and founded the Banque Générale Privée, which had the right to issue banknotes (paper money), and put his idea into practice. In 1719 the bank was renamed Banque Royale, with the regent as its principal shareholder. The royal seal increased the bank's credibility, and, not letting this opportunity pass, Law started to print huge quantities of banknotes.

At the same time, the bank acquired the Mississippi Company (renamed Compagnie d' Occident), which did business in the expansive Louisiana Territory of North America (not to be confused with the U.S. state of the same name), which then belonged to France. The Mississippi Company became a center of speculation, capturing the imagination of the public with the supposedly vast gold reserves of Louisiana and the promise of exorbitant profits that would be generated by the company's trade with France's colonies. In addition, the company was granted the right to collect all direct and indirect taxes in France. The company's share price, which stood at 500 *livres* in January 1719, rose to almost 10,000 *livres* by the end of the year!

The end came in mid-1720. The issuance of an excessive amount of banknotes caused inflation, and an increasing number of people sought to exchange their banknotes for gold.* Moreover, as is usually the case, the great expectations surrounding the fabled gold deposits of Louisiana were not fulfilled. In July 1720, almost fifteen people died in front of the bank as they tried to convert their banknotes into gold, and the bank was forced to announce that it was unable to make any such exchanges. Law's creation collapsed. In just a few days, hundreds of millionaires turned into paupers. By the end of the year, all had been lost, and Law was forced to flee the country. The "Mississippi bubble," as it went down in history, caused a huge financial crisis in France and seriously impaired the public trust in paper money and the country's banking system.

The frenzied ride of the Mississippi Company coincided with the emergence of the South Sea Company bubble in Britain, whose bursting in 1720 brought many investors to ruin. In both cases, the rapid increase in the supply of credit from newly established banks was instrumental to the creation of the bubble.[6] Since the stockholders of these two companies included investors from various European countries, the repercussions of the crises reverberated all over Europe.

THE WONDER OF THE IRON ROAD

The railway was born in England around 1830, and the Manchester-Liverpool line became the first commercially successful railroad.[7] The railway was one of the greatest technological innovations of all time, and its diffusion unified the globe, drastically reducing distances. Journeys that

---

* *Initially, each banknote corresponded to a certain quantity of gold, and its holder could exchange it for gold.*

took weeks in the pre-railway era could now be completed in a few days, or even hours. The railway was seen as "the very symbol of man's triumph through technology."[8] Soon, the expectations surrounding the potential and the prospects of this novel technology gave rise to an investment frenzy that swept Britain in the early 1840s.

The country's businessmen, being the greatest beneficiaries of the Industrial Revolution, had accumulated huge sums of money that they desperately sought to invest. The railway presented a golden opportunity, and the new communication medium of that time, the newspaper, played a decisive role in raising expectations. The railway mania was fanned by a growing number of railway papers such as the *Railway Express*, the *Railway Code*, and the *Railway Standard*.[9] Moreover, the creation of organized stock markets enabled even small savers to buy shares. What really mattered for investors was that they could purchase these "gold bearing" shares by depositing an amount equal to just 10 percent of their value, actually obtaining call options on stock. In other words, the shares were bought on credit.

Dozens of investment firms focused on the development and operation of railway networks sprang up everywhere. Their shares were promoted as "risk free" investments, and many hundreds of small investors, as well as many Members of Parliament, bought in, using not only all their savings but also money that they borrowed. At the peak of their growth, in 1844–1846, these investment firms constructed thousands of kilometers of railways. But these railways did not correspond to any actual need.

The crash landing would soon come. Near the end of 1845, the Bank of England raised interest rates, discontinuing the flow of ample investment-speculative capital to railways. The rise in stock prices was over, to be followed by a steep fall. All investment in the construction of new lines froze, dozens of companies went under, and shareholders lost their fortunes.

THE PANIC OF 1873

No one learned their lesson. It took a mere thirty years for the debacle of the 1840s to be forgotten and for a new investment fever to spread, once again centered on railways.

This time, though, the consequences were much greater and wider. Historians believe that the crisis of 1873 was the Victorian equivalent of the Great Crash of 1929; it is also considered to be the first really global financial crisis.

The inglorious end of the 1848 revolts* that shook Europe's old regimes from the ground up was followed by a period of unprecedented economic growth. A wind of optimism blew around the globe, and the strong growth rates made many people believe in the "new" economy's potential for unlimited expansion.

The revolutions in transport and in communications brought on by the railway and the telegraph, respectively, led to the first wave of globalization, giving a huge boost to trade. Distances were brought to nothing, expanding the boundaries of the commercially exploitable world. At the same time, new liberal legislation swept away old barriers, leading to full openness in international trade.

Optimism about the future abounded. Investors from Britain and Europe, full of confidence and certainty about tomorrow, invested heavily in railways and in other ambitious projects in the U.S. and many Latin American countries. The rapid growth of the railways caused big rises in the prices of metals and other commodities, spurring the growth of heavy industry. In addition, war reparations paid by France to Germany after the

---

* The European Revolutions of 1848, were a series of political upheavals throughout Europe in 1848. It remains the most widespread revolutionary wave in European history, but within a year, reactionary forces had regained control, and the revolutions collapsed.

Franco-Prussian War (May 1871) fueled a large speculative boom in the property and stock markets of Germany and Austria.[10]

Once again, a painful end came—this time in 1873, when the illusion of unlimited growth was shattered. Many thousands of "miles of American railroads collapsed into bankruptcy," along with banks, investors, and other large industrial enterprises, as metal prices plummeted. "[A]lmost half of the blast-furnaces in the main iron-producing countries of the world stopped,"[11] owing to the drop in demand.

In May 1873, the Vienna stock exchange crashed, and the New York Stock Exchange was closed for ten days. In the next years, "German share values fell by some 60 per cent."[12]

1929: THE GREAT DEPRESSION

The Great Depression, which began in 1929, is one of the few financial crises that have been deeply etched in our collective memory, and its specter still scares us. The size, severity, duration, and consequences of the Great Depression cannot be compared to anything either before or since.

A few months prior to the collapse of the New York Stock Exchange, there was no doubting the growth potential of the American economy and the stock market. This had been preceded by a speculative binge, based on ample liquidity and a firm, universal belief that one could become infinitely rich through the stock market.

Investment trusts were the ostensible great innovation of that time, attracting the interest of small investors, and these trusts were instrumental in the creation of the bubble. However, the big push forward was, once again, provided by ample liquidity and easy credit. In the spring of 1927, the Federal Reserve System of the U.S. reduced interest rates. The market was flooded with cheap money, the majority of which was channeled to the stock market. Brokers, firms, and retail investors borrowed excessively in order to invest—actually, to gamble—even more, driving share prices higher and higher. Government officials, esteemed university professors, bankers, market pundits, and respectable businessmen spared no opportunity to trumpet the strong growth prospects and the huge development potential of the economy.

The first disturbances in the stock market came in September 1929. Irving Fisher, a renowned professor of economics, wrote in *The New York Times* that "there may be a recession in stock prices, but not anything in the nature of a crash." However, this recession was not contained, and Thursday, October 24, 1929, also known as Black Thursday, has gone down in history as the day of the crash of 1929. As professor John Kenneth Galbraith writes in his book *The Great Crash, 1929,* "by eleven o'clock the market had degenerated into a wild, mad scramble to sell."[13]

Despite some coordinated efforts to support the market, the results were poor. A few days later, total destruction ensued. Tuesday, October 29, 1929, was the worse trading day in the history of the NYSE (till then), and an increasing number of people started to realize that the mechanics of incessant rise could also work the other way around. "In a single day, the rise in values of the entire preceding year had been erased [and a] few weeks later, $30 billion of 'wealth' had vanished into thin air."[14]

While everything was falling apart, the powerful (till yesterday) market pundits kept mumbling assurances that the economy remained sound and its prospects positive. But soon the panic started to spread in commodity markets as well as in the real economy.

The crisis plunged the U.S. economy into a deep recession and quickly affected many countries. Many economists believe that one of the main causes of the Great Depression was the infamous gold standard.* The central banks, in their effort to defend the gold standard, proceeded to large interest rate increases, leading to the collapse of their countries' economies. Economic activity came to a standstill.

The crisis had devastating effects on developed and developing countries alike. International trade shrank, unemployment soared, production declined, incomes were radically curtailed. In 1933, the U.S. GDP was one-third lower than in 1929, and thirteen million people (one in four) were jobless and living under terrible conditions. In Britain, unemployment rose to 26.6 percent in 1931, and in Germany it exceeded 33.7 percent. The Great Crash put an end to the early era of globalization, as most countries adopted policies aimed at restricting international trade and imposed strict controls on capital flows. This climate of international suspicion, introversion, and control that prevailed throughout the 1930s changed only after World War II.

THE DEBT CRISIS OF LATIN AMERICAN COUNTRIES

In the 1960s, the countries of Latin America, especially Brazil, Argentina, and Mexico, became the focus of investor interest thanks to their high growth rates. The boom in commodity prices gave a great boost to the commodity-rich economies of this region.[15]

Foreign banks, especially American ones, rushed to exploit these favorable conditions, offering low-interest loans. Debt capital provided a further boost to economic development, while strong economic fundamentals encouraged banks to infuse fresh capital into the countries of the region. For a while, everything seemed to be right as rain.

---

* The gold standard was an exchange-rate system based on gold. Each country determined a fixed exchange rate of its national currency against gold. In theory, gold was convertible to currency and currency to gold at this fixed price. The standard imposed monetary restrictions, thus limiting the issuing capacity of monetary authorities.

However, the gradual deterioration of economic conditions, especially following oil price hikes in 1973–1974 and a rise in interest rates, stemmed the flow of capital to the countries of Latin America, making it difficult for them to service their debt. The problem was exacerbated by the devaluation of the local currencies against the dollar. Given that the countries of the region borrowed in dollars, the devaluation of their currencies made debt servicing impossible.

In 1981, stock markets were rattled by concerns over the ability of the region's countries to service their debt, and a few months later these concerns were justified: In August 1982, Mexico's Secretary of Finance, Jesus Silva-Herzog, announced that the country would no longer honor its debts. "Within a few months the crisis had spread through most of Latin America."[16] Banks stopped extending new loans to the countries of the region and resorted to portfolio restructuring in order to prevent panic from spreading in the entire banking system. The discontinuation of foreign capital inflows caused shocks in the economies of the region, leading to many years of recession with high unemployment and reduced output and incomes. This tough period in history is known as *"La Década Perdida"* ("The Lost Decade") of Latin American countries.

JAPAN'S LOST DECADE

Japan is also haunted by its own "lost" decade. In the mid-1980s Japan began to see particularly high growth rates. Driven by ample liquidity, itself the product of the central bank's low-interest policy and great expectations regarding the country's prospects, a huge speculative bubble emerged in the property and stock markets. According to the prophecies of that time, Japan would soon become the greatest economic and technological power on the globe, leaving the U.S. on the sidelines.

On December 29, 1989, the Nikkei index rose above 39,000 points, from 10,000 points just a few years earlier. House prices doubled and commercial property prices trebled. The country's market capitalization—the total market value of all stocks—exceeded that of the U.S., "which had twice Japan's population and more than twice its gross domestic product."[17]

The unraveling began in 1990, when the Bank of Japan started to increase interest rates in order to curb speculation. In early 1991, the party came to an abrupt end: The stock market crashed and, at the same time, the property market bubble burst. The economy was trapped in low growth rates and stagnation, and the dynamism was never regained, despite the fact that the central bank reduced its interest rates to zero and the government spend huge sums to boost the economy.

The 2000s became Japan's Lost Decade as the fall in the stock exchange continued. In 2009 the Nikkei index stood at 7,050 points, the lowest level of the past 27 years.

THE ASIAN TIGER CRISIS

The economic "tigers" of Asia—Hong Kong, Taiwan, South Korea, Singapore, Thailand, and so on—were considered for quite a few years to be models of economic growth, showing impressive rates that ranged from 8 percent to 12 percent per year. Everybody was enchanted by the Asian economic miracle. The countries of the region were lauded not only for their fast growth but also for their effective fiscal policies, monetary stability, and substantial increase in savings. There was not a single cloud on the horizon.

The opening of the financial sector facilitated the inflow of foreign capital, while high economic growth acted as a magnet for foreign banks and investors. Just as in the previous cases, the new funds accelerated growth, which in turn attracted new debt capital. However, out of all this optimism and these great expectations gradually rose a huge property and stock market bubble. "By early 1996 the economies of Southeast Asia were starting to bear a strong family resemblance to Japan's 'bubble economy' of the late 1980s."[18]

The usual crash landing occurred in July 1997. The trouble erupted as a result of the devaluation of Thailand's currency (the baht), the move causing a panic that would soon become a full-blown financial crisis, dragging along the economies of other East Asian countries. Just as in Latin America, the situation was exacerbated by the pegging of local currencies to the dollar. The authorities of these countries tried to react and, in a bid to support their national currencies, increased interest rates and spent their dollar reserves. However, high interest rates were not enough to contain the panic or to attract foreign capital. The sudden and sizable increase in the cost of money not only failed to save local currencies but caused the bankruptcy of many local industries, which were unable to honor their debts.

The crisis left the world shocked, as it involved economically advanced countries that, in theory, were free of problems. As a result of globalization, capital fled at unprecedented speeds, causing markets all over the globe to plummet.

THE ATHENS STOCK MANIA

By early 1997, more and more Greeks were discovering the charm of the stock market. Just as the Dutch had done 400 years ago, the Greeks found a "surefire" and "fast" way of becoming rich.

After many years of fluctuating in a narrow range from 750 to 1,100 points, in autumn 1997 the General Index of the Athens Stock Exchange closed at 1,688.51—a historical high. The prospect of hosting the 2004 Olympics, the anticipation of European economic support as part of the Community Support Framework, and Greece's progress toward joining the Economic and Monetary Union (EMU) were the key factors that fueled optimism regarding the future of the Greek economy. The bull run in the stock market was sustained, gaining even more speed in March 1998, when the drachma joined the Exchange Rate Mechanism of the European Monetary System.

The steady rise in share prices created the illusion that stocks provided a fast, easy, and safe way of making money. The large capital gains attracted more and more fledgling investors in search of a sure deal. Everybody was buying shares. Nationwide TV stations interrupted their normal programming in order to broadcast news live from the Athens Stock Exchange, and regional TV and radio stations aired live broadcasts of the entire trading session. Various nobodies, totally clueless about stocks and stock exchanges, emerged as stock trading experts, setting up investment firms and Firms for the Reception and Transmission of Orders. The country was possessed by an unprecedented mania, and during each ASE trading session all activity would cease, as everybody traded in stocks and counted their gains. In just a few days you could double your money!

Back then, there were no derivative financial products in Greece, nor the option of margin trading. So another "creative" idea was put into practice, which injected lots of borrowed money in the stock market: the so-called trading on air. Brokerage firms, taking advantage of the lack of a regulatory or supervisory framework, allowed their good clients—initially— to buy shares without paying, using their stock portfolio as collateral for these "open" purchases. Soon brokerages and investment firms, striving to attract new client-investors, were in a race to see who would offer the largest margin of trading on air. The mania reached its peak in September 1999 when the General Index of the ASE reached 6,355 points, its all-time high. Then came a precipitous fall. In the end, the capital gains, profits, and assets of the fledgling investors, which had been to a great extent based on air, proved, indeed, to be nothing but thin air: By March 2003, the General Index had crash-landed at 1,467 points, registering a loss of almost 77 percent.*

THE BUBBLE OF THE "NEW" ECONOMY

In the 1990s, the Internet came into our lives for good, creating new astonishing capabilities and huge business opportunities. It was hailed as a groundbreaking technological innovation, comparable to the advent of the railroad in the nineteenth century.

In 1995 the NASDAQ index of high-technology companies embarked on a bull run, rising from 800 points to almost 1,500 points by 1998. The party had just begun. Then came the onslaught. Dot-com companies, which were made out of nothing and did business in the virgin market of the Internet, popped up like mushrooms, and their share prices skyrocketed. Venture capitalists, mutual funds, banks, and investors from all over the world jostled to see who would get to invest more in order to secure a seat on the train of perpetual Internet-based growth. A reduction in the Federal Reserve's rates in 1998 provided a further boost to liquidity and fueled the speculative boom. In 1999 the NASDAQ high-tech index soared, and in early 2000 it broke the 5,000-point barrier. Companies with far-fetched plans promised absurd profits, and overnight their shares were publicly traded at many hundred millions of dollars, and in some cases billions of dollars.

---

* This fall was nothing compared with the one that would follow some years later during the fiscal crisis that hit Greece. On Tuesday, June 5, 2012, the ATHEX Composite Index (as the General Index was renamed) fell to 476.76 points amid political uncertainty and widespread fears of a possible exit from the euro zone.

Venerable journals and newspapers, such as *Forbes* and *The Wall Street Journal*, emphasized the great prospects of the new economy and encouraged investment in the companies of the tech sector, in the same manner that, in the past, other venerable publications had touted the great prospects of the railroad. Everybody could get rich—provided that they bought shares in the new economy.

In January 2000, America Online (AOL) acquired the mighty Time Warner, a company whose roots could be traced back to 1920. The merger, which was later described as one of the worst in history, was not based on actual capital but on a stock swap. This is how many new-economy firms, exploiting their exorbitantly high valuations, managed to take over blue-chip companies.

The spectacular rise was followed by an equally spectacular fall, and by mid-2002 the high-tech company index had fallen to 1,200 points. Many hundreds of advanced technology companies were wiped out, and five trillion dollars evaporated as a result of the crash. For example, the new AOL-TimeWarner company had a market capitalization of $350 billion just after the merger. A few years later, it was at $29 billion.

At the same time, many cases of accounting fraud were uncovered, the most striking being that involving WorldCom, which employed creative accounting to inflate its profits in order to fuel the rise of its share price. Confidence was shaken, and the U.S. Securities and Exchange Commission imposed heavy penalties on Citigroup and Merrill Lynch for misguiding investors through their valuations and analyses.

3

A VERY FAMILIAR PATTERN

Times may change, technology may transform our lives, new knowledge and experience may be added to our collective wisdom, and progress may seem astounding and undisputed. However, free-market societies are repeatedly caught in painful crises. Periods of exuberance and growth are always followed by decline, depression, and despair—again and again.

Who is to blame? We have seen that economic science ignores crises, considering them to be more or less isolated incidents. Experience, though, is painting an entirely different picture. What's really impressive is not how often crises erupt, but how similar they are. As we saw above, irrespective of era or situation, an extremely familiar pattern emerges.

Typically, crises are preceded by large-scale speculative episodes, but this does not mean that all speculative episodes lead to wider economic crises. When economic conditions are favorable, all things new—new technologies, new capabilities, new ideas—intrigue people and capture the imagination of investors. Innovation, or what passes for innovation, creates expectations and attracts capital. Capital pushes prices upward, fulfilling existing expectations and creating even greater ones. The sustained rise in prices attracts new investors, whose entry accelerates the bull run.

A key feature of each speculative episode is easy access to money. On various pretexts, the faucets of liquidity are turned on, and either directly through the banking system or indirectly by means of financial "innovations," everybody gains easy access to cheap money. Money freely flows into the economy and the party is in full swing.

Everything seems perfect, everybody is making money, and the sky seems to be the limit. Profits enhance self-confidence, and individuals, certain about their abilities, undertake new risks. More and more bankers, academics, entrepreneurs, distinguished analysts, and journalists agree that "this time is different": that the market exuberance is fully justified by "new" developments that ensure the further growth of the economy. Success makes people gullible, and all kinds of greedy, base little people, as well as common crooks, find fertile ground for action.

Profoundly confident in their knowledge and ingenuity, investors march on. As a matter of fact, this very knowledge—or, to be more precise, this supposed knowledge—quite often leads to the most irrational moves and the most spectacular disasters. When the speculative episode is still unfolding there is no room for dispute. Those who dare utter their concerns about the state of the economy and the level of indebtedness face public ridicule and are branded as foolish doomsayers. Only optimism is acceptable.

What's really amazing is not the fact that *Homo economicus* never learns from his mistakes, but how consistently we humans repeat the same mistakes again and again. From the tulip mania that swept Holland in the 1600s to the new-technology mania that took over the U.S. in 1990s, few things seem to have changed in the way we act and behave.

Every time, we go down the same path firmly certain that this time the situation will be different. Only one thing is certain, though: the end, the forced (and in most cases brutal) landing in reality. Moreover, the end comes in the same way every time. At some point the flow of debt money is interrupted, some prudent or lucky players leave the game, and panic and collapse ensue. Animal spirits roam unfettered.

However, people, and especially economists, pay very little attention to history and the teachings of the past. Economic theorists unabashedly continue to put all their intellectual efforts in building theories of a fine-tuned ideal universe, dominated by rationality, equilibrium, and confidence in the efficiency of markets.

If nothing else, history teaches us to be humble.

GOLDFISH MEMORY

A major contributor to instability is our extremely short economic—and not only economic—memory span. People quickly forget past troubles. "When the danger is over, God is forgotten," as a wise proverb says. As we have seen, it took a mere 30 years to forget the railroad debacle of the 1840s: In 1870 there was a new investment rush, once again centered on the railways.

When the same (or nearly the same) situation emerges after a certain time period in a different environment, we tend to gaze at them through a lens of optimism, to see them as totally new and different. Every crisis is succeeded by another one, right? But we are caught unawares every time, as if the new crisis were a unique, novel phenomenon that had never before occurred.

According to certain neuroscientists, we humans have a tendency to view the future with optimism, expecting things to change for the better. Optimism seems to be hardwired into the human brain.[19] The young are especially optimistic. A few years are enough to infuse society with a new batch of young people (many of whom are economists), full of self-confidence and entirely certain of their knowledge and skills. These people become the executives of banks, international organizations, and companies, or they launch new business initiatives. "The contempt of risk," Adam Smith wrote, "and the presumptuous hope of success, are in no period of life more active than at the age at which young people choose their professions."[20]

This new batch of young people are barely aware of past crises and believe that the mishaps of previous generations will not affect them. After all, no school of economics has ever offered courses like "The History of Financial Crises" or "Failure and Economic Policy." All schools of economics teach and disseminate certainties.

THE MAGNET

In each speculative episode we can find something new or something that seems to be new: some instrument or great opportunity that captures the imagination and gives rise to great expectations. This "new," innovative thing acts as a magnet, attracting capital that puts the wheels of speculation in motion. The "new" thing creates expectations; expectations attract capital; capital generates returns; and returns attract new capital. And the cycle starts again. In 1830 it was the unlimited potential of the railroad—and a hundred years later, the magic of investment trusts stoked the speculative orgy that led to the Great Depression. Later, the magnets were the huge growth opportunities of certain economies, like those of Latin America in the 1960s and the "Asian tigers" in the 1990s. In 2000, investors were intrigued by new-technology companies and the amazing potential of the "new" economy.

Innovation may indeed be real, as in the case of the railroads or the Internet, but it also may be ostensible, like tulips in Holland or securitization in 2007 (when loans were transformed into "fresh" money). It barely matters if innovation is actual or ostensible. In each speculative episode, expectations skyrocket, losing all touch with reality.

THE ACCELERATOR

Money is the great accelerator. And since money is in short supply, periods of prosperity see the emergence of various "creative" ideas, designed to satisfy the appetite of both the economy and the investors. Either in an organized manner—through borrowing and financial innovation—or in an impromptu manner—as with the "air" transactions of the Athens Stock Exchange in 1999—the market is injected with huge sums of money. The magic word is *leverage*.

Leverage amplifies results. Like the lever, which turns a small force into a larger one, leverage—borrowing—multiplies the purchasing power of each individual or organization. Using leverage, banks, firms, investment funds, and individual investors multiply their capital by factors of ten, twenty, fifty, or more. In 1845, investors could buy options on railroad shares at only 10 percent of their value. In 1928, it was the innovative investment trusts' turn to generate capital out of thin air. Today, leverage is affordable to everyone. Any private investor can speculate in currency, stock, and commodity markets with a small capital investment of $50,000 or $100,000, buying or selling positions that exceed the value of his or her money by one hundred, two hundred, or more times. In other words, with $100,000 an investor can take a $20,000,000 long or short position on the Dow Jones Industrial Average. Borrowed money flows freely.

It is no use talking about the huge flows of capital managed by commercial and investment banks, as well as the army of investment funds and large investors, which not only are instrumental to the creation of bubbles, but also exacerbate instability through the rapid movement of capital.

Quite often, supposedly conservative and wise central bankers are hidden behind large speculative episodes. Central banks can encourage or discourage borrowing by increasing or decreasing the interest rate, thus determining the supply of money in the economy. Two years before the crash of 1929, the U.S. Federal Reserve reduced its interest rates by a wide margin, and the dot-com bubble also was preceded by a large interest rate reduction. But even after the bursting of the new-economy bubble, the Fed, in an effort to soften the effects of the crisis, reduced its rates to almost zero, thus stoking the crisis of 2007.

As William McChesney Martin (1906–1998), the longest-serving chairman of the Fed, once said, the job of the central banker is to "take away the punch bowl just as the party gets going."[21] In reality, though, the central banks quite often not only fail to take away the punch bowl, but pour more alcohol into it.

IT IS COMPLICATED…

We have seen that innovation (or perceived innovation) attracts capital, capital generates returns, and returns attract new capital. Everybody gains, and the economy grows quickly. This is what economists call a virtuous cycle.

The problem is that most people do not realize that their success is driven not by their talent, but by the rising tide. They confuse having money with having skill. They firmly believe that their profits are the result of their intelligence—that they are ingenious, more capable and more clever than others. The more money they make, the more their belief in their supreme abilities is confirmed, and they take even greater risks. Investors continue to purchase shares or property, firms absorb other firms and diversify into new sectors, banks "give away" loans, small entrepreneurs take big steps, contractors build houses and malls, and so on.

All these are based on the miracle of leverage. New debt capital flows into the economy, driving prices even higher and rewarding the players with huge profits. The economy and the values are inflated, along with people's egos. Money is the yardstick of success. The more money people make, the more clever and capable society considers them to be. As Veblen said, in our modern "civilized" world men exhibit their strength and superiority through the accumulation of money and its lavish display.

Of course, when the high tide is over and the low tide sets in, leverage becomes a bludgeon that beats to death even respectable titans, like the late Lehman Brothers. As Warren Buffett said, "It's only when the tide goes out that you learn who's been swimming naked."

ALL THE THINGS WE THINK WE KNOW

Knowledge and the ability to accumulate and transfer knowledge from generation to generation constitute a unique, invaluable asset of human-kind. However, knowledge may sometimes lead us down dangerous paths. As money can be confused with skill, so can knowledge fill people with excessive self-confidence and arrogance concerning the extent and adequacy of their knowledge.

Even experts quite often overestimate their capabilities and fall prey to the illusion that their knowledge enables them to swim safely in even the deepest and most dangerous waters. In a nutshell, they think they know more than they actually do. A legendary case in point is the collapse of Long-Term Capital Management (LTCM), a fund management firm created in 1993 by the prominent economists Robert Merton and Myron Scholes. Both avid supporters of orthodox economics, the two shared the 1997 Nobel Prize in Economic Sciences for developing a method by which to determine the value of options. On the basis of this method, they created complex trading strategies that used even more complex mathematics and were supposed to eliminate risk. They invested in various geographic regions at leverage ratios of up to 50 times. Through 1997, LTCM showed enviably high returns.

However, the Russian financial crisis of August 1998 soon spread to all markets. Contrary to the predictions of the two academics and the standard risk management models, global markets moved together in the same direction: down. In just a few days, the much-touted LTCM lost not only the high returns of the previous years, but its entire capital ($4.6 billion). In September 1998, the Fed was forced to move in and bail out the firm in order to reduce the risk of a possible contamination of the banking system and to quell anxiety in the markets. It turned out that the two Nobel Prize winners did not know all they thought they knew.

More about the knowledge trap, which creates the illusion that we know more than we actually do, in the following section.

TRINKETS AND MIRRORS

At the beginning of my career as a journalist, in 1996, I worked for the *Exousia* newspaper. Initially the newspaper was extremely popular, but it soon went south. The beginning of the end was marked by an unheard-of offer:* Readers were given the opportunity to get a house of their own by collecting coupons. The offer caused a stir, but it took no deep analysis to conclude that it was financially unsound. A few months later the newspaper shut down and its readers were left holding worthless coupons. Some years later, the same publisher launched a new newspaper, which promised a new car to any reader who collected the requisite coupons. During that period I came across an old colleague from *Exousia* who told me he was collecting coupons in order to get the car. I was flabbergasted. "But," I asked, "do you really believe there is even the slightest chance of getting a new car with coupons?" Yes, he did. "The publisher has no other option," he told me confidently, "because if he fails again to make true on his offer and give away the cars, he will lose all credibility and be ruined!" As I anticipated, the offer was never realized.

People are easily impressed, and when great expectations take over, rationality goes flying out the window. This is plain foolishness, a short-circuit of reason, that can afflict even the most intelligent people. Sadly, this happens very often. The prospect of making a large, fast, and effortless profit, such as getting a car with coupons or investing in Louisiana gold or the dot-com marvel, creates such great expectations that it boggles the mind. Looking forward to huge gains, people reshape the facts to make them fit their expectations. It is the same when we buy a lottery ticket: We never consider that the possibilities of winning are just seven in a million, but we do think about how our life is going to change with the five million dollars of the New Year's Lottery. And we keep on hoping until the end.

The Dow at 40,000, The Road to Financial Freedom: Your First Million in Seven Years, No Fear of the Next Crash: Why Stocks Are Unbeatable as Long-Term Investments, The Courage to Be Rich—these are just a few of the books that sold millions of copies during periods of exuberance. Trinkets and mirrors are still doing an excellent job, even today.

---

* In Greece, many newspapers, striving to attract new readers, offer CDs, books, DVDs, even coupons for the purchase of items at supermarkets, in every issue.

For years, Bernard Madoff's clients were happily sailing along the seas of high returns, and nobody considered the possibility that these returns were bogus, the result of fraud. Bankers, institutional investors, the media, and many others heaped praise on this wizard of Wall Street, justifying the unjustifiable. Like people in love with someone who is obviously not interested in them (as sadly noted by their close friends), they keep on thinking up impossible excuses and reshaping the facts to make them fit their desires.

BASE LITTLE PEOPLE

Corruption and fraudulence are also integral parts of the inconvenient reality. The world is rife with crooks and greedy, base little people who will do anything in order to make more money.

"Who is buying these crappy subprime loans?" asked a fund manager in 2006. "Who's the idiot?" "Dusseldorf" was the calm reply of a high-ranking trader with Deutsche Bank in the United States. "Stupid Germans. They take rating agencies seriously. They believe in the rules."[22]

In 2008, Jérôme Kerviel, a trader with Société Générale, caused the French banking giant losses of $6.5 billion, throwing it into great trouble. Kerviel had been systematically breaking the rules—a practice that was tolerated, he claims, by his superiors—gambling huge sums of money on derivatives.[23]

In 2006, a bank in California lent "a Mexican strawberry picker with an income of $14,000 and no English…every penny he needed to buy a house for $724,000."[24]

Enron, one of the largest and most powerful U.S. companies, suffered a leg-endary failure in 2001. A bunch of base little people, including a person named Andrew Fastow*, Enron's CEO, and a few greedy Arthur Andersen auditors, committed the greatest corporate fraud of all time. Fastow was stealing from Enron and using accounting fraud to report increased profits, misleading shareholders and investors. All this occurred with the seal of approval of Arthur Andersen, then one of the top accounting firms in the United States.

In 2003, the investigation on the collapse of WorldCom, one of the shiniest stars of the new economy, revealed that Bernard Ebbers, the company's CEO, had been consistently fiddling with accounting data in order to report increased profits and assets, which he had inflated by $11 billion.

WorldCom lost the honor of being the greatest accounting scandal in U.S. history in 2008, when Bernard Madoff's incredible scam came to light. Delivering absurdly good and consistent results for a long time, Madoff's fund managed many billions of dollars under complete secrecy— ostensibly to prevent other funds from copying its models. Madoff was considered to be one of the most reliable money managers in the world. In the end, it was proved that he had been faking his returns and that his firm was actually the greatest Ponzi scheme ever, to the tune of $65 billion! The respectable, above-suspicion Madoff was found guilty of 11 federal offenses and was sentenced to a total of 150 years in prison.

---

* Andrew Stuart Fastow (born December 22, 1961) is an American businessman who was the chief financial officer of Enron Corporation, an energy trading company based in Houston, Texas, until the U.S. Securities and Exchange Commission opened an investigation into his and the company's conduct in 2001. Fastow was one of the key figures behind the complex web of off-balance-sheet special purpose entities (limited partnerships which Enron controlled) used to conceal their massive losses. Fastow served a six-year prison sentence for charges related to these acts.

Apparently, the distance from John Law to Bernard Madoff is not so big as we think.

IRRATIONAL EXUBERANCE

When people enjoy the sunny days of summer, they hate being told about the possibility of a harsh winter. Only optimism is acceptable. Shortly before the Great Crash, in March 1929, Paul Moritz Warburg (1868–1932), president of the International Acceptance Bank, warned that if the orgy of unrestrained speculation did not stop immediately, there would be a collapse. As he pointed out, the crash not only would be disastrous for the speculators, but would cause a widespread recession throughout the entire U.S. economy. Nobody took him seriously. Some called him old-fashioned; others accused him of having sorted the market. In the following months, as the stock market rally continued unabated, the newspapers made frequent and always ironic references to him.[25]

The term *irrational exuberance* was used in October 1996 by Alan Greenspan, then chairman of the Federal Reserve, to warn investors about the excessive rise in stock prices, especially those of the new economy. At that time, the Dow Jones Industrial Average stood at 6,000 points. A few months later the index reached the 7,000 mark, and the party had not even started yet. "You can't fight market forces," admitted Greenspan* in *The Age of Turbulence*, quoting Robert Rubin.[26] It appeared Greenspan had learned his lesson, and he neither spoke again about the stock market nor tried to put the brakes on stock prices.

---

* Robert Rubin, Secretary of the Treasury in the Clinton administration, had advised Greenspan not to meddle with the stock market. He believed that federal financial officials should not make public statements about the stock exchange. He had given three reasons for this: a) There is no way to be certain whether a market is overvalued; b) you can't fight market forces; and c) anything you say is likely to backfire and hurt your credibility.

When things go well, no one wants to listen to the naysayers. On September 1, 1999, while the Greek stock market party was in full swing, the then governor of the National Bank of Greece, Theodore Karatzas, stated, "If we wish to preserve the health of the stock market, we need coordinated interventions from the stock market and supervisory authorities, to ensure that stock values somehow correspond to reality."[27] On the day he said this, fifty stocks had closed at the maximum permitted fluctuation level (the so-called limit-up) and the General Index had closed at 5,205 points. No one listened to Karatzas. A few weeks later the index broke the 6,400 point mark.

The same thing, more or less, is what happened in 2007. The scant warnings from a few analysts and professors, like Claudio Borio of the Bank for International Settlements (BIS) and Raghuram Rajan of the University of Chicago in 2004, as well as from Nouriel Roubini in 2006, were ignored.[28]

Sadly enough, during the sunny days not even the guardians of the system would listen. In May 2000, Harry Markopolos, a securities industry executive, submitted a report to the U.S. Securities and Exchange Commission concerning Madoff's unorthodox tactics and inexplicable returns. These were followed by four more reports, with new evidence about the irrational success of the mighty Madoff, but no one, not even Markopolos's friends, would believe that the respectable Madoff could be stealing.[29] Only when the tide went out with the 2007 crisis did we learn who had been swimming naked.

4

THE 2007 CRISIS*

In case you wonder what the mistakes of people who lived in 1630, 1870, 1929, or 1960 have to do with us and our modern world, the experience of the 2007 crisis may give you an answer.

In 2008, the global economy came very close to total destruction. The United States, the metropolis of the free market, came face to face with the collapse of its banking system and, by extension, its entire economy. A few years before it would have seemed inconceivable, almost absurd, that the modern economy could be at the brink of a disaster similar to the Great Depression, which had shaken the world 80 years earlier. But the inconceivable did happen.

Conventional wisdom says that the sole culprit for the financial crisis that broke out in the summer of 2007 and almost went out of control in 2008 was the banking system: a handful of greedy bankers and the toxic investment products they created and sold all over the world.

---

* The financial meltdown is sometimes referred to as the crisis of 2007 and other times as the crisis of 2008. In fact, it began in the summer of 2007 and almost went out of control in the autumn of 2008, when Lehman Brothers collapsed.

In a few words, the story is as follows: Around the mid-2000s all moderation went out the window. Greedy bankers, blinded by exorbitant bonuses and other extraordinary benefits, went on an unprecedented tear: They lavishly gave out housing mortgages, even to people without jobs and income, and they pooled these crappy loans, securitized them, and created investment products, which were then sold all over the world. This financial alchemy of turning loans into cash was implemented for many years and was treated as a wondrous innovation.

Naturally, the stream of debt capital that was channeled into the property market drove housing prices up and led to the creation of a bubble. Sometime in 2007, the bubble burst and mortgage loans stopped being serviced, dragging down the investment products that had been based on securitization. Because these products had been sold all over the world, the crisis in the U.S. housing market was rapidly transmitted, almost causing the collapse of the financial system and the global economy.

In general, the conventional narrative of the crisis contains truths, but it represents only the tip of the iceberg. It reflects just part of a complex, dynamic reality that nurtured the crisis and finally brought the world's economies face to face with the greatest recession seen since the end of World War II.

Banks are obviously to blame for the crisis, but they are not the only culprits. A large part of the blame must also go to regulators, political leaders, rating agencies, human greed, and many, many others. Unfortunately, one of the main culprits is economics.

THE ROOTS

The macroeconomic imbalances that had been quietly developing for many years without being dealt with were the first stone in the edifice that led to the crisis of 2007. On one hand, countries such as China were pursuing a large-surplus policy while, on the other hand, nations like the United States ran big deficits. China, having learned the lessons of the Asian crisis of 1997, which put the countries of the region in a dire position because of the pressures exerted on their currencies, adopted a policy aimed at the accumulation of increased foreign currency reserves to avoid finding itself in such a position. Emphasizing exports, China accumulated huge reserves, which at the time of writing (June 2014) exceeded $4 trillion. However, China did not utilize this wealth to improve its citizens' living standards and to boost internal demand. China used its trade surplus to purchase U.S. Treasury bonds, providing the United States and, by extension, American consumers with ample liquidity.

To cut a long story short, the Chinese lent money to the United States, and the United States bought cheap Chinese industrial products in bulk. As a result, China's exports account for 60 percent of its economy, while in the United States domestic consumption accounts for 70 percent of the economy.[30]

Other Asian countries followed in China's footsteps, as did petroleum-producing countries that, helped by soaring oil prices, used their huge surpluses to purchase sovereign bonds and other securities, mainly from the United States and other developed economies. Mass investment in U.S. securities flooded the market with liquidity, causing interest rates in developed countries to fall to 1 percent or 2 percent. In turn, low interest rates led to rapid credit growth, and a large part of this debt was channeled to the property market, raising housing prices to exorbitant levels. In the ten years from 1996 to 2006, house prices rose 92 percent in real (adjusted for inflation) terms, whereas the rise in real prices from 1900 to 1996 had been only 27 percent.[31]

This money did not flow only into the property market. Low interest rates spurred investors to incessantly pursue new investment opportunities with the aim of improving their returns. The prices of shares, commodities, and precious metals rose sharply; this time, though, the windfall, the "magic" innovation, came from the field of complex financial products.

A GREAT DEVICE

The fabulous tool of securitization was first put to use in the United States during the 1970s, but its roots reach back to the New Deal, a series of policies and measures implemented by President Franklin D. Roosevelt from 1933 to 1936 as a way to counter the Great Depression and strengthen business activity. Securitization had been viewed as an innovative liquidity-enhancing instrument.

By means of securitization, banks were able to create a "basket" of housing mortgages extended to households and issue bonds based on this basket that could be resold to investors. Typically, the bank kept part of the profits and the bond buyers collected the revenues from the repayment of the mortgages as interest. Given that the basket comprised many hundreds of housing loans, the risk of default was very small, and these products were considered to be rather safe. Securitization revolutionized banking operations as it magically turned loan obligations into highly liquid assets. In other words, it generated money out of nothing!

This process had many advantages. Instead of waiting 20 or 30 years for the repayment of the housing loans they had extended, the banks could immediately turn a handsome profit. They also obtained capital for the extension of new loans and shook off the risk of default—that is, non-repayment of the securitized loans. The buyers of these products expected a steady flow of income, having, in essence, invested in the property market, a market that was rather safe according to conventional wisdom. Hefty profits were also reaped by various middlemen, mostly investment banks that were involved in the creation and sale of these products. Thus a new device was created, a device that was very lucrative for the banks and would soon find its field of glory.

The process also seemed to have significant advantages for the borrowers and, in general, the economy. Borrowers benefited from the excess liquidity; moreover, owing to this increased liquidity and the transfer of lending risk to third parties, the banks established looser lending criteria, doling out loans more easily to more people. Contractors benefited from the property market boom, and governments reaped great gains as well, as prosperity and high growth rates were credited to their wise economic policies and supreme capabilities. These innovative investment products, which were based on the dark magic of securitization, had been steadily gaining ground during the 1980s; however, it was in the 1990s that their great liftoff began.

Blinded by this groundbreaking innovation, both theorists and market people paid very little attention to a rather crucial shift that had occurred in banking operations. Traditionally, banks would lend money and wait for the repayment of the loan. The loan would be carried on its books throughout its entire life. If a bank systematically made mistakes or turned a blind eye in approving loans to ineligible borrowers, these loans would go bad and the shareholders would incur heavy losses. But securitization changed all this. A bank could extend loans and resell them to third-party investors. This way, the investor not only bought the loan, but also bought (without realizing it) its default risk. In the end, a bank could give out loans without being particularly concerned about the borrower's solvency.

ALL FOR DEMOCRACY!

The shadow of responsibility for the 2007 crash lies not just on the banks and their managers but also on the political leadership of that time, which not only failed to prevent the tragedy but, on the contrary, was instrumental in creating the crisis. The political leadership's mistakes in regard to macroeconomic policy and the supervision of the system were very big indeed, but they pale in comparison to the opportunistic subsidization of the U.S. housing market.

In the 1990s, both Democrats and Republicans embarked on a bidding war over how they would make it easier, not only for the average American but for every citizen, even the poorest ones, to get a home. It was populism and cheap talk in all their glory. Nonetheless, this war between the two parties was not waged with government money and policies for boosting employment or reducing inequality. It was waged with other people's money: the money of the banks (which were, in the end, bailed out with the taxpayers' money).

In the name of democracy, and in order to make housing affordable to minority or low-income citizens, the United States introduced laws that forced banks to loosen their criteria for assessing potential borrowers' ability to fulfill their future obligations. This selective implementation of rules that should be totally inviolable contaminated the core of banking operations. It is indeed telling that, in mid-2000, the Congress passed legislation that forced Fannie Mae and Freddie Mac* to allocate 50 percent of their total mortgage loan portfolio to families with incomes below the average income of their region of residence. Getting a home loan became a piece of cake. So, by the end of 2004, only 14 percent of mortgage loan applications were rejected, as compared with 29 percent in 1998.[32]

The spigots were turned on for everybody, with financial products providing the greatest push: In 1991, investors bought subprime loans amounting to $10 billion. In 1997 these loans exceeded $60 billion, in 2003 they

---

* In 1938, as part of the New Deal, the United States established the Federal National Mortgage Association, also known as Fannie Mae. Its purpose was to secure funds for the extension of housing loans. In 1970, the Federal Home Loan Mortgage Corporation (Freddie Mac) was established as a rival to Fannie Mae in order to boost competition and improve market conditions and the situation of households.

exceeded $332 billion, and in 2007 they stood at a hair-raising $1.3 trillion.[33] All this money inflated both the property market and the American economy.

Moreover, the U.S. tax reform of 1986, which permitted the deduction of mortgage loan payments from taxable income, gave a strong incentive for more borrowing. Many people rushed to buy a home, while existing homeowners took new loans (for repairs, refinancing, etc.) to benefit from the tax break. The total volume of mortgage loans increased tenfold between 1974 and 2000, reaching $7 trillion at the end of 2000. By 2008 mortgage loans stood at a total of more than $14 trillion.[34]

WHEN THEORY CAN SERIOUSLY HARM REALITY

With the fall of the Berlin Wall in 1989 and the subsequent total collapse of the Soviet Union, it became evident that the rival economic system, central planning, not only was less efficient than capitalism but was—without exaggeration—a primitive economic system. It seeped failure from all sides. In retrospect, the question is not why the Soviet empire collapsed so fast, but why it hadn't collapsed sooner.

Although correct, this conclusion had fatal ideological repercussions, as most people took the failure of socialism as a measure of the success of capitalism and the free market economy. Margaret Thatcher's motto that "there is no alternative" seemed to be finally and irrevocably verified. By ironic coincidence, the fall of the Soviet Union was followed by 15 years of astonishing global economic growth, which was, to a great extent, the result of the imbalances described above. All this created the illusion that capitalism had entered a new historical phase of continuous and consistent growth and that the free market was the solution to everything (just as in 1873).

In 2003, professor Robert Lucas, winner of the Nobel Prize in Economics, declared that the central economic problem of depression prevention had been solved, for all practical purposes.[35]

Neoclassical economists took these illusions and, using their sophisticated models and mathematics, turned them into irrefutable certainties. Eugene Fama "demonstrated" the efficiency of free money and capital markets and their ability to always determine the right prices. Robert Lucas "demonstrated" the rational decision-making behavior of economic units. Paul Samuelson "demonstrated" that speculation is a stabilizing factor in markets, imposing discipline and correcting any excesses and imbalances. At the same time, a series of new, advanced models—such as VaR, a method of assessing possible losses a credit institution may incur—filled bank managements with overconfidence in their ability to measure and monitor risk. This illusion of control encouraged the further assumption of risk.

"The rule books [are] out of date,"[36] said President Bill Clinton on every occasion in the mid-1990s. "There is now a debate, a serious debate in this country, about whether there is a maximum growth rate we can have over any period of years without inflation."[37] The president wanted to see where the economy's "rocket" would go.

Alan Greenspan, Fed chairman from 1987 to 2006 and chiefly responsible for the supervision and regulation of the banking system, paints a superb picture of blind faith in rationality, market forces, and the efficiency of self-regulation in his book *The Age of Turbulence*. The book was written shortly before the outbreak of the 2007 crisis, when optimism had peaked, and offers an unadulterated view of the arguments and beliefs of neoclassical economics. As Greenspan wrote:

> [T]he first and most effective line of defense against fraud and insolvency is counterparties' surveillance. For example, JPMorgan thoroughly scrutinizes the balance sheet

of Merrill Lynch before it lends. It does not look to the Securities and Exchange Commission to verify Merrill's solvency…As good as some bank examiners are in promoting sound banking practice, they have little chance of uncovering most fraud or embezzlement…Protective of their own shareholders, these lenders [i.e., the banks] have incentives to monitor hedge fund investment strategies very closely…[Banks were] much better situated and staffed…to understand what other banks and hedge funds were doing as compared with the "by-the-book" regulation done by government financial regulatory agencies… The world is moving too fast for political and bureaucratic dawdling…Markets have become too huge, complex, and fast-moving to be subject to twentieth-century supervision and regulation…Financial regulators are required to oversee a system far more complex than what existed when the regulations still governing financial markets were originally written. Today, oversight of these transactions is essentially by means of individual-market-participant counterparty surveillance. Each lender, to protect its shareholders, keeps a tab on its customers' investment positions. Regulators can still pretend to provide oversight, but their capabilities are much diminished and declining… Since markets have become too complex for effective human intervention, the most promising anticrisis policies are those that maintain maximum market flexibility—freedom of action…Regulation, by its nature, inhibits freedom of market action, and that freedom to act expeditiously is what rebalances markets…In today's world, I fail to see how adding more government regulation can help.[38]

Under the ideological dominion of neoliberalism, in the 1980s the United States and other countries saw the beginning of the gradual deregulation of markets, which gained momentum in the 1990s. In the name of modernization and liberalization, the authorities embarked on the deregulation of the financial system, leaving banks, to a great extent, uncontrolled. Policymakers fervently believed that banks could be more properly and efficiently supervised by their peers than by "dawdling politicians and bureaucrats."

FROM THE INVISIBLE HAND TO THE INVISIBLE BANKS

In 1933, with the Great Depression in full effect, the United States passed the Glass-Steagall Act, which set barriers between commercial banks (which accept deposits and extend loans) and investment banks (which buy and sell securities, with their activity connected to the markets). The law aimed at enhancing transparency, putting an end to practices that caused conflicts of interest, and reducing the risks faced by commercial banks, which managed household savings. The ultimate goal was to create a more stable and resistant banking system, capable of weathering "harsh winters" more easily. Nonetheless, as time went by, the 1929 debacle started to fade in memory, along with the experience of the past.

Decades later, under the exuberance of strong economic growth and the ideological dominion of neoliberalism, deregulation began. Markets were efficient and had to be set free from the bonds of inefficient government.

The first step was taken in the 1980s, when the Fed allowed commercial banks to trade in certain securities. In 1996, the Fed more than doubled (from 10 percent to 25 percent) the initial threshold of the profits commercial banks could derive from securities operations,[39] and in 1999 the Gramm-Leach-Bliley Act repealed the 1933 legislation, allowing banks to extend their operations to all areas of the market. This brought down the protective barrier that had been built between commercial banking and investment banking, as well as insurance operations. Banks could freely acquire other institutions in order to provide integrated services, which allowed them to expand at will. Moreover, the new legislation left in the shadows, beyond any control, the greatest bulk of derivative financial products* and new, "innovative" products and instruments.

The icing on the cake came in 2004, when the U.S. Securities and Exchange Commission permitted the loosening of rules that governed the banks' leverage ratios (i.e., the participation of debt capital in the banks' balance sheets). Subsequently the banks released many billions of dollars (from reserves kept for emergencies), which were, without any hesitation, used to fuel the economy's rocket. Gradually, banks increased their leverage ratios from one dollar of equity for every ten dollars of debt, to ratios of 1 to 20, 1 to 30, or even 1 to 50! The banks continued to assume more and more risks, while the supposed security offered by advanced risk assessment models encouraged extremely reckless decision making.

In order to slip away from the anachronistic—according to mainstream neoliberal views—regulations, the banks exerted strong pressure in all directions, resorting, at the same time, to unorthodox practices in a bid to follow the letter, but not the spirit, of the law. As regulation became looser, the opportunities to employ more "flexible" tactics increased. The aim was to maximize short-term profits, even if it was achieved by increasing exposure to risk. Nouriel Roubini describes the banks' "purposeful evasion of regulations in pursuit of higher profits" with the term "regulatory arbitrage."[40]

Soon the traditional banking system became much larger and less capitalized, found itself in waters considered dangerous until recently, assumed increased risks, and operated under reduced supervision. This was coupled with the development of new "shadow banks"—nonbanking mortgage

---

* In finance, a derivative product is a contract whose value depends on the value of some other, underlying asset.

loan firms, special structured investment product firms, hedge funds, special mutual funds, private equity funds, and so on. Although they operated in the way traditional banks did (borrowing short-term and investing in long-term and illiquid assets), they were subject to absolutely no supervision. By 2007, shadow banks had become much larger than conventional commercial banks!

This led to the creation of a giant banking system—or, to be more precise, as Minos Zombanakis[†] said, to the transformation "of the [global] financial system into a giant lottery."[41] European and American banks were inextricably linked through a vast web of transactions. In 1990, global flows of money stood at around $2 billion a day; in 2008, they exceeded $130 billion a day, a 6,000 percent increase. Finance "became the biggest industrial-scale moneymaking machine the world has ever known."[42] In 2008, the volume of trading in derivative products in nonregulated markets stood at $672 trillion. The banking sector became, as they say, "too big to fail."

The banks' unprecedented economic power and the seemingly huge success of their entire sector significantly increased their influence. Admittedly, the banks and their managements were not doing everything they wanted, but it is rather certain that they were doing many of the things they wanted.

The dominance of the financial sector over all the other sectors of the real economy was the result of the "obvious policymaker bias in favor of the rich financial sector. In the past few years most U.S. Treasury secretaries have come from Wall Street. This way the banks were enabled to direct part of the policy according to their wills, disposing of any criticism from regulators or the public."[43]

[†] Zombanakis is a banker and financial adviser with a long and rich career in international banking. He has been recognized for his major role in the creation of the euromarkets for dollars, the markets for syndicated loans, and the London Interbank Offered Rate (LIBOR).

THE GREAT FEAST

Steve Eisman is one of the few money managers who earned many hundreds of millions of dollars from the 2008 crash, perceiving from early on that there was something rotten in the state of securitization and subprime lending. One of the reasons he decided to short-sell* structured products, as well as shares of banks with lots of skin in the property market game, was the banks' incomprehensible (as he perceived it) tactic of lending large sums to low-income individuals.

One day in the mid-2000s, Eisman's housekeeper asked his advice regarding the purchase of a townhouse. He was very impressed. The price was absurd, but the banks were giving her a no-money-down option mortgage! A little later, he got a phone call from the baby nurse he'd hired to take care of his twin daughters; she told him that she and her sister owned six townhouses. How did that happen? After they bought the first house and its value rose, "the lenders came and suggested they refinance and take out $250,000—which they used to buy another." When the value of the second house rose, they bought a third, and so on.[44]

Houses were turned into small mints that coined money for everyone. The banks, using as their rationale the fact that the loans were secured by mortgages, gave out hundreds of millions of dollars, in violation of all banking regulations.

The great feast was in full swing. Everyone bought increasingly dear houses, using less and less of their own money. Everything was founded on the miracle of lending. And after everyone with a job—even poor immigrants—had gotten a loan, the banks started to lend even to jobless or no-income individuals. So-called liar loans were given to borrowers lying about their finances and providing absolutely no evidence about their

---

* Short selling is the tactic of borrowing shares and then selling them through the stock exchange, anticipating a fall in their price.

financial status. These were the infamous NINJA loans, named for "no income, no job, and no assets."[45] Naturally, household borrowing in the U.S. took off: "The household-debt-to-disposable-income ratio went from 65 percent in 1981 to a staggering 135 percent by 2008."[46]

Irrational exuberance also led to other incredible excesses, the most distinctive being the absurd levels of remuneration paid to banking executives (the "golden boys"). "In 2005 the big five firms"—Goldman Sachs, Morgan Stanley, Merrill Lynch, Lehman Brothers, and Bear Stearns—"paid $25 billion in bonuses; in 2006 they paid $36 billion; and a year later, $38 billion."[47] In 2008, the bonuses paid by Deutsche Bank and Goldman Sachs stood at nearly 60 percent and 50 percent of revenues, respectively.[48]

These exorbitant bonuses further encouraged risk-taking and the use of leverage at an unheard-of scale. Everyone believed that, thanks to the use of advanced mathematics, risk was under control. Even the most irrational behaviors were justified under the notion that markets are efficient and people are rational. There was no possibility of error.

Moreover, new forms of securitization emerged: complex structured products such as CDOs (collateralized debt obligations). The structure and makeup of the CDOs were so complex that few people were able to comprehend them, and most of these products were extremely difficult to mark to market (to value on the basis of their current market price). CDOs were created by mathematicians with a very limited knowledge of economics and were purchased by economists with a very limited knowledge of math.

No one missed the party—not even rating agencies, the supposedly independent guardians of the system's credibility. Standard & Poor's, Fitch, and Moody's dipped their hand in the honey jar, unable to resist the temptation of easy money. On the eve of the 2007 crisis, they made more than half of their profits by handing out AAA ratings to dangerous, toxic products. How could they do this? Let's say that a bank created a basket of loans that included, for example, BBB-rated subprime loans. The end product could manage to get a higher rating than its components, thanks to increased dispersion—that is, by containing thousands of loans from all the U.S. states. According to statistics, there had never been a simultaneous drop in house prices in all states in the entire history of the country. For example, prices might fall in New York, but go up in California or in Texas. So, according to the rating agencies' rationale, an investment product that was based on securitization and included loans extended in many different states was much less risky that individual mortgage loans. A huge investment mechanism was built on the rating agencies' assessments and reassurances that these products were safe, and these toxic products were sold to banks, pension funds, institutional portfolios, and other investors all over the world, spreading the virus that finally caused an unprecedented financial pandemic.

THIS TIME IS DIFFERENT

Today everything seems obvious and more or less predictable. With hindsight, everyone agrees that a violent crash was inevitable.

In 2006, though, everything was different. The financial system was expanding fast, economies were growing at high rates, and politicians reaped the fruit of their efficient government. There was not a single cloud on the horizon.

In the beginning of 2007 almost everyone was unconditionally optimistic about the prospects of the global economy. The period 2002–2007 saw the greatest average global economic growth rate of the past 40 years. With economies growing by an average annual rate of 5 percent, more and more people embraced the belief that the troublesome phenomenon of the business cycle had vanished.

Technological progress, new knowledge, and the successful handling of various minor crises filled policymakers with confidence in the ability of economics and its models to foresee situations and get them under control. With time, the excesses, mistakes, failures, and follies of the past were forgotten.

Humanity was living the Golden Age, the Great Moderation, when neither loose monetary policy nor the persistence of low interest rates gave rise to any inflationary pressures. Nor did they disrupt growth as anticipated. This unparalleled and persistent macroeconomic stability made lots of people believe that macroeconomic risks had been drastically contained.

This time—said economists, bankers, entrepreneurs, and politicians—it was, indeed, different. Ben Bernanke, Fed chairman from 2006 to 2013, said in 2004 that one of the most remarkable features of the economy during the past 20 years, and more, was the substantial reduction of macroeconomic instability.

The advent of China on the economic stage, and the emergence of new major markets, such as Brazil, India, Russia, and the Middle East, strengthened the illusion of stability and created a steadfast certainty in the future and the capabilities of the global economic system. Nothing could threaten this new state of "utmost bliss."[49]

This time it was different! The unprecedented rally of U.S. house prices was not a bubble, said both economists and politicians with certainty, as the rise in prices was fueled by the growth of the economy, the steady inflow of foreign capital, and financial innovation. The boom in share prices was also different this time, since it was based on the unprecedented growth of U.S. productivity. Even the over-indebtedness of the

United States was considered to be justified in light of the new economic situation.

Everything seemed to be ideal. Those few who voiced concern about the dangerous path the global economy had taken—such as economists Nouriel Roubini and Raghuram Rajan—were considered excessively pessimistic or were accused of betting on destruction or of failing to understand the new situation—just like Paul Warburg in 1929!

We were living the longest period of uninterrupted economic growth in the United States, with the lowest jobless rate of the past 30 years. What could go wrong?

THE BEGINNING OF THE END

Behind the facade of unshakable optimism, things were much different. Beginning in early 2006, the ratio of nonperforming mortgage loans started to rise at an accelerating pace, and in mid-2006 house prices in the U.S. ceased to increase for the first time in many years.[50] Then prices started to fall. This development was, to a great extent, the result of the gradual increase of the Fed's main intervention rate*, which had risen to 5.25 percent in 2006, from 1 percent in 2004. Liquidity remained abundant, although loan servicing costs increased dramatically. At the same time, the property market, overheated in previous years, reached a saturation point. In an economy where a family's baby nurse had become the owner of six townhouses, there simply weren't any more buyers.

---

* The rate of exchange, either high or low, at which a country's national bank must buy or sell its own currency in order to return it to the same value that it had before

In December 2006, Fitch, the rating agency, warned that in 2007 a large number of subprime mortgage borrowers would face increased difficulty in repaying their debt, as a result of the rise in interest rates. By the end of 2006, almost ten firms and small banks operating mainly in the subprime lending market had gone belly-up. The bubble in the U.S. property and mortgage lending markets had started to burst, but no one yet seemed to care. As already discussed, at the beginning of 2007 almost every-one was still unconditionally optimistic about the prospects of the global economy.

Banks such as Citibank, Bear Stearns, Merrill Lynch, and Lehman Brothers remained heavily involved in the subprime housing loan market. As for-mer Citigroup CEO Charles Prince told the *Financial Times* in June 2007, referring to liquidity, "As long as the music is playing, you've got to get up and dance. We're still dancing."[51]

In February 2007, HSBC announced losses of $10 billion as a result of its U.S. operations. By March 2007, more than fifty organizations had become insolvent, and in early April, New Century Financial, the second-largest subprime loan provider, met the same fate. That summer it was an open secret that Bear Stearns, the investment bank, was in a dire situation as a result of its exposure to subprime loans. In August, BNP Paribas, one of France's largest banks, announced it would unwind three of its mutual funds that had invested in mortgage lending products, since it was impossible to make any reliable valuation of their assets. In September 2007, panic swept the United Kingdom over the situation of Northern Rock, with TV broadcasts showing the long queues formed outside the bank's branches by alarmed depositors waiting to withdraw their money en masse. The image was shocking. This was the first bank run to occur in the U.K. since 1860!

THE EARTHQUAKE

In December 2007, the situation was ameliorated through the coordinated initiative of five central banks to enhance liquidity in the banking system. Unfortunately, this was just a short respite.

In February 2008 Northern Rock was nationalized, and in March, Bear Stearns—the fifth-largest bank on Wall Street—was acquired by JPMorgan for $240 million. This was actually a bailout, since the acquisition required government money in order to be finalized. One year prior to the acquisition, the market capitalization of Bear Stearns had stood at $18 billion. Alarm and uncertainty started to spread, and in April 2008 the IMF estimated that the cost of the crisis could exceed $1 trillion. The IMF's estimate was nothing but a shot in the dark; because the banking sector—both official and shadow—had grown so uncontrollably in the preceding years, no one knew (or could figure) the real dimensions of the problem.

In July, the U.S. government was forced to provide finance to Fannie Mae and Freddie Mac, and shortly after that, on September 7, 2008, it announced that it would bail them out. Both companies had guaranteed mortgage loans worth $5 billion. According to the U.S. treasury secretary, Henry Paulson, the debt levels of the two companies posed a systemic threat to financial stability. In other words, they were too large to fail.

However, government intervention gave rise to severe criticism in the United States, since it contradicted the prevailing paradigm of the free market and its ability to self-heal through the process of creative destruction. The issue of moral hazard, i.e., our tendency to assume more risks when we know that, even if things go wrong, we will be rescued, started to become imperative.

And Lehman Brothers was sacrificed in the name of moral hazard. On September 10, the bank announced very high losses, and on September 15, after a botched effort to find a buyer, it filed for bankruptcy. On the same day, Bank of America announced the acquisition of Merrill Lynch. Two historic investment banks were erased from the map.

The decision to let Lehman pay for its own sins was designed to be a response to the issue of moral hazard. As a matter of fact, Henry Paulson and his staff believed that Lehman's failure would help restore confidence. What followed, though, was a devastating earthquake that almost led to the complete breakdown of the financial system. Confidence evaporated, and for some time the fall of capitalism emerged as a possible outcome.

On September 16, AIG, the insurance giant, which was heavily involved in the credit default swap (CDS) market, was nationalized, something unheard of in U.S. history. In order to contain panic and save the last living investment banks—Goldman Sachs and Morgan Stanley—these firms were converted to bank holding companies so they could gain access to the ample liquidity of the Fed. All talk about moral hazard went out the window.

In the days that followed, the crisis dominoes continued to do their devastating work in Europe and the Middle East. The situation in those parts of the world was not very different from what it was in the United States. Property and stock market bubbles, as well as excess dependence on lending, were universal phenomena.*

THE SPECTER OF THE GREAT DEPRESSION

The financial crisis was instantly passed on to the real economy. With the banking system in bad shape, the abrupt reduction of credit had an immediate and drastic impact on all businesses, as well as on trade.

---

* In 2008, ING's leverage stood at 49 to 1, Deutsche Bank's at 53 to 1, and Barclay's at 61 to 1. The leverage of the failed Lehman Brothers had stood at only 31 to 1.

By the end of 2008, the entire U.S. automobile industry, once the country's industrial engine, had, for all intents and purposes, gone bankrupt. General Motors (GM), Ford, and Chrysler received government aid in order to be able to remain standing, and in 2009 GM and Chrysler were temporarily taken over by the government.*

In 2008 and 2009, world GDP fell for five quarters in a row for a cumulative drop of 5 percent. Global trade contracted by 20 percent, economic activity shrank dramatically, and unemployment soared to record levels. By early 2009, the markets had sunk to the lowest levels in 15 years.

The global economy was in a state of dangerous turbulence, and there was a clear danger that it might spin out of control. The specter of the Great Depression of 1929 loomed once again. The scale and intensity of the crisis were far beyond any government's individual capacity to react effectively, and the high degree of interconnection among economies made it practically impossible to insulate any of them from the wider global environment.

This unprecedentedly dangerous situation required a commensurate response. Finally, albeit belatedly, policymakers realized that the only way out of the crisis was coordinated global action.

On April 2, 2009, at the G-20 meeting in London, British Prime Minister Gordon Brown presented a $1 trillion plan for rescuing the global economy. The scale and extent of this intervention had no precedent and helped defuse the crisis. The vessel was once again under control.

However, the deep recession and the erosion of confidence left deep scars in all economies; scars that can be clearly seen even at this writing, in early 2014.

---

* In November 2010, there was a public offering of General Motor shares, reducing the U.S. government's stake in the company from 61 percent to 26 percent. The aim was to sell all the company's shares to the private sector. As far as Chrysler is concerned, in July 2011 Italy's Fiat completed the purchase of the entire U.S. government stake, gaining full control.

THE MORAL OF THE STORY: MORE OF THE SAME

The end was violent and painful and had a dramatic effect on the lives of many millions of people all over the world.

In the end, the nonchalance of the Great Moderation, the illusion that business cycles had disappeared and that the global economy had entered a new historical phase of uninterrupted growth, imposed a huge cost in terms of money, energy, and human suffering.

The great crisis of 2007 shocked the academic community. The sudden downturn of the U.S economy and the fierce repercussions of the crisis all over the globe had been utterly unexpected.

In hindsight, the violent disruption of nonchalant growth seems prescribed, crystal clear, inescapable. Does anybody seriously believe that we can tame business cycles? That we can eradicate financial crises? That we can harness the passions and urges that drive us to excess? That we can utilize our accumulated knowledge and experience in order to lead economies to a permanently high plateau?

Alas, modern economic history is rife with such certainties—or, more precisely, illusions. Swept by the euphoria of success, all people, trained or not, specialists or not, believe that "this time is different"—that new knowledge, new technologies, and new economic conditions guarantee perpetual growth.

The path that led to the 2007–2008 debacle and the conditions that prevailed during the precrisis period not only were "not different this time" but proved to be shockingly similar to the crises of the past. Each crisis seems to replay itself, following the same pattern. We (ir)rational people insist on repeating the same mistakes that lead to ruin.

Once again, the 2007 shock had been—for various reasons—preceded by an economic boom. Once again, the lessons and the experiences of the past were forgotten. Once again, an innovation gained magical and unlimited capabilities in people's minds. Once again, lending was used immoderately. Once again, ample liquidity led property, stock, and other asset prices to soar. Once again, most people mistook the coincidental generation of large profits—because of the business cycle—for their own supposedly superior skills and talents. Once again, base little people defrauded other people consciously and systematically, in order to get more money and more power. Once again, the most specialized and the most trained believed they knew much more than they actually did. Once again, the warning voices were ignored or considered to be excessively pessimistic. Once again, most people were certain that this time was different.

Once again, though, reality came to crush human pride and foolishness. Finally, once again, in the crisis of 2007 nothing was all that different.

PART THREE

HUMAN, VERY HUMAN

Far out in the uncharted backwaters of the unfashionable end of the Western Spiral arm of the galaxy lies a small unregarded yellow sun. Orbiting this at a distance of roughly ninety-eight million miles is an utterly insignificant little blue-green planet whose ape-descended life forms are so amazingly primitive that they still think digital watches are a pretty neat idea.

This planet has—or rather had—a problem, which was this: most of the people living on it were unhappy for pretty much of the time. Many solutions were suggested for this problem, but most of these were largely concerned with the movements of small green pieces of paper, which is odd because on the whole it wasn't the small green pieces of paper that were unhappy.

Douglas Adams, The Hitchhiker's Guide to the Galaxy

1

HOMO SAPIENS

*"But men may construe things after their fashion,
clean from the purpose of the things themselves."*
William Shakespeare, Julius Caesar, *Act 1 Scene 3*

Economic science and the mainstream economic model are trying to tame the world of action and, using the advanced navigation tools they have developed, to soften any tensions and lead economies to growth along a smoother and more scientifically controlled course. However, this aspiration is continually and persistently undermined by reality. As we have seen, crises never cease to refute human certainties.

The biggest problem of models is reality, and the great rival of *Homo economicus* is *Homo sapiens*, this mysterious creature that, some five million to six million years ago, embarked from some part of Africa on a course that gradually led to its global domination. Man is the only species that managed to break free from the bonds and limitations of its natural environment and, more or less, place nature under its control.

Homo sapiens, as we all deeply know, is not a cold-blooded, calculating machine that computes the satisfaction drawn by each individual action, but is much, much more. It is a creature of complex intellectual and mental processes and moods, and its dynamic interaction with both the social web and the environment leads to the most intricate and unpredictable reactions and behaviors. We are not dealing with humans as individuals, but with people who interact with other people.

Reason is, by all means, a major parameter of our behavior, but it is not the only one. The are many other things beyond the marvelous world of thought. The senses, the processes of memory and perception, the way decisions are made and problems are solved, our intelligence, disposition, and emotional world, even thought itself, are complex and puzzling functional structures that are barely understood. Human behavior is so dynamic and complex that it is doubtful whether we can definitely and fully understand it, let alone fit it into forecasting models.

For that matter, how can we model free will, the fact that human behavior not only depends on external stimuli but is also the result of choices determined by each individual's will, each individual's psyche? How can we model temper and emotional fluctuations? How can we fit passions or ideologies into a model? Or complex social relations? Or luck?

As shown by hundreds of experiments, our daily behavior doesn't even approximate the concept of rationality. As a matter of fact, it has no aspect that remains unaffected by emotions, urges, fallacies, illusions, biases, and other tricks of the mind and the senses. Failures and bad judgments are the rule, not perfection. We humans may have been endowed with reason, but we are not models of reason, as economists would have it.

We should never forget that man is just another biological species that, like any other species on this planet, is concerned primarily with survival and reproduction.

THE MYSTERY OF THE BRAIN

What should I eat? What should I wear? Should I go out or stay at home? Should I read or watch TV? These are only a few of the questions the brain responds to at any given time. Apart from such quotidian issues, the brain is often called to decide on complex problems that require strenuous mental effort.

However, most functions of the brain are performed outside the bounds of consciousness. Automatic processes are incessantly running in the background, making us discern sounds, comprehend speech, see, smell, taste, walk, talk, create memories.

When we see a friend we immediately recognize her. We "have not the slightest impression that billions of nerve cells have digested the signals from [our] eyes and distilled them into the wisdom of perception."[1] When we walk, thousands of calculations set up the muscle tone for each step, determine our position in space, and carry out the necessary adjustments.

Those amazing three pounds in your skull[2] are solely responsible for human uniqueness. Certainly, all species are unique, but humans are totally different from any other earthly creature. The comparison with our closest relatives, the chimpanzees, is overwhelming. We share 98.6 percent of our genetic material with chimpanzees, but the mental differences between humans and chimps are huge.

Only humans are able to transfer complex information and accumulated knowledge from generation to generation. Complex language and the development of writing provided us with the ultimate evolutionary advantage and made it possible to develop culture, science, and arts. No other species on the planet possesses cognitive mechanisms that allow it to probe deeper, to see below the surface.

That said, what is the brain, and what exactly is its function? This is a very tough question. Even today, after decades of analytical research and the revolution of neuroscience, many areas of the brain remain obscure and inaccessible. Our knowledge remains limited, and scientists still confront great mysteries—for example, how memories are formed or what schizophrenia is or how, exactly, sleep works.

The way the brain drives our thoughts and actions remains elusive. One of the greatest mysteries faced by neuroscientists is "how a thought moves from the depths of the unconscious to become conscious."[3]

With the development of neuroscience, many of the things we thought we knew about the workings and the structure of the brain were overturned by new findings, and the solution of a puzzle about how the brain works frequently gives rise to even more perplexing mysteries. Scientists acknowledge, with a little bit of melancholy, that it will not be possible in the foreseeable future to attain full knowledge about the nature and operation of the brain.

For most people, the word *brain* refers to thinking, to grand ideas and higher mental processes; however, this kind of analytical thinking is just a small part of the brain's daily functions. The brain is dedicated neither to analytical thinking nor to grand ideas and philosophy. Its main concern, its primary work for thousands of years, has been to guarantee the individual's survival and reproduction, and over the millennia this has been achieved not through conscious thought, but through the brain's autonomous functions—functions that are mechanically, unconsciously executed. In its striving to ensure survival, the brain is barely interested in truth or strict logic.

The bulk of the brain's work has to do with nondeliberate mental processes that are incessantly executed and lie beyond the control of our consciousness. No one dies from forgetting to eat or drink. Even when we are trying to solve a complex problem or are immersed in an intellectual masterpiece or are madly in love, the brain, responding to the body's chemical signals (hormones, neuropeptides, etc.) and regardless of our conscious self, will send the appropriate directions regarding the need to get food or water.

Many other critical functions are reflexive, without even the smallest participation of the brain. If our hand accidentally touches a sizzling object, it will automatically move away—on the spinal cord's direction. There is no way the pain will go unnoticed if, for example, we forget ourselves in front of the TV. The pain signal is rapidly transmitted and the hand is immediately withdrawn, without any conscious thought.

Of course, possessing a brain is not just a human privilege; all species of the animal kingdom are equipped with this valuable organ. Even the brain of a mosquito or a cockroach is continuously performing complex calculations. In our age, despite computers' immense computing power and the achievements of artificial intelligence, scientists cannot create robots capable of coordinating their limbs and determining their position in space as effectively as, for example, a cockroach.

This mysterious, enigmatic organ constitutes our being and produces amazing intellectual results. This is not to say, however, that the brain is perfect or infallible.

THE DARK PATHS OF MEMORY

"We use memory all the time, in everyday living as well as when we are studying."[4] Assisted by memory, we automatically recognize faces, objects, behaviors, functions, and so on, and without it we wouldn't be able to do many things. In general, memory comprises two qualitatively different types of storage: short-term memory, which fades fast, and long-term memory,[5] for preserving knowledge and experiences that we carry inside us for the largest part of our lives.

Memory is one of the greatest enigmas scientists confront as they strive to explain the nature of perception and thought. How are memories shaped? How accurate are they? What are the causes of mnemonic errors or absentmindedness? How can we lose our car keys but never forget how to drive? What causes the "short circuits" that make us forget the names of very familiar people?

Memory is rife with ambiguities and remarkable inconsistencies that put its reliability to question. We humans tend to have better recollection of initial and most recent data or observations. Experiments have shown that when people are read a list of twenty words and then are asked to write down those they remember, the most-recalled words are those at the beginning and the end of the list. In-between data are "erased." Memory, both short- and long-term, has limitations.

Most people believe that as soon as you experience an event and form a memory of it, this memory will remain unchanged. This is a mistake. Memory does not depend only on what actually happened, but also on the meaning we attach to events, how we interpret them. As part of an inspired experiment, psychologists read the following list of words to a group of volunteers: *bed, rest, awake, tired, dream, wake, snooze, blanket, doze, slumber, snore, nap, peace, yawn,* and *drowsy.* A few minutes later, the participants were asked to write down the words they had been read. Almost 40 percent of the respondents recalled having heard the word sleep, which was not included in the list! It had been fabricated by their brain. All words of the list were associated with sleep, so the brain created a false memory, believing that the word *sleep* had been read.[6]

When we perceive something, we extract the meaning only from what we see, instead of encoding everything in perfect detail. Such encoding would be a meaningless waste of energy.[7] Out of thousands of pieces of information around us, the brain filters and selects only those sufficient to interpret and understand the facts. It is not designed to seek the truth and nothing but the truth, but only to understand what is going on—to make sense of events and make swift decisions. Quite often, the meaning that the brain attaches to an event affects the memory that is being formed.

Psychologists William Brewer and James Treyens conducted the following experiment: They led certain students to an office and asked them to wait there for a minute. A few moments later the subjects were led to another room and were asked to write down a list of everything that they had seen in the office as they waited. Almost all the subjects recalled the things we usually find in a typical office (desk, chairs, shelves, etc.). However, 30 percent also remembered seeing books, and 10 percent recalled seeing a file cabinet, neither of which were present in the waiting room. Their memory reconstructed the contents of the room on the basis of both the objects that were actually there and objects that the subjects expected to find, or believed they should find, in an office.[8]

The brain takes over and processes external stimuli so they make sense and fit our beliefs. In other words, it constructs its own version of reality. When two people fervently disagree on how an event played out, it is not necessarily the case that one of them is deliberately lying; it is just that each person's mind is stubbornly supporting its own version, its own "truth."

In the 1930s, psychologist Frederic Bartlett studied the way people forget, as well as "the manner in which they organize and distort the memories they retain." In his experiments, one person read a story to another person, this person tried to repeat it from memory to a third person, who tried to recite it to a fourth one, and so on. The most notable finding of this experiment was not that the stories became more and more unintelligible with each reproduction, but that the narrators added or deleted facts, distorting the stories to fit their existing beliefs, knowledge, and emotions.

Bartlett showed that "people do not simply remember scattered but accurate fragments of their original experiences."[9] Distortions become certainty, and people firmly believe they remember exactly what happened.

The impressions that are created are powerful, and we are easily misled into certainties. In a relevant experiment, a group of people were read a list of names and then were asked whether they had heard more names of men or of women. The majority of the subjects replied with certainty that they had heard more names of men. In fact, more women's names had been read; however, the men's names that had been read included more famous ones, such as Richard Nixon, which made a deeper impression.[10]

In our age, there is no doubt that "memory is imperfect and susceptible to distortion and loss."[11] Memories, no matter how evidential they may be, become less and less accurate with time. In order to fill in any gaps, the brain uses false memories or mixes up similar memories of other events, in order to preserve the recollection's meaning and coherence.

So beware of your memories, and of all those who swear to tell the truth and nothing but the truth. Especially when they are witnesses in a courtroom.

ALL THE THINGS WE THINK WE SEE

We may admit that we were wrong or that we don't remember something well, but it is very hard to question something that we have seen. Personal experience creates a sense of irrefutable knowledge and certainty. "But I saw it with my own eyes," we say with ardor and conviction.

In reality, though, our perception of the visual world is limited, and what we actually see is much less than what we think we see. The brain focuses on specific fields, those it is interested in, ignoring other situations, even when these play out in front of our very eyes.

In the late 1990s, cognitive psychologists Christopher Chabris and Daniel Simons conducted the following experiment: Using students from Cornell University, as actors, they shot a short film showing two teams of people moving around and passing basketballs. One team wore white shirts and the other wore black. Then they showed the film to groups of students and asked them to—silently—count the number of passes made by the players wearing white while ignoring any passes by the players wearing black. When the film ended, the volunteers were asked to report how many passes they had counted. The answer did not matter, as the only purpose of the counting exercise was to keep the subjects engaged with a task that demanded their attention. "[W]e weren't really interested in pass-counting ability," Chabris and Simons wrote in their book, *The Invisible Gorilla.* "We were actually testing something else: Halfway through the video, a female student wearing a full-body gorilla suit walked into the scene, stopped in the middle of the players, faced the camera, thumped her chest, and then walked off, spending about nine seconds onscreen…Amazingly, roughly half of the subjects in our study did not notice the gorilla!"[12]

Since then, the invisible gorilla experiment has been repeated and checked many times, with generally the same result. This error of perception, the inability to notice something unexpected, is called by psychologists "inattentional blindness." When we focus we devote our attention to a particular area, and we tend not to notice unexpected objects, even when they are conspicuous and appear in front of us.

As a matter of fact, contrary to our intuitive belief that we can think and do many things at the same time, the "brain can think consciously about only one thing at a time" and all "other decisions are being made automatically."[13]

In the early 1980s, NASA research scientist Richard Haines was working on "head-up display" technology for aircraft, which involved projecting critical instrumentation directly on the windshield of a plane, in front of the pilot. According to Haines's thinking, this would help pilots have all the information required for landing the planes right in front of their eyes, to avoid any distraction. After many hours of practice, experienced pilots were tested on a simulator. To the researchers' great surprise during the landing trials, in spite of having visual contact with the instruments and the runway, many of the pilots failed, while approaching the runway, to see another plane accidentally enter the runway (as per the simulation scenario). Actually, quite a few pilots drove their aircraft straight into the "invisible" plane. They "never saw the large jet on the ground turning onto the runway right in front of them."[14]

As part of another experiment, a university professor informed his students that an experiment would be conducted, and those interested in volunteering should go to the eighth floor and fill out a form. Those who went stood at a counter and started filling out the forms. Then, the "experimenter who had been talking to them ducked down behind the counter—ostensibly to file away some papers—and a different person stood up."[15] The new person continued to give information. Most of the students missed the change!

There are endless examples. Even geometric shapes presented in a certain manner, or a photo shown from different angles, can short-circuit the brain and create illusions. However, we all firmly believe that we can see and accurately perceive everything that happens around us.

THE POWER OF EXPECTATION

Another inconvenient angle on the concept of human rationality concerns expectations and their inexplicable influence. Deep faith in something can lead to results that cannot be explained, at least not rationally.

The perplexing power of expectation is vividly reflected in the placebo effect. *Placebo*, which in Latin means "I shall please you," is the term used in medicine to signify simulated, or otherwise medically ineffectual, treatments—usually plain sugar—given to patients suffering from various diseases or conditions. It is a great mystery, but a large fraction of patients are always cured by taking sugar or plain water. The mere expectation of taking a medicine has a healing effect. Today, approval of a new medicine by the competent authorities requires proof that it offers statistically better healing percentages than a placebo.

There are reports concerning dramatic improvements in the health of patients suffering even from incurable diseases, such as cancer, who took plain water as medicine. In 1950, in California, Sandra Levy of the University of Pittsburgh described the case of a terminally ill cancer patient who was treated with the drug Krebiozen. After being given the drug, the patient "underwent an amazing remission and began to lead a perfectly normal life." A few months later, though, certain reports were published, claiming that Krebiozen did not have any therapeutic value. Immediately the patient relapsed, and his doctor, in desperation, gave him pure, distilled water, telling him it was a special, pure form of Krebiozen with strong healing effects. To the doctor's great surprise, the patient recovered, but two months later an official government report on Krebiozen's ineffectiveness was published, sending the man to his grave.[16]

Expectations, the things we expect to happen, are quite often more influential than fact and reality.

In 2008, the journalist Gene Weingarten won a Pulitzer Prize by conducting an impressive social experiment, which was published in the *Washington Post*. The experiment was conducted with the assistance of world-class violinist Joshua Bell. On Friday, January 12, 2007, just before 8 a.m., carrying a case that held his violin worth almost $3 million, Bell arrived at the L'Enfant Plaza station of the Washington Metro. He picked a nice spot between the entrance and the escalator, took his violin out, opened his case so that passers-by could throw some money in, and started playing classical pieces, continuing for almost 43 minutes. While he performed, 1,097 people went through the station, most of them hurrying to work. How many of them actually stopped? Only seven passers-by, of which one did indeed recognize Bell. How much money did he get? Excluding the $20 placed in the case by the person who recognized him, Bell collected a total of $32![17] Really, who could expect that a world-class virtuoso would be playing his violin at a Metro station? No one. Many of the same people who passed him by would gladly have bought a high-priced ticket to attend one of the famous violinist's concerts.

Expectation can be an inexhaustible source of strength. A small army unit got lost in the Alps while executing a maneuver. In the next days there was heavy snowfall, compounded by avalanches. Everyone considered the soldiers dead. A few days later, though, the unit showed up unharmed at an impossible spot. Amazed, the general staff asked the leader of the unit to explain how the soldiers managed to orient themselves under such harsh conditions. The leader replied that one of the soldiers was carrying an old map that helped them find their way. General staff officers inspected the document and found that the lifesaving map had nothing to do with the Alps, but depicted a mountainous region in the Pyrenees.[18] So, equipped with the wrong map but with lots of expectation, the soldiers were saved.

Economics also provides a very characteristic example of the arbitrary effect expectations can have. When optimism is on the rise and positive expectations predominate, people tend to disregard bad news and over-react even to the most trivial good news. In contrast, when pessimism and negative expectations are rife, good news is ignored and every piece of negative information is overstated. Facts are altered and reshaped through the distorting lens of expectation.

We believe what we want to believe.

DRIVEN BY BELIEF

When people speculate and make estimates, they are systematically influenced by their beliefs and biases regarding the world and reality. We interpret the world on the basis of the "little boxes" we have in our brains. When we hear that someone works as a lawyer or a doctor or a musician or a civil servant, we unconsciously form an image of how this person is dressed or behaves, based on beliefs we have formed through our past experiences.

In 1959, American psychologist Abraham Luchins (1914–2005) showed how primacy effects can activate beliefs, which have a decisive impact on human judgment. He gave research participants a description of a student called "Jim," whom they were asked to describe as extroverted or introverted. The description consisted of two parts:

Jim left the house to get some stationery. He walked out into the sun-filled street with two of his friends, basking in the sun as he walked. Jim entered the stationery store, which was full of people. Jim talked with an acquaintance while he waited to catch the clerk's eye. On his way out, he stopped to chat with a school friend who was just coming into the store. Leaving the store, he walked toward school. On his way, he met a girl to whom he had been introduced the night before. They talked for a short whole, and then Jim continued to school.

After school, Jim left the classroom alone. Leaving the school, he started on his long walk home. The street was brilliantly filled with sunshine. Jim walked down the street on the shady side. Coming up the street toward him, he saw the pretty girl whom he had met on the previous evening. Jim crossed the street and entered a candy store. The store was crowded with students and he noticed a few familiar faces. Jim waited quietly until he caught the counter man's eye and then gave his order. Taking his drink, he sat down at a side table. When he finished the drink he went home.

One group of research participants were given the text as it was given here, starting with the paragraph that highlighted Jim's sociable characteristics, followed by the second description. The other group was given the text the other way round, starting with the second paragraph, which focuses on Jim's solitary characteristics, followed by the first paragraph. According to the result of the experiments, although both groups received the same information, those who first read "the sociable description judged Jim to be an extroverted character, while those who first read the unsociable description judged him to be an introvert."[19]

Kahneman and Tversky outlined the following character: "Linda is thirty-one years old, single, outspoken, and very bright. She majored in philosophy. As a student, she was deeply concerned with issues of discrimination and social justice, and also participated in antinuclear demonstrations." Then they asked the participants in their experiment which of the following alternatives was most probable:

a) Linda is a bank teller.

b) Linda is a bank teller and is active in the feminist movement.

About 85 percent to 90 percent of the respondents chose the second option, "contrary to logic."[20] The above experiment was conducted in many universities, with the participation of undergraduate students who, at least in theory, use—or try to use—cold, analytical logic.

Certain stereotypes, such as "outspoken," "deeply concerned with issues of discrimination and social justice" and "participated in antinuclear demonstrations" led the vast majority to classify Linda as a feminist. Most important, the irrational answer of the participating students did not result from a situation that favors intuitive judgment (e.g., time pressure), but was the result of analytical thinking.

The brain prefers acting fast to thinking, probing, and being precise. It aims at reaching fast conclusions, based on the things it already knows and the beliefs it has formed, instead of subjecting each new experience to analytical, logical scrutiny in order to select the most rational interpretation.

2

SOCIAL LIFE

Various studies have shown that humans spend, on average, 80 percent of their waking time in the company of others, and that they average six to twelve hours per day in conversation with other individuals.[21] "Our bodies and minds are not designed for lonely lives."[22] We are social to the bone.

Our brain exists mostly for dealing with social issues and not for contemplating the vastness of interstellar space or reaching optimum economic decisions. The absence of human company has serious detrimental effects, even on our health. Medical studies have shown that "healthy volunteers exposed to cold and flu viruses got sick more easily if they had fewer friends and family around them."[23]

A lot can be said about how and why we are social to the bone. Anthropologists, neuroscientists, evolutionary biologists, psychologists, and others quarrel about the reasons and the causes. In any case, no matter what the reasons, society and social relations constitute the most important aspect of our life—an aspect that, as we saw in Part One, has been stricken from economics. According to the beliefs of academic economists, there is no society—that is, relations among people—but only relations between people and goods. Like Robinson Crusoe's world before the arrival of Friday.

In reality, though, there are not just individuals, but individuals in constant interaction with other individuals. Sociability and social networks have ancient genetic roots: They are written into our DNA. We seek out friends, not just mates.[24] There is almost no human activity that is cut off from society and other people. We are incessantly affecting, and being affected by, others. We eat in the company of others, go out in the company of others, work in the company of others, enjoy our vacation in the company of others, play in the company of others, and so forth. Even the most asocial people maintain some sort of social cycle.

The degree of our happiness depends not on some internal, objective happiness-gauging mechanism, but on the incessant comparison of our situation to that of the people around us. For most people, improving one's living standard is not enough; it has to be better than, or at least equal to, that of their neighbors. Well-to-do individuals living in an immensely rich neighborhood may feel miserable when they compare their situation to that of their richer neighbors. In 1995, researchers asked a group of graduate students and staff members at the Harvard School of Public Health which situation would make them happier: earning $50,000 a year while their peers were paid $25,000, or earning $100,000 while their peers were paid $200,000. The majority chose the lower salary.[25]

Our behavior is not determined only by our inner self, but also by an uninterrupted, dynamic interaction with all the things that shape our social environment: the people around us, our living standards, our educational and financial status, the institutional and regulatory framework, and so forth.

As Keynes said in regard to investors, most people's everyday behavior is not based on what they really want or believe in, but on an effort to stand up to other people's expectations. We have role models, we admire other people, we are influenced by friends and acquaintances, and we—consciously or unconsciously—imitate behaviors.

It is amazing how an idea, a behavior, or an action can, through the social network and the endless social chain (a friend of a friend and so forth), influence individuals that live thousands of miles away from the starting point. And similarly, it is amazing how our everyday life may be affected by people whom we neither have met nor are ever going to meet in our lifetime.

Certain psychologists argue that the evolution of humanity's higher intellectual facilities was a response to the complexity of social life.[26]

IMITATION AND SOCIAL NETWORKS

Where's the rationality when, out of the blue, everyone wears All Star sneakers? Or energy bracelets? Why do we choose this or that brand of blue jeans? Why do people in the city of London dress more or less the same? Or why do people in Camden Town dress the same, albeit different from how city people dress? Why does Saturday night clubbing impose a dress code? Why do people from different places speak in different accents?

People imitate other people, either voluntarily or involuntarily. Actually, we are mimicking machines. Many studies have shown that newborns less than 72 hours old can imitate facial expressions accurately.[27] Newborns are naturally capable of imitation.

Mimicry and simulation constitute a powerful learning, socialization, and civilization diffusion mechanism. We learn by watching and repeating other people's actions. My three-year-old son repeats the words he hears and includes them in his vocabulary without comprehending their precise meanings. Comprehension comes with time.

It is not only children who imitate their parents' behavioral patterns. All people, irrespective of age, are continually imitating others. Imitation help us become accepted in social groups. We adopt facial expressions, manners of speech, vocabularies, accents, inflections, emotional responses, and various—good and bad—habits of friends, relatives, even strangers. Couples who have been together for many years not only are alike in the sense that they behave similarly, but in some cases seem to adopt each other's facial features. The face of the one resembles the face of the other.

Neuroscientists have identified certain neurons,* called mirror neurons, that are unconsciously fired when we see another person perform an action.[28] So we may unwittingly cross our legs or scratch our head or yawn immediately after another person around us has done the same.

Imitation, or mimicry, is rather widespread in nature. Certain species imitate other species' features as a survival strategy. Some butterflies taste bad. They are usually brightly and distinctively colored, so that birds can easily recognize them and avoid devouring them. Other species of butterfly that do not taste bad mimic the coloring and shape of nasty-tasting butterflies well enough to fool birds.[29]

One of the weirdest phenomena, which scientists have been studying for many decades now, is the widowhood effect. When a person dies, the likelihood of his or her partner's dying in a year's time is doubled.

This phenomenon has wider implications. What happens to our intimate partner or a friend or a colleague can deeply affect us. For example: Your wife loses her job and suffers a breakdown, a condition that soon has an impact on your mood. In turn, your own bad mood may affect that of your mother—who lives in another city—as well as the mood of some of your

---

* Neurons are the nerve cells that are the structural parts and functional units of the nervous system. An adult's brain comprises almost 100 billion neurons, each forming 1,000 to 10,000 synapses with other neurons—an inconceivable structure!

coworkers. Thus, social association has put a domino effect in motion. Your wife's poor disposition may ultimately affect the mood of a butcher who lives and works in a another town many miles away, simply because he happened to serve your bad-tempered and quarrelsome mother.

Our life is embedded in complex social networks that affect us and are affected by us. But how are these networks formed? Which is their purpose? How do they operate, and to what extent do they affect our lives? Social scientist and physician Nicholas Christakis studied the amazing invisible power of social networks and how they shape our lives. He dealt with the issue of obesity in the United States and tested the assumption that obesity can spread from person to person like a contagious disease. As he pointed out, "The spread of obesity is not simply a matter of monkey see, monkey do." Rather, "normative influences are at work."[30] The results of his research were impressive: The risk of obesity is 45 percent if a person's friends are obese, 25 percent if this person's friends' friends are obese, and 10 if his friends' friends' friends—people he probably doesn't even know—are obese. Only when we reach the fourth level—one's friends' friends' friends' friends—is there is no longer a relationship.[31]

As Christakis noted, as years go by the network changes, yet it has consistency, memory, and resilience that allow it to persist across time. People die and new members are added, turning social networks into "living things." These networks are superorganisms that show or evince behaviors or phenomena that are not reducible to the individuals composing them. Their workings are complex, and they seem to possess a collective wisdom, like a flock of birds that pool their collective knowledge and manage to cross many hundreds of miles to migrate to a tiny speck in the Pacific.[32]

American social psychologist Solomon Asch (1907–1996) conducted a series of experiments demonstrating the immense power of social pressure on individual judgment. Asch studied groups of nine people, eight of whom were his confederates and one of whom was actually the subject.

Asch asked the entire group to answer a sequence of twelve questions, and the subject "would hear most of the others' answers before giving his own answer before the group." The correct answers were obvious, but Asch's confederates deliberately gave wrong answers to seven of the twelve questions. Faced with a group of people who were unanimously giving wrong answers, "a third of the time the subjects caved in and gave the same wrong answers as had been given by the confederates."[33]

Herd behavior is based on the individual's inclination to attune to the majority of other people in his or her environment. This deeply rooted psychological tendency of people to behave like a herd is more distinct in situations of danger.

Social networks can facilitate the swift spread of ideas, beliefs, stereotypes, perceptions, habits, rumors, emotions, behaviors, fads, and so on. Spreading information is an ancient mechanism for informing and protecting people, but also for deceiving them.

Social networks have a decisive impact on economic life: More often than not, they set off extreme fluctuations in stock exchanges and markets, lead to the dominance or the extinction of products, cause panics, and so on. "Financial panics may result from the spread of emotions or information from person to person."[34] Your friend's friend, who has an acquaintance whose cousin works for X bank and told him that next Monday Greece will default,* may lead you to the decision—unthinkable till yesterday—to withdraw your money from the bank. The economists who studied the behavior of Irish depositors at a New York bank during two panics in the 1850s found that "social networks were the single most important factor in explaining the closure of accounts."[35]

---

* In 2010, Greece was caught in the maelstrom of a fiscal crisis, and default was avoided only thanks to European aid. Until the middle of 2012, the possibility of a Greek default was an everyday news item. Thus, in the three years from 2010 through 2012, bank deposits fell—owing to fears of a default—by $120 billion (a drop of almost 40 percent).

FRAUDULENCE AND FRAUDSTERS

In Part Two of this text, we met base little people, such as A. Fastow (Enron), B. Ebbers (WorldCom), and B. Madoff, who, for the sake of short-term profit, power, and short-lived fame, systematically defrauded society, violating laws and regulations.

The list of fraudsters is endless and includes all types of people, from petty thieves to respected judges, university professors, scientists, politicians, bankers, businesspeople, and so on. Moreover, an unknown number of fraudsters manage to escape the tentacles of the law and live among us, enjoying a respectable life.

One legendary case is that of Cyril Burt (1883–1971), who was considered to be one of Britain's most important educational psychologists. Burt claimed that intelligence is heritable, and his views were instrumental in the adoption of intelligence testing to determine educational access. However, when professor L.S. Hearnshaw, a great admirer of Burt, embarked on writing his biography, he found out, by carefully examining the British psychologist's work and papers, that his hero had manipulated evidence to make them fit his theories.[36] In other words, he had committed fraud.

Fraud and treachery are not mere dark digressions in human behavior that are related only to a problematic, maladjusted minority. Quite the contrary: They constitute a key aspect of social life. Setting common criminals aside, fraudulent behaviors are much more widespread and common than we realize: the doctor who recommends a cesarean section instead of natural childbirth in order to collect a larger fee; the taxi driver who doesn't follow the shortest route; the journalist who emphasizes a trivial—albeit impressive—detail to capture the attention; the soccer player who fakes injury to gain a free kick, and so forth. Deception is all the little white lies all of us use every day, sometimes to make our lives easier, and other times to gain some edge.

According to studies, obstetricians in areas with declining birthrates are much more likely to perform cesarean-section deliveries. This means that "when business is tough, doctors try to ring up more expensive procedures."[37] It is no coincidence that Greece, a country addicted for many years to fast and easy money, is number one in cesarean-section deliveries in Europe. Fifty-three percent of Greek women give birth by cesarean section, while the corresponding rate for the Netherlands is just 13 percent.[38]

If you believe that only schoolchildren cheat at exams, think again. In 1996, the United States adopted high-stakes testing in elementary and secondary education. According to the new education policy, a school with low scores would be placed on probation and, in case performance was not improved, would "face the threat of being shut down, its staff to be dismissed or reassigned." In contrast, schools that did well were assigned bonuses "for teachers who produced big test-score gains," which in certain states, such as California, amounted to $25,000. Soon it became evident that teachers were highly vulnerable to temptation. Many teachers, either to get the bonus, conceal their inadequacy, or avoid being reassigned, were systematically breaking the rules like common crooks. Certain teachers illegally obtained copies of the test the previous day and were preparing their students. Others gave students extra time to complete the test. Most teachers, though, simply changed the students' answers, filling in the correct ones!*[39]

In the spring of 1987, seven million children suddenly "vanished" in the United States. What was the reason? A simple change in a tax rule: "Instead of merely listing each dependent child, tax filers were now required to provide a Social Security number for each child." Thus, one in ten dependent children in the United States disappeared overnight.[40]

---

* In the end, the U.S. Department of Education caught—and fired—the cheating teachers. It developed an algorithm that identified unusual fluctuations in student performance between grades. When an A student got a C the next year, or vice versa, this student was placed on probation, in order to ascertain any "creative contribution" on the teacher's part.

In March 2012, almost 36,000 disabled individuals "vanished" in Greece, having failed to register with a census that was conducted in order to ascertain who was really entitled to social benefits and who had been cheating society.

Deceiving the enemy in the battlefield is the quintessence of strategy in times of war. The general who deceives his opponent is, of course, considered a hero, not a cheat. General Rommel was a German Nazi marshal, but owing to his skills, he enjoyed the admiration and respect of both friends and foes and was nicknamed the Desert Fox. Sun Tzu* stresses that war is based on deception. "When able to attack," he wrote, "we must seem inactive; when we are near, we must make the enemy believe we are far away; when far away, we must make him believe we are near."[41]

Deception is ubiquitous, says the neuroscientist Michael Gazzaniga. It "begins in the morning when women put on makeup (to make themselves more beautiful or appear younger) and perfume (to mask their own odor)." Men also put on deodorant, dye their hair, wear toupees, or "brush their thin hair across their bald spots."

In the real world we all deceive, and we all lie. Inadvertently, parents begin from a very early stage to "train" their offspring in the skill of lying: When Grandma or some other person sends an unwelcome present to the little child, the parents intervene and make the child speak with Grandma over the phone to thank her and tell her how much he or she loved the present. The sincere honesty of children is unacceptable! Similarly, in the world of adults, when one is a guest at a friend's house, it is very rude to tell the hostess that the food she prepared is tasteless. The food is always splendid, even if it's barely edible!

---

* Sun Tzu was a Chinese general who lived around 500 B.C. His work *The Art of War* had a deep influence on Chinese and Japanese—as well as Western—military thinking.

Not only do we lie to each other, we also lie to ourselves. Self-deception rules. Almost 100 percent of high school students rank themselves as having a higher-than-average ability to get along with others, while 93 percent of college professors rank themselves above average at their work.[42] We humans have more self-confidence and self-esteem than we deserve.

Various types of deception, as survival strategies, can also often be encountered in nature. Black-headed gulls nest in large colonies with nests only a few feet apart. It is quite common for a gull to swallow one of the neighbor's chicks whole while its neighbor is away fishing. This way, the cheating gull "obtains a good nutritious meal, without having to go to the trouble of catching a fish, and without having to leave its own nest unprotected."

"Emperor penguins in the Antarctic stand on the brink of the water, hesitating before diving in, because of the danger of being eaten by seals. If only one of them would dive in, the rest would know whether there was a seal there or not." So they wait patiently for another bird to dive—and even, as researchers have observed, "try to push each other in."[43]

3

THE KNOWLEDGE TRAP

Knowledge, learning, and education are the key ingredients of civilization, progress, and human development. This is an arduous and long process.

Through ceaseless, persistent, and painful trial and error, beginning circa 10,000 B.C., hunter-gatherers gradually domesticated certain animals (dogs, sheep, swine, cattle, horses), turned wild species of plants and trees to cultivable ones (grains, legumes, olive trees, and so on), and managed to produce a surplus of food. Managing these extra stocks of food required more complex forms of organization, and gradually they formed permanent societies (communities, kingdoms, etc.). The existence of complex social structures facilitated technological progress, and technology led to the creation of even more complex social structures. Thanks to the unequaled advantage of speech and the development of writing, humankind created more complex structures (a sovereign's commands could be transmitted in writing to the farthest corners of the kingdom) and became capable of transferring knowledge and experience from generation to generation.

By means of writing, humans were able to precisely record and disseminate collective knowledge. However, writing was not just a method of recording things, but much more: It somehow created logic. "Speech is too fleeting to allow for analysis," writes the American journalist James Gleick in his book *The Information*. "Logic descended from the written word, in Greece as well as India and China, where it developed independently."[44]

Thanks to the development of writing, humanity managed to break its bonds with mere experience (see, hear, narrate) and wander in the realms of what we call advanced knowledge. Mathematics, too, followed from the invention of writing.[45] Writing was instrumental to the scientific revolution, since it would be impossible to develop science without written culture.

Knowledge, the nucleus of civilization, is a mighty force. Quite often, though, knowledge—or, to be more precise, what we firmly believe is infallible knowledge—can get us into great trouble.

We often find ourselves at that dangerous point where the knowledge we have accumulated makes us overconfident and makes us "think that we understand much more than we actually do." This is something that the American-Lebanese professor Nassim Taleb calls "Platonicity." According to Taleb, the "Platonic fold" is "the explosive boundary where [what we think we know] enters in contact with messy reality, where the gap between what you know and what you think you know becomes dangerously wide."[46] And this is where the trouble begins.

Sadly, our education and the knowledge we accumulate fill us with arrogance and unfaltering certainties. We overestimate what we know and cast away what we don't know. We puff ourselves up for every personal achievement (which we always attribute to our exceptional skills, knowledge, and superior mental capacity) and rationalize our every mistake, our every misjudgment or erroneous decision, all of which are attributed to bad luck, some external obstacle, and so on. Everything good that happens is attributed to our intelligence and skills, while all our failures and mishaps are blamed on third parties or misfortune.

In the Western world, educational systems, from primary education to universities, stigmatize mistakes. Mistakes are never taught—only successes and conventional wisdom. But mistakes have much more educational value. Without them it is impossible to become creative and succeed.[47]

Success, progress, and development neither materialize out of nowhere nor are the product of enlightened inspiration (with a very few exceptions). They require hard work, toil, and painstaking implementation of the trial-and-error process.

HIGH-LEVEL FOOLISHNESS

Arrogance is deeply rooted within ourselves. Ancient Greeks believed that Delphi was the center of the world and Earth the center of the universe. This geocentric view, which in its various versions was supported by many civilizations, remained irrefutable for centuries.

Until the Middle Ages, the world considered it to be self-evident that all celestial bodies orbited the Earth. So great was the certainty that Earth was the center of the universe that astronomers developed highly complex geocentric models in order to explain the movement of celestial bodies. The heliocentric (sun-centered) hypothesis of Copernicus, which was developed in the 16th century and explained the movement of celestial bodies with much simpler and precise calculations, sparked an uproar and took many decades to be accepted.

---

* Copernicus's groundbreaking book, *De Revolutionibus Orbium Coelestium Libri VI,* was published in 1543 and caused a great reaction, not only among church leaders but among many scientists of that time. It was included in the Index of Prohibited Books of the Roman Catholic Church, were it remained listed until 1835.

Today, all these things may sound quaint; deep down, though, an anthropocentric view of the universe still persists.

As Adam Smith wrote, "The overweening conceit which the greater part of men have of their own abilities, is an ancient evil remarked by the philosophers and moralists of all ages."[48] Quite often, arrogance and self-complacency stem from knowledge or, to be more precise, from the things we think we know.

It is amazing how much nonsense has turned, over time, into irrefutable scientific certainty. High-level foolishness!

Up to 1850, doctors viewed washing their hands as a meaningless and unnecessary task. As a result, 25 percent of the women that gave birth in public hospitals died from childbed fever. Of the 620,000 men who died during the American Civil War (1861–1865), nearly 400,000 died not on the battlefield but in hospitals, as a result of infections caused by the doctors' dirty hands and the lack of sanitation.[49] It took many decades before doctors and nurses finally accepted the importance of personal hygiene.

In 1949, the Portuguese neurologist Egas Moniz was awarded the Nobel Prize for his contribution to the development of the lobotomy. According to Moniz's research, the adverse effects of serious mental disorders, such as schizophrenia, immediately vanished in people who underwent lobotomy. True, the procedure did make some symptoms of schizophrenia go away; however, the side-effects (which were initially ignored) were disastrous. In 1951, 20,000 lobotomy operations were performed in the United States alone. Little by little, a series of scientific studies shed light on the grave side-effects of lobotomy and threw doubt on the effectiveness of the process, leading to its decline and, finally, to its abandonment. Lobotomy was forgotten, but Moniz kept his Nobel Prize.

In the mid-1950s, when lobotomy was falling out of fashion, psychiatrists developed another "miraculous" cure: electroshock therapy.* Psychiatrist Donald Ewen Cameron, a distinguished scientist who had served as president of the American, Canadian, and World Psychiatric Associations, claimed that by inflicting an array of electroshocks, "he could unmake and erase faulty minds, then rebuild new personalities." How could he do that? By means of tape-recorded messages. Cameron's patients, "shocked and drugged into an almost vegetative state," were forced to listen to these messages for sixteen to twenty hours a day for weeks.[50]

In the late 1950s, a new class of "miraculous" pharmaceuticals, benzodiazepines, was discovered and became the basis of Valium. Valium was considered to be a perfect and totally harmless drug, and doctors prescribed it lavishly: for insomnia, for all forms of anxiety, for epileptic seizures, for backache, and so on. "In 1975, 100 million prescriptions for Valium and related drugs were filled in the United States alone." Valium was the magic pill that helped more and more people overcome their problems—until, in the mid-1970s, the magic vanished into thin air. Various studies started to produce alarming findings, and it was finally realized that "benzodiazepines, like so many of the wonder drugs of former times, can be addictive."[51]

One of the best-known tragedies of medicine concerns the "magic" drug thalidomide. Thalidomide was considered to be effective and safe and was heavily prescribed during the 1950s and the early 1960s for the treatment of insomnia, cough, common colds, and headaches. It was even used for alleviating morning sickness in pregnant women. A few years later, doctors found out that the drug caused very serious genetic defects. The

---

* Electroconvulsive therapy (ECT), also known as electroshock, is now a valuable and safe healing tool of modern psychiatry. Today it is administered on the basis of specific indications and in accordance with specific treatment protocols, in a patient-friendly and painless manner (the patient is first given an anesthetic), with the purpose of treating serious mental disorders, not reprogramming people.

miraculous hypnotic and antiemetic pill was proved to be a teratogen, as a result of which 10,000 babies all over the world were born with shortened limbs or limbs that were missing altogether.

The list of errors has no end. In the mid-1960s, for example, specialists claimed that mothers' milk had nothing more to offer than milk prepared in laboratories. Many people paid dearly for the specialists' certainty: Years later, research showed that those who were not breast-fed as infants had increased risk of developing a number of diseases. Moreover, it was found that breastfeeding reduced the risk of breast cancer among mothers. For another example, quite some time ago, tonsils were considered to be useless tissues that were removed for almost no reason. A few years later, research showed that people who had their tonsils removed ran a higher risk of developing throat cancer.[52]

High-level foolishness leaves no discipline untouched. In the past 20 years, many airliner crashes, with many hundreds dead, were caused because properly trained and fully specialized mechanics changed certain maintenance protocols, believing certain procedures to be redundant. Or they were caused by the mistakes of top engineers who designed new, state-of-the-art, and supposedly much safer airplanes. The *Mayday* documentary TV series, also known as *Air Crash Investigation(s)*, provides an abundance of relevant examples.

In Part Two of this text, we discussed the debacle of Robert Merton and Myron Scholes, the economists and holders of a Nobel Prize in Economic Sciences. They believed that, thanks to their advanced mathematics, they had put risk under control, when suddenly, in August 1998, the Russian crisis instantly evaporated all the assets of their much-touted Long-Term Capital Management fund.

In May 2012, while the wounds of the financial crisis were still open, JP Morgan, the largest bank in the United States, shocked markets by announcing trading losses of $2 billion. The company's management said the losses were caused by "errors," "sloppiness," and "bad judgment."[53]

The key assumption on which subprime lending and the securitization industry leading to the 2007 crisis had been based was that housing prices in the United States could never show any significant overall fall, as never before in the country's history had property prices declined simultaneously in all states. Highly paid and highly specialized executives, graduates of the best economic universities in the world, firmly believed that housing prices could not simultaneously decline all over the United States.

THE IRRESISTIBLE CHARM OF NARRATIVE

How did Egas Moniz (lobotomy), Donald Ewen Cameron ("reprogramming" the brain through electroshock), Robert Merton (Long-Term Capital Management), and many, many more manage to persuade the scientific world, as well as society at large, that their findings could work wonders? The answer is complex. However, it is certain that, among many key factors, the decisive one was their ability to tell great stories: to tidy up evidence, to connect facts, to synthesize phenomena and impose a logical coherence, creating a cogent narrative.

Narrative has an irresistible appeal to people, probably because it speaks mainly to affect. The brain, as we have seen, is designed to process facts in a manner that makes sense. Linking information and incorporating it into narratives makes it easier not only to understand, but also to memorize. By means of the narratives and logical patterns it creates, the brain can retain an immense volume of information and data that it would otherwise be unable to remember.

For example, a string of letters such as:

C-N-N-F-O-X-N-B-C-C-N-B-C-B-B-C-M-T-V

might be far outside the limits of our memory's capacity. It is very difficult to memorize these letters precisely and to remember them over a few days' time. However, if we break this string of letters into a more familiar pattern, everything changes:

CNN-FOX-NBC-CNBC-BBC-MTV[54]

This second string can be easily held in our memory and transferred to others for a long period of time. Prior to the advent of writing, ancient Greeks related from memory the Homeric epics, legends, and other heroic narratives, passing them from generation to generation. They had developed mnemonic devices based on similarities, contradictions, or close connections.[55] The meter, the formulaic redundancy, served as an aid to memory. "Its incantatory power made of the verse a time capsule, able to transmit" these heroic narratives across generations.[56]

The novelist E.M. Forster pointed out, in 1927, the crucial difference between the statements: "The king died and then the queen" and "The king died and then the queen died of grief."[57] The second statement is more comprehensible and can be recalled more easily, despite the fact that it includes an extra piece of information—the queen's grief—as compared with the first. This happens because by adding the cause of the queen's death we give plot and cohesion to the statement. We create a story, a narrative that makes much more sense than an indefinite, causeless death. Our brain is better able to comprehend an event when it can link it to a cause. An event's inclusion in a narrative makes the hard task of memorizing much easier.

As part of an experiment, subjects were asked to estimate the odds of the following two scenarios: First, a massive flood somewhere in America in which more than a thousand people die. Second, an earthquake in California causing massive flooding, in which more than a thousand people die. Most subjects selected the second scenario to be more likely.[58] However, the first scenario is actually much more likely to happen, since it is much more general and abstract. It includes the entire country—including California—and speaks generally of a flood that could have many causes (earthquake, heavy rainfall, the collapse of a dam, etc.). The irrational selection made by the subjects to this experiment illustrates the mind's powerful tendency to seek causality among events, as well as the irresistible charm of narrative. Stories stick. Data do not stick as easily.

Narrative can be useful; more often than not, though, it can be deceptive and become a powerful weapon in the hands of certain charismatic narrators. Politicians mesmerize crowds and govern with many words but very few deeds. Economists, using the heavy seal of mathematics, talk about how they have harnessed risk. Analysts, presenting a plausible narrative, predict this or that course of events with certainty. Lawyers tell nice stories, reframing facts and evidence, in order to make the jury sympathetic to their clients, and so on.

Karl Popper, the great philosopher, stated that in fact "there is no history of mankind, there is only an indefinite number of histories of all kinds of aspects of human life. And one of these is the history of political power. This is elevated into the history of the world."[59] It is impossible to approximate with any scientific accuracy the conditions that prevailed 100, 500, or 4,000 years ago or to reconstruct the facts. What history records are certain narratives that concern great and strong realms and important people. The accuracy and objectivity of these narratives are, at best, highly dubious.

IN RETROSPECT

Media figures, politicians, scientists, analysts—all of us, with no exception—have the ability to rationalize everything that happens in our life, to find meaning, reason, and cause in the way events unfold. This happens because the brain abhors confusion and cannot tolerate the unknown. So, in every single case, it will find the meaning and make the necessary connections so it seems that events are intertwined. In retrospect, everything makes sense. In a classic experiment, subjects listened to music while watching Christmas lights blinking. Most respondents erroneously believed that the two were synchronized.[60]

As the American journalist Robert Wright points out, "The brain is like a good lawyer: Given any set of interests to defend, it sets about convincing the world of their moral and logical worth…Like a lawyer, the human brain wants victory, not truth."[61] When information reaches the conscious mind, the brain, this great omniscience, will be called to make sense out of it.

An experiment conducted on a split-brain patient showed how unscrupulous the omniscient brain can be in its effort to carry out its task. Neuroscientists showed the patient (both of whose brain hemispheres functioned, but without communicating with each other) two pictures: a chicken claw to his right visual field, so the left hemisphere saw only that, and a snow scene to the left visual field, so the right hemisphere saw only that. Then the scientists asked the patient to choose from an array of pictures presented to him. He chose a picture of a shovel with his left hand and the image of a chicken with his right. When asked why he chose these two pictures, he said that it was very simple: "The chicken claw goes with the chicken, and you need a shovel to clean out the chicken shed." The left brain, the great omniscient, had not seen the snow scene, but had to offer an explanation for choosing the shovel.[62] And it effortlessly found this explanation. Our brain functions in a way that can rationalize literally everything!

Before the crisis of 2007, economists, analysts, and journalists argued with ease and certainty that the economic exuberance of the 2000s was fully justified. A few months after the shock of reaching the brink of economic collapse in 2008, they used equally irrefutable arguments, with the same ease and certainty, to explain why the crisis had been inescapable. Both before and after the crisis, everyone was brimming with certainty.

The tragic terrorist attacks of September 11, 2001, in the United States, which caused the deaths of almost 3,000 people, have been deeply etched into the collective memory. A few hours before the attack such a thing was inconceivable, impossible. A few days later, the globe was teeming with explanations offered by all kinds of experts (and of course including dozens of conspiracy theories) regarding the causes of this inconceivable act of terrorism.

When we assess something that has already transpired, no matter how rare or improbable an event it is, in retrospect it always seems plain and predictable. No matter what has happened, our brain will find the reasons to substantiate it.

THE THINGS WE DON'T KNOW

The achievements of science and technology are more than simply amazing. What to mention first? Man setting foot on the moon decades ago? The robots (Spirit and Opportunity) that explored the surface of Mars? Cosmology, which studies the birth of the universe? The decoding of the DNA sequence? The achievements of medicine and pharmacology, which allow us to live a longer and better life? Or the cars, the TVs, the air conditioners, the computers, the mobile phones, and the abundance of other goods that make our lives easier and are affordable even to society's lowest-income groups? The list of achievements has no end. The knowledge that we have accumulated in each field has no precedent. Equipped with applied mechanics, mankind seems capable of achieving the impossible. We just need to aim at it.

Nevertheless, the moon also has a dark side: all the things we don't know, the things we tend to push out of the limelight, to cast into the darkness. We have already spoken about the mysteries of the brain. Since ancient times, doctors have been able only to conjecture about what schizophrenia is. We do not know how the menstrual cycle, which is amazingly precise in most women, is timed and controlled by the body. Cancer is another unsolved puzzle; despite extensive research, many forms of this disease remain incurable. The causes of Alzheimer's disease remain unknown. Why can't we predict earthquakes? Even the common flu has not been eradicated, causing thousands of deaths each year. Notwithstanding mankind's undisputed progress, the list of the things we don't know is still long.

There is a striking asymmetry between knowledge, such as the conquest of the moon or the decoding of the DNA sequence, which fills us with self-confidence and, unfortunately, quite often with arrogance, and non-knowledge, such as the inability to eradicate cancer or predict earthquakes, which is cast away into the shadows. We puff ourselves up for our mental abilities, which have allowed us to form theories regarding the Big Bang and the creation of the universe, while, at the same time, we are unable to systematically predict the weather. What we don't know is just as important as what we do know.

But the omniscient brain is embarrassed by, and does not tolerate, ignorance and incomprehension. So, it focuses on the visible side of the moon.

If we were indeed rational, we would more often contemplate the things we don't know and we would be more cautious regarding our abilities. We would be more modest. And, by all means, we wouldn't attribute a negative connotation to the word *humble.*

---

* Humble are those who are aware of their insignificance, of their frailty. The word, however, also denotes those who are low in rank, quality, or station.

4

THE POWER OF EXPERTS

Adam Smith highlighted the importance of specialization in the modern world (remember his excellent example of the pin factory). Since then, the world has become increasingly specialized, and scientists focus on more and more limited subjects, which they know almost perfectly. Our era is the apotheosis of specialization.

That said, in addition to its positive aspects (productivity gains, enhanced innovation, etc.) specialization also has some negative ones. Scientists and practitioners may benefit a lot from delving into a subject, albeit lose a lot in terms of broadness of spirit.

Excessive specialization at the expense of general knowledge, what we call culture and education, leads to individuals who are scientifically/professionally perfect, though socially incomplete. Our knowledge has become much better, but more limited. Sadly enough, many universities are currently creating highly specialized yet ignorant people, unable not only to express an opinion, but even to understand how the world beyond their own field of expertise works.

A microsurgeon may perform delicate operations on the little fingers of a months-old infant and be, nonetheless, unable to tell the difference between a deposit and a bond. Or she may not have any clue of what the French Revolution was. A physician may list the bones of the hand from memory but be completely unaware that just a few decades ago, certain irrefutable medical certainties ("washing one's hands is meaningless") caused the deaths of thousands of people. A physicist may understand the fine concepts of quantum physics but find it hard to grasp elementary social issues. Even worse, a graduate of the business administration department of a school of economics may be an expert on issues pertaining to a firm's operation but have a limited understanding of macroeconomics.

The overspecialization that dominates our era gives specialists great power. Feeling insecure about making our own judgments, we seek expert opinions on everything: how to raise our kids, how to take care of our diets, how to treat our significant others, how to dress, and so on. We are peculiarly addicted to experts, in order to cope with everyday life.

Most times, expert opinion is accepted as irrefutable fact. Experts are people who know the solutions and are lent almost magical qualities by society, which obeys their dictates as if mesmerized. Expert opinions are not critically evaluated and are very seldom put to the test. When a person say something, his degree of specialization is more important than what he actually says. Moreover, the more obscure and specialized the jargon an expert uses, the more prestige he enjoys and the more important he (or she) seems in the eyes of the many.

THE MAGIC OF THE WHITE COAT

According to psychiatric reports, people who experience highly stressful situations show immediate, spectacular improvement as soon as a doctor shows interest in their condition. Two or three simple questions, showing that the doctor understands the problem and empathizes, are enough to provide the patient with immediate relief.

What would you think, though, if you were told that even the sense of physical pain—in other words, how much we hurt—is a very relative thing? Jon Levine, from the University of California, set out to find out how personal contact can alleviate pain. Levine took healthy volunteers who had just had their wisdom teeth extracted and told them he was going to inject them with a painkiller to reduce their pain. In reality, Levine was injecting them with a placebo. He divided the volunteers into two groups. One was given the injection by a computer-controlled automatic pump, without any doctor or nurse present. The second group was given the injection by Levine himself, complete with white coat, stethoscope, and meticulous administration of the medication. Remember, both groups were given a placebo. Afterward, Levine asked the patients to judge their level of pain on a numerical scale. The differences between the two groups were more than striking. "Those who were ministered to by the faceless computer had little alleviation of pain. But those who had the personal care of a doctor suffered much less."[63] Without being given a real drug, patients felt less pain at the mere sight of the white coat, simply because an expert took care of them.

Just as in the depths of Africa the dances, incantations, and colorful masks of the shamans drive away pain and make the patient feel better, in our modern era the doctor's white coat apparently retains some magical powers.

The influence of specialists—of any authority—on the individual is immense and may lead to unthinkable acts. The studies carried out by American social scientist Stanley Milgram (1933–1984) caused shock and awe. His experiments were conducted at Yale University with the participation of two people and the experimenter. The actual subject of the study was asked to assume the role of a teacher; the second person pretended to be a learner but in fact was, along with the experimenter, one of Milgram's associates. The experimenter instructed the supposed teacher to administer an electric shock to the learner each time the latter gave the wrong answer to a mnemonic test, and to increase the voltage after each mistake. Of course, no actual electroshock was administered, but the learner pretended to be in pain. The learner eventually claimed to be in great agony and asked that the electroshock be stopped. If the "teacher" hesitated to continue and asked guidance from the experimenter, the latter gave one of the following instructions: 1) Please continue; 2) The experiment requires that you continue; 3) It is absolutely essential that you continue; or 4) You have no other choice, you must go on. The experimenter guaranteed that the electric shock would not cause any permanent damage to the learners and asked the "teachers" to continue administering it, stressing that he personally assumed all responsibility. An eerily large number of the subjects who played the teacher's role continued to administer the electric shocks, despite the fact that the learner was screaming in pain and asking to be relieved.[64] The fact that a specialist assumed all responsibility, providing assurances that there was no danger, was enough to make the subjects ignore the tangible reality: They were torturing another human being.

Obedience to authority is deeply rooted within us, starting from the way we are raised as children ("Always listen to your parents [your grandma, your teacher, etc.]") and extending through society's hierarchical structure.

Television and the media have magnified the power of experts: Professor X or doctor Y or psychologist Z said it. In 2011–2012, hosts of economics professors all over the world explained with certainty why the euro was doomed to fail. Others, though, believed the euro crisis would hasten the political union of European Union member states, a view that, apparently, has been borne out by subsequent developments (banking union, etc.). As if disagreements among experts were not enough, conventional wisdom changes almost every year. The consumption of liver by children is sometimes thought to be dangerous, and at other times is said to be necessary for the development of the brain. The same applies to whether babies should sleep on their stomach or on their back.*

Expert studies highlight the advantages of consuming red meat. Other studies claim that the consumption of meat is linked to heart disease and certain forms of cancer. In general, there are experts for every taste, capable of providing strong arguments to support even the most implausible views.

GIBBERISH

"Sound is the change in the specific condition of segregation of the material parts, and in the negation of this condition;—merely an abstract or an ideal ideality, as it were, of that specification. But this change, accordingly, is itself immediately the negation of the material specific subsistence; which is, therefore, real ideality of specific gravity and cohesion, i.e.—heat. The heating up of sounding bodies, just as of beaten or rubbed ones, is the appearance of heat, originating conceptually together with sound."[65]

What do you think of the above statement? We humans are frivolous beings that are attracted by spectacular phenomena. We are easily impressed, and we seek to impress others any way we can. In addition, we are impressed not so much by arguments as by the identity of the person who presents them (the power of experts).

If I told you that this statement was one of my own attempts at complex thinking, you would probably sneer at my ravings. If, however, I told you that the above statement belongs to Hegel, the great German philosopher,

---

* In her book *Raising America: Experts, Parents, and a Century of Advice About Children*, Ann Hulbert documents the contradictions and inconsistencies of expert opinions on child-rearing over time.

then you would be much more restrained in your criticism. You would read the passage again and again, trying to find some meaning. Even if you ultimately failed to do so, you would probably assume it was your fault that you could not grasp the profound meaning of the text, despite the fact that the great philosopher (also) wrote things that could be dismissed by many people as gibberish.

Specialized terms and difficult words that are not used in everyday life have an irresistible charm and add an aura of spiritual superiority. Yale University psychologist Jeremy Gray devised the following clever experiment to demonstrate the power of intricately formulated babble. Gray gave volunteers the following text to read:

> *Researchers created a list of facts that about 50% of people knew. Subjects then read the list and noted which ones they already knew. They then judged what percentage of other people would know those facts. When subjects knew a fact, they thought that an inaccurately large percentage of others would know it, too. For example, a subject who already knew that Hartford was the capital of Connecticut might think that 80% of other people would know it, even though only 50% actually do. The researchers call this finding "the curse of knowledge."*

Then, Gray asked the volunteers to choose between a bad and a good explanation for the "curse of knowledge." The bad explanation claimed this: "This 'curse' happens because subjects make more mistakes when they have to judge the knowledge of others. People are better at judging what they themselves know." The good explanation stated: "This 'curse' happens because subjects have trouble switching their point of view to consider what someone else might know, mistakenly projecting their own knowledge onto others." It should be noted that Gray designed the answers so that the first explanation does not actually tell anything about the phenomenon, whereas the second, the good explanation, exhibits a strong logic and seems to provide a satisfactory explanation.

Most of the volunteers who participated in the experiments rated the good explanation as more satisfying, dismissing the first one as irrelevant. Nonetheless, everything changed when a completely irrelevant, yet impressive, piece of information about the human brain was added to the first explanation: "Brain scans indicate that this 'curse' happens because of the frontal lobe brain circuitry known to be involved in self-knowledge. Subjects make more mistakes when they have to judge the knowledge of others. People are much better at judging what they themselves know."[66] After this impressive, scientific-sounding piece of information was added, the subjects rated the bad explanation as more satisfactory than the good one.

In 1996, Alan Sokal, professor of mathematics at University College London and professor of physics at New York University, submitted a paper full of well-written, pompous nonsense, for publication in the scientific journal *Social Text*. Sokal wanted to see if it was possible to have a nonsensical paper published simply because it appeared to be serious and "flattered the editors' ideological preconceptions." The article, ponderously titled "Transgressing the Boundaries: Towards a Transformative Hermeneutics of Quantum Gravity," was published unedited in the journal in the summer of 1996, causing a stir in the academic community.

Today, all the high-risk "synthetic" investment products that wreaked havoc in 2008 are known as "toxic" products. But in the 2000s, the buyers of those products—insurance funds, institutional investors, banks, etc.—were purchasing "collateralized mortgage obligations" (CMOs), "collateralized debt obligations" (CDOs), and "collateralized loan obligations" (CLOs). Junk had been adorned with fancy words, designed to convey a feeling of security and certainty.

So, beware of eloquent, elaborate, pompous, and ponderous analyses. Setting aside the lofty pursuits of philosophers, all things that pertain to the world of real action can be phrased in a manner that is simple, clear, and understandable to the average person. When public discourse is rife with obscure concepts, specialized expressions, and jargon, watch out: Someone wants either to impress us with trinkets and mirrors or to mislead us through a pompous narrative.

5

DECISION MAKING

We are making decisions all the time, from small, everyday matters, such as what to eat and what clothes to wear, to very important issues that may affect our entire life, such as what profession to follow and if (or when) to have children.

Unfortunately, many decisions are irrevocable, and those that can be revoked may incur a huge cost. For example, if you study to become a lawyer and then realize that law is not your thing, a new beginning in another profession will require extra effort and time, and the three- or four-year investment in obtaining your law degree may lose its value. Similarly, if in 2005 you decided to put your savings in Citicorp stock in the belief that investing in a financial giant was the safest and most efficient choice, today, more than seven years after the 2007 crisis, you would still show losses of almost 90 percent.* Time cannot be reversed.

If you retired in 2004 and placed your lump-sum retirement benefit in bonds of a member state of the mighty euro zone, to make sure you'd sleep easy at night (since states do not default), today you are probably realizing

---

* In early 2007 the price of Citibank shares stood at $550 (adjusted for the reverse split that took place); by early 2009 it had fallen to $10. Today, in June 2014, the company's stock is trading at $49.

that things are not exactly that way. The "haircut" of Greek government bonds, through the voluntary public sector involvement (PSI) scheme, led to losses of more than 50 percent for all holders of Greek sovereign debt.

Decisions are made under conditions of uncertainty and entail risk. There are no guarantees or assurances that the outcome will be this, that, or the other. In 1921, the economist Frank Knight (1885–1972) made a distinction between uncertainty, which cannot be measured, and risk, which can be quantified and measured with the help of statistics.[67] Uncertainty includes, for example, a devastating earthquake, a major terrorist attack, a deadly tsunami, a fatal flu epidemic, and so on. Risk is something that can be assessed on the basis of statistical observations; for example, the probability of heads or tails when tossing a coin or the probability of winning at the slot machines of a casino. The decision-making process is complex and dynamic, and we do not have the slightest idea of how many things, big or small, affect it. As we have seen, expectations, feelings, emotions, beliefs, knowledge, experiences, misapprehensions (narratives, impressions, our interpretation of events, etc.), the influence of friends (and the friends of these friends), and a host of other things that we may not even suspect play a decisive role.

Decisions are reached through the interaction of emotions and logic, but the exact process is not clear. As we will see below, whenever we lack sufficient data or information about something and we need to make a decision, we tend to be affected by random or irrelevant elements.

THOUGHT, INTUITION, AND EMOTION

Psychologists divide the process of thinking into two systems: System 1 corresponds to what we consider to be, and conceive of as, intuition; System 2 corresponds to complex analytical thinking.[68]

System 1, as described by Daniel Kahneman* in his book *Thinking, Fast and Slow*, operates automatically and quickly, makes associations, and is capable of handling many facts simultaneously. It is based on emotions, impressions, and biases and has a strong emotional content. It operates with little or no effort and no sense of voluntary control. It is what makes us act swiftly and effectively, even under the most pressing situations. System 1 is perfect for reaching quick decisions; however, whether these decisions are correct or rational may be a different story altogether. Quite often, intuitive action leads to persistent, repeated errors.

System 2 is what we consider to be, and conceive of as, thought. It is analytical, linear, and progressive; requires time and effort; employs rules; and is based on judgment. It deals with tough problems that require strenuous mental activities and complex calculations. It follows a logical sequence, which allows us to revisit previous stages of thought and correct mistakes. System 2 leads more seldom to errors and even more seldom to systematic, repeated mistakes, as individuals learn from their errors and improve themselves.

In short, System 1 is superior in terms of speed but is inferior in terms of quality, while the qualitative superiority of System 2 (fewer errors) is costly in terms of time and effort. To a great extent, human behavior is determined by the interaction of these two systems. The interaction among personal, social, and emotional factors leads to the preponderance of logic in certain cases and to the preponderance of emotion in others. Speed is crucial in our everyday life. Most times we must immediately reach a decision; whether this is the most appropriate one is of secondary importance.

According to Kahneman, when we think about our own self we identify it with thought, with our consciously thinking self that makes choices

---

* Daniel Kahneman and Amos Tversky (1937–1996) are considered to be pioneers for their research regarding decision making. In recognition of their work, Kahneman received the Nobel Prize in Economic Sciences in 2002, six years after Tversky's death.

and decisions (System 2). However, the great star of our everyday lives is something that goes unnoticed, something that flies under the radar of consciousness: System 1, intuition, which "is effortlessly originating impressions and feelings that are the main sources of the explicit beliefs and deliberate choices of System 2," thought.[69]

So even when we try to employ cold logic to contemplate an issue and reach a purely rational decision, we will probably fail to do so. Many independent studies have shown that we humans rush to rely on the first argument that satisfies our opinion. As we have seen, humans rely mainly on pleasant narratives, on plausible stories. "A plausible narrative is sufficient to dictate the corresponding verdict choice, testimony inconsistent with this narrative is disregarded."[70] Just one story/narrative is enough to persuade the logical system that things are exactly that way, to lead to the formation of a strong opinion and to corresponding actions.

The contribution of emotions to the decision-making process is decisive. Emotions such as joy, fear, disgust, anger, sorrow, surprise, and contempt, are omnipresent. Even though we like to think of ourselves as being able to make nonemotional decisions, emotions are always lurking in the background, and emotion is the ultimate arbitrator of an action.[71] Likes or dislikes, contempt, instant anger: Quite often, these things ultimately determine an action. Emotion is the great catalyst, while the omniscient brain will simply find the necessary logical arguments to justify any action.

Gazzaniga believes that we humans are apparently not yet comfortable with our rational, analytic mind: "In terms of evolution, it is a new ability that we humans have recently come upon, and we appear to use sparingly."[72] Given this, economists may take heart: There is indeed hope that, thousands of years in the future, *Homo economicus* may actually gain flesh and blood!

FAST AND DIRTY

We have seen how System 1—intuition—helps us reach swift decisions. Swiftness in decision making is more crucial for our everyday survival than the actual quality of the decisions. A correct decision at the wrong time is a wrong decision.

Through experience, we humans are unconsciously creating rules, on the basis of which we solve everyday problems and reach fast decisions. Psychologists have given these rules of thumb, which work pretty well in most situations, the name *heuristics*.[73] Heuristics help people simplify difficult and complex problems and handle them in a fast and efficient manner. Many people, though, say that the way heuristics work is not only fast but also dirty, pointing to the fact that they quite often lead to repeated errors. "People," write Tversky and Kahneman, "rely on a limited number of heuristic principles which reduce the complex tasks of assessing probabilities and predicting values to simpler judgmental operations."[74] Generally speaking, heuristics are very useful but often lead to serious systematic errors.

The errors related to heuristic strategies are not easy to identify and deal with, since their operation depends on the computing processes of the brain that have developed during thousands of years of human evolution. As Thorstein Veblen so insightfully noted more than 100 years ago, deep inside us are primitive emotions related to millions of years of evolution. Consider this: Everyone easily learns to be afraid of snakes, but it is impossible to teach a child to be afraid and cautious of flowers!

We humans have many innate fears: fear of strangers, fear of being taken by surprise, fear of falling into a void, and so on, many of which are unfounded. A six-month-old infant is afraid of loud noises and sudden movements. Lab rats (that have been born and raised in a safe environment) show reactions of fear when smelling a cat, despite the fact that they have never in their lives encountered such an animal.

Little children and grownups share an instinctive fear of the dark. This is, more or less, the case in all civilizations. When we are in an unknown environment, such as a forest, and we hear a strange sound or see something move toward us, we automatically assume a defensive stance, or we move away as quickly as possible; we never stop to consider whether it is actually a wild beast that is coming to get us, or simply a shadow. Obviously, our most contemplative ancestors (if they indeed existed) would not have managed to survive for long (and disseminate their genetic material) if, at any potential danger, they stopped to think whether the danger was real or not. The only survivors were those who reacted immediately, quickly running away from the potential danger without wasting a single second on analytical thinking.*

When we go through an episode of intense fear, the pupils of our eyes dilate (so that we can see better), the heart beats faster (more blood means more available energy), our breathing quickens (the body needs more oxygen), the skin sweats (evaporating perspiration cools the muscles), and our hair is raised (a purely primitive reaction). All these reactions are triggered by the autonomic nervous system, and our conscious self has absolutely no way of assuming control over them. The most impressive thing is that these involuntary reactions are manifest in exactly the same manner in other animals that experience fear, from chimpanzees to mice.

There are more such mechanical actions in our life than we ever suspect, and they are instrumental in shaping our behavior.

When we stand in the queue to buy, let's say, bread, we do not analyze the pros and cons of each type of bread. We simply decide on the spot, either because we

---

* More on fear and the neuroanatomical background of fear can be found in *The Emotional Brain: The Mysterious Underpinnings of Emotional Life*, by Joseph E. LeDoux.

recall some taste we savored in the past or because at that precise moment some characteristic, such as shape, color, or smell, draws our attention. Or we simply choose what the person in front of us has chosen (mirror neurons in action).

Even major business decisions, where the evidence is not enough to produce a straightforward yes or no, are based on intuition or, even worse, on the mood, bad or good, of the person or people making these crucial decisions at that specific time.

If for every decision we undertook a detailed analysis of advantages and disadvantages, costs and benefits, as well as alternatives, we would remain inactive for hours, and we would be able to complete only a limited number of actions.

As mentioned above, speed is crucial. However, speed has its price. In order to carry out the tough task of day-to-day survival and provide quick answers, the brain quite often "lies" to us, overlooks parts of reality, reconstructs facts, and leads us to repeated errors. As we have seen, we all consider ourselves to be capable and smart, and we believe we can make nonemotional, purely rational decisions; in practice, though, everywhere and always, under the radar of the conscious mind, emotions are guiding our choices.

This inconvenient and dark side of human behavior should be acknowledged and remembered regularly, especially when the sirens of success are singing the sweet tunes of pride and arrogance.

ANCHORING

An especially powerful heuristic that is often employed when making decisions is anchoring. Whenever people have insufficient information about a certain value they are called to estimate, or when they have to make a decision on the basis of limited information, they hold on to—they anchor themselves to—any available information, even random numbers.

As part of a classic experiment, subjects were asked to give their best guess of the percentage of African nations in the United Nations. Before that, they had been asked to spin a wheel of fortune (like the ones used in game shows) marked from 1 to 100. The experiment showed that if the wheel stopped at a small number, the subjects tended to guess an equally small number of African U.N.-member nations. Conversely, if the wheel stopped at a large number, they gave a much larger number of nations.[75] Remember the experiment we saw in a previous section, the one with the chicken, the snow scene, and the shovel.

In another famous experiment, participants were asked to consider the four last digits of their tax registration number. Then they were asked to make a guess of the number of physiotherapists working in New York. Once again, those with large tax registration numbers overestimated the number of physiotherapists, and the people with smaller numbers underestimated.

Northcraft and Neale asked real estate agents and business school students to estimate the value of a particular house. These estimates included an appropriate advertising price, i.e., a reasonable price for buying the house, as well as the lowest offer. Some participants were given a high listing price as a starting point, while others were given a lower price. The researchers found that "in all cases, the estimates were heavily dependent on the listing price which the research participants had been given. Those who were given a high listing price made higher estimates than those given the low listing price."[76]

FRAMING

The decision-making process is greatly affected by the way a problem is formulated. Quite often, the solution we choose or decision we make depends not so much on the problem *per se*, but on how we perceive it. In other words, the same problem may be given many different and conflicting solutions by the same individuals, depending on the way it is presented to them.

The way a problem is presented may fool even specialists. A group of statistics undergraduates were given a simple statistical problem that was not phrased in a statistical manner: "Assume that you live in a town with two hospitals—one large, the other small. On a given day 60 percent of those born in one of the two hospitals are boys. Which hospital is it likely to be? Many statisticians made the equivalent of the mistake (during a casual conversation) of choosing the larger hospital, when in fact the very basis of statistics is that large samples are more stable and should fluctuate less from the long-term average—here, 50 percent for each of the sexes—than smaller samples"[77] Many students chose the seemingly obvious, namely that the largest probability lies with the hospital where more babies are born, overlooking a fundamental rule of statistics: The smaller the sample, the more unstable the result. (Conversely, the more the sample size increases, the more we approach the average.) The experiment showed that a large number of people specializing in statistical issues made the wrong choices.

In another study, volunteers were asked to choose between two courses of action to combat a serious disease that was expected to kill 600 people. One group of volunteers was told that option A would result in saving 200 lives, while if option B was selected there would be a one in three chance of saving everyone and a two in three chance of not saving anyone. The second group of volunteers was given exactly the same options, but phrased differently. Instead of hearing that 200 would be saved with option A, they were told that 400 would die. Similarly, option B was phrased as offering a one in three probability that no one would die and a two in three probability that all 600 people would perish. Seventy-two percent of the first group of volunteers chose option A, but only 22 percent of the second group made the same choice.[78] Phrasing exactly the same problem in a different way had a decisive effect on the participants' perception and led to completely different decisions.

6

ON PREDICTION

"For the gods perceive future things, ordinary people things in the present, but the wise perceive things about to happen."

Kavafy, Philostratos, *Life of Apollonios of Tyana,* viii, 7*

In the previous sections we saw how our way of thinking, our senses, and our emotions are actively involved in an extensive, unconscious conspiracy that makes us believe that we perceive, understand, and control much more than we actually do.

Totally certain that we fully comprehend everything that happens and feeling that we have the situation under control, we move even further and try to make predictions about tomorrow or even the distant future. But harsh reality never ceases to belie our unfaltering certainties and our predictions.

We are spending a great deal of time, energy, and money and using our greatest minds to understand what is going on around us and to plan for the future; however, the most improbable reality still pops up under our nose and takes us by surprise. The United States used to spend billions of

---

* Translated by Edmund Keeley/Philip Sherrard

dollars and employed leading academics, scientists, analysts, and opera-tives to scrutinize the Soviet Union. They monitored and analyzed every-thing. And all this manpower, with its vast resources and cutting-edge technology, was completely surprised in the winter of 1989. The fall of the Berlin Wall and the rapid unraveling of the Soviet Union had not been predicted by anyone. "No world power had ever disintegrated so totally or so rapidly without losing a war."[79]

In order to cope with the discrepancy between the things we predict and the chaos of reality, we have developed a highly efficient self-deception and mutual-deception mechanism. Whenever a prediction of theirs is verified, experts attribute this to their knowledge, skills, and sophis-ticated tools. But when their predictions fail, blame is laid on circum-stances, bad luck, and so on. The same is true on the personal level: Our successes are the result of our ability, our failures are caused by others or by ill luck.

In the late nineteenth century, French physicist and mathematician Henri Poincaré (1854–1912) made an astounding discovery, overturning ideal-ized Newtonian certainties. According to classical physics, a closed system (a few interacting bodies, isolated from outside forces) is in perfect order and is fully predictable (a pendulum will swing back and forth eternally). As Poincaré showed, in the case of a closed, stable system that contains only two bodies, such as the sun and the Earth, the orbits can be precisely determined and Newton's equations can be solved exactly. However, by simply adding one more body, such as the moon, we render Newton's equations unsolvable. Their solution requires a series of approximations. Poincaré showed that with even the very smallest perturbation, some or-bits behave in an erratic, even chaotic way. His calculations showed that a minute gravitational pull from a third body might cause a planet to wob-ble and weave drunkenly in its orbit and even fly out of the solar system altogether."[80]

But Poincaré's findings were relegated to the fringes, as the scientists of that era were not yet ready to explore and discuss approaches outside the field of Newtonian physics.

Darwin was also initially treated with suspicion when, in 1859, he published his historic, revolutionary book *On the Origin of Species*, refuting the belief in the individual creation of each species and upsetting the notion of a perfectly designed, benign natural world. It was Darwin who introduced the concepts of probability, chance, and uniqueness into scientific discourse. [81]

Chance and microstates (which interact, producing macrostates) prevail, leading the evolution of life on this planet—and our day-to-day lives as well—along highly complex and unpredictable paths.

Reality is a dynamic, chaotic system, affected by a huge number of variables that overwhelm any computing capacity. "The more microstates that are associated with a given macrostate, the less we are able to say with precision about the individual components of the system."[82]

Quite often, the predictions of certain analysts/experts are verified. But this is a far cry from systematically making accurate predictions. In a pool of many thousands of experts who make myriad predictions about the future, some of these predictions are bound to be verified. I am not talking about some kind of lottery; I am talking about the coincidental alignment of an expert's view with reality. Some alternative pathways are corroborated by fact. These predictions draw attention and make the headlines.

The more unusual or nonlinear these verified predictions are, the more of a sensation they make. When these heretical predictions are borne out, then the dissident prophets are deified. But most predictions simply slip into oblivion.

A YESTERDAY-LIKE TOMORROW

Expert predictions are rarely based on well-thought-out analyses or on an inspired combination of facts, data, and experience that leads to conclusions. There are very few analyses that try to reach below the surface, seeking out deeper causes and roots, in order to reach conclusions and formulate meaningful predictions.

Usually, predictions are projections of yesterday into tomorrow. Economists make some assumptions, for instance that the GDP will grow by 6 percent in the next three years, that interest rates will range around 3 percent, and that inflation will average 2 percent, and use these assumptions to extrapolate the fundamentals of an economy or a business three years into the future. These assumptions are based on history and the data of previous years (more about the economists' predictions in the next section).

Climate change experts observe the evolution of temperatures and other climatic data during, let's say, the past 50 years, and make a projection into the (unknown) future, predicting disasters and natural calamities. It is so naively simple. Based on limited knowledge and experience, we are trying to predict the potentially infinite paths of the future. Even though we are not even able to predict tomorrow's weather with some reasonable certainty, we are under the illusion that we can estimate climatic developments 10, 20, or 30 years ahead.

But what happens if tomorrow, or in the year 2020, scientists develop a new technology that will drastically alter, for example, the energy sector? Remember the reasoning of the Reverend Thomas Malthus, who, on the basis of what he knew, predicted famine and devastation. He claimed that the exponential growth of populations could not be covered by the linear growth of food production. There would not be enough food for everyone. Malthus was not delusional. Given the knowledge of the 1800s, he was absolutely right. However, the future is not determined by today's and yesterday's knowledge, but by tomorrow's achievements, which are impossible to know and incorporate into our predictive models. Technology is the most crucial parameter and has a decisive effect on the evolution of social and economic life. Malthus could not imagine the technological revolution that was to come.

The predictions of the Club of Rome* are another example of erroneous estimate. The group's 1972 book, *The Limits to Growth*, included a simulation model that (in Malthusian fashion) warned about the devastating effects of rapid population growth, given finite resources. None of these predictions has come to pass.

The future cannot be predicted, simply because no one can foretell nor even conceive of technological progress.

The great paradox is that, at the same time we acknowledge our inability to predict the development of new technologies, we venture forth with long-term "scientific" predictions on a series of issues whose outcomes depend exclusively on technological progress.

Taleb uses a story about a turkey to warn us about the problem of induction, in other words, of knowledge that is based on (limited) experience. Consider a turkey being raised in the yard of a farmhouse in the U.S. Midwest. It is well fed and always has a warm and safe place to spend the night. With every passing day, the turkey becomes firmer in its belief that the people of the house love it and look out for its best interests. The days pass uneventfully, and the turkey feels happy and safe. But on the afternoon of the Wednesday before Thanksgiving, something unexpected happens, something unthinkable based on the turkey's experience, putting

---

* The Club of Rome is a global think tank that deals with a variety of international political issues. Founded in 1968 at Accademia dei Lincei in Rome, Italy, the CoR describes itself as "a group of world citizens, sharing a common concern for the future of humanity." It consists of current and former heads of state, UN bureaucrats, high-level politicians and government officials, diplomats, scientists, economists and business leaders from around the globe.

a violent end to its beliefs about the intentions of its human masters (who had been so diligently taking care of it).

If tomorrow were a continuation of yesterday and the course of events were linear, then ancient Greece or the Roman Empire would dominate the Mediterranean Basin. Or, to avoid going that far back in history, the Chinese and British empires would not have met with such inglorious demises.

Progress is neither as linear nor as predictable as many people think.

THE THINGS TO COME

In the winter of 1940, the French had a haughty attitude toward Germany's increasing hostility. They thought it was the other nation's problem, not their own. They firmly believed that France was invincible and secure from the Germans. Their confidence was founded on the Maginot Line, a long line of fortifications at the Franco-German border that was thought to be impregnable. However, this impressive defensive line did not deter the Germans from launching an offensive against France in May 1940. Contrary to predictions, the German army strolled across French soil and in just a few weeks was marching triumphantly in the streets of Paris. Hitler simply outflanked the mighty fortification, invading through Belgium, and forced the French to a dishonorable surrender without a fight. The "impregnable" Maginot Line had been constructed on the basis of the experiences and lessons of World War I.

Success fuels complacency, and complacency leads to failure. On Sunday, June 22, 1941, Germany invaded the Soviet Union, predicting that a few weeks would be enough to achieve the objectives of the operation and destroy Soviet forces. On July 3, encouraged by the initial successes of the

German army, general Franz Halder (1884–1972) confidently declared, "It is no exaggeration to say that the Russian campaign has been won in fourteen days" A few months later, the campaign took a turn, and the Soviet Union became a vast grave for German soldiers, marking the beginning of the end for Nazism.

In the late 1860s, metal industry experts believed that the only metals with "a serious economic future" were those that had been known since ancient times, such as iron, copper, lead, gold, and silver. They claimed that the novel metals of that time, such as manganese, nickel, cobalt, and aluminum, did not seem "destined to play an important role as their elders."[83] Reality, as determined by technological progress, surpassed the estimates of these experts by far.

Let's consider something much simpler and more controlled, like the construction of a building. The construction of the famous Sydney Opera House, which was designed by the Danish architect Jørn Utzon, had a budget of $7 million (Australian). It was begun in 1960 and its completion was expected in 1963. In the end, the opera house opened its doors to the public ten years later with a cost exceeding $100 million (Australian). In 1883 Antoni Gaudí undertook the design and construction of the famous Basilica of the Sagrada Família in Barcelona, and in 1886 he stated that the work would be completed in ten years. The project is still unfinished, and the aim of the Spanish government is to have all work done by 2026, the centennial of Gaudí's death!

In the 1980s, all analysts (and U.S. policymakers) gazed at the Japanese economic miracle with awe, and everybody agreed that Japan would soon become a new superpower. In contrast, the United States was in decline, its industry waning, its poor fiscal condition leaving little room for optimism. Indeed, in 1969, when Japan showed very high growth rates, the futurist Herman Kahn published *The Emerging Japanese Superstate*, predicting that it would be the world's leading economy by the year 2000.[84] In the late 1970s, Ezra Vogel's best-seller, *Japan as Number One*, caused a stir. All this proved to be hot air. By the late 1990s, contrary to all pompous predictions, Japan had become an outworn economy, while the United States, spearheaded by new technology, was the uncontested global power. Japan not only didn't become number one as experts predicted, but was trapped in a painful recession, the infamous Lost Decade discussed in Part Two.

At the end of the 1990s, the greatest challenge for biologists was to determine the number of genes in the human genome. Some top geneticists estimated that the number of genes ranged from 80,000 to 100,000. However, in September 1999, Incyte Genomics estimated the number at almost 140,000, and some biologists claimed it did not exceed 50,000. Ewan Birney, a geneticist at the European Bioinformatics Institute, decided to start a peculiar betting pool for the world's top researchers: They could bet on their predictions regarding the final gene count. Initially, 338 biologists took part in the pool; the average estimate was 66,050 genes and the highest stood at 153,478. By 2002, another 115 biologists had entered the bet; their average estimate was only 44,375, and the lowest estimate stood at 25,747 genes. The final number of genes remains uncertain, but the most accepted value has dropped to 19,599, much lower than the experts' lowest estimate (25,747).[85] In short, not even one of the 453 leading biologists in the world managed to come up with a correct estimate. To make matters worse, the researchers even failed to predict how soon they would be able to count the genes: They believed that the issue would be resolved by 2003.

In early 2000, one of the most popular subjects of public debate was climate change. Tons of pages were written, and hundreds of experts explained the disastrous consequences of the melting of Arctic sea ice, as well as the dramatic impact of the greenhouse effect on our lives. In 2007, the BBC presented the predictions and estimates of American scientists who believed that "northern polar waters could be ice-free in summers within just five to six years." "Arctic Summers Ice-free 'by 2013'" was the headline.[86] What did actually happen? In the summer of 2013, contrary to the scientists' predictions, the Arctic ice sheet not only had not disappeared, but had grown by 29 percent—an unthinkable change! Following this completely unexpected development, some eminent scientists estimated that the world may be possibly heading for "a period of cooling that will not end until the middle of this century."[87] The above error does not mean that human activity has no grave effect on the environment and that there is no reason for worry. Quite the contrary. Nonetheless, it shows that climate change unfolds in a much more complex way than we think.

But let's leave experts aside and think about one ordinary day in our own lives. How often does the day unfold without a care, without any incident, without any setback? Skeptics are requested to prepare a detailed daily schedule and try to follow it to the letter. Reality is too complex and dynamic to be under our control. Of course, there are countless examples of people who have done very well in predicting situations and actions. However, this should not lead us into certainties. More often than not, things follow a course much different from the one we initially aim for.

We should always keep in mind Yogi Berra's aphorism that "it's tough to make predictions, especially about the future."* This should be taught in all economic universities. As we will see in the following section, apart from economic theory, the predictions made by economists are also barely related to reality. And whatever little relation exists could be attributed to chance.

---

* Legendary American baseball player and coach. This quote is also attributed to the physicist Niels Bohr, as well as to Mark Twain.

7

THE ROLE OF CHANCE

"The happy man is he who…is neither puffed up, nor crushed, by the happenings of chance."

Seneca, *On the Happy Life*

In the summer of 2002, almost 45 students from the Russian city of Ufa were chosen for a two-week educational trip to the Costa Daurada area of Spain, near Barcelona. The trip was part of a UNESCO program and involved the most talented students of this Russian city. The kids were aged 10–15 and had been distinguished for their performance in learning, sports, and arts.

In the end of June they traveled by train to Moscow in order to board a flight to Barcelona. Owing to a mistake on the part of the travel agency that organized the trip, the students were transported to the wrong airport and missed their flight. Two days later, on July 1, 2002, everything was settled and the students boarded Bashkirian Airlines flight 2937, bound for Barcelona. Sadly, the students, along with the other passengers of flight 2937, never reached their destination. At 11:35 p.m., as the plane flew over the German-Swiss border, it collided with a DHL flight, leading to the deaths of the passengers and the crews of both aircraft.[88] Such accidents are unthinkable in the airline industry.

Chance is omnipresent in life. Some people have tons of luck. Others are simply unlucky, and some others, like the students from Ufa, are never given the opportunity to test their luck. Some people survive incredibly difficult operations, while others die from very simple procedures as a result of unthinkable medical errors. Some people are given immense riches by luck, and others are given poverty. Some are given happiness, other misery. Luck never discriminates: Many extremely smart and talented people have to deal with tragically bad luck, and society is rife with lucky idiots. A moment of absentmindedness, a misjudgment, an ill-thought-out decision, a bad moment is enough to bring the end: In Greece, traffic accidents claimed the lives of 861 people in 2013 alone.[89]

Life is full of events that shouldn't normally have transpired. In September 2000, 81 people met a tragic death in the shipwreck of the *Express Samina* ferry, just a few miles out of the port of Paros, Greece. In August 2005, the passengers and crew of Cypriot Helios Airways flight 522, a total of 121 people, died when the plane crushed just outside Athens. The aircraft had been flying for hours on autopilot, with the pilots and passengers unconscious after a disastrous combination of errors and omissions that "normally" should not have occurred.

Chance does not only have to do with matters of life and death. You attend a social gathering (which bores you to death and you wish you had avoided) and you meet the love of your life. While on vacation, you meet an executive from a huge multinational company and, out of nowhere, you are offered a major professional opportunity. You fail at an interview for a job you considered very desirable, and a few weeks later you are presented with an unbelievable opportunity that, had you been chosen at the previous interview, you would have been unable to exploit. Chance rules our lives much more than we tend to realize.

Business giants disappear and new empires are built from scratch. In the 1970s, Roy Raymond faced a problem: He felt embarrassed whenever he had to visit a lingerie shop to buy a present for his wife. So he came up with the idea of creating a firm that would make men feel comfortable buying lingerie and would also offer mail order options. Following lots of relevant research, Raymond opened the first store of the well-known Victoria's Secret chain in 1977. To open the store, Raymond took a $40,000 loan from a bank and borrowed $40,000 from his parents. In 1982, only five years after its formation, the company had a turnover of many millions of dollars and Raymond sold it for $4 million. Two years later, in 1984, he launched a second business venture: My Child's Destiny, a chain of baby and children's stores. This venture, though, did not share the success of Victoria's Secret: The new company went under in 1986. In contrast, Victoria's Secret continued to grow rapidly in the hands of its new owners, and by 1990 it was the largest lingerie chain in the United States, with a value of many millions of dollars. In August 1993, Raymond committed suicide, jumping from San Francisco's Golden Gate Bridge; he was only 46 years old. The value of L Brands, the parent group of Victoria's Secret, amounted to almost $16 billion as of June 2014.

There are smart young people who get their postgraduate degrees in banking and just two or three years later receive bonuses amounting to hundreds of thousands of dollars, as was the rule prior to the financial crisis. But other, even smarter young people get their postgraduate degrees in banking and two or three years later not only haven't found the great jobs they dreamed of, but, owing to the crisis that radically altered the situation in the banking sector, find it difficult even to repay the bank loan that financed their studies.

Children from families with high educational backgrounds and income levels become criminals, while children from families facing lots of problems (low income, violent parent behavior, alcoholism, drug abuse, etc.) turn, against all odds, into model citizens.

There are soccer matches in which overwhelmingly superior teams find it impossible to score, and matches in which the much weaker team scores a goal out of nowhere and "steals" a victory. And there are some unbelievable sequences of events in which soccer teams with long traditions and high-quality players in perfect physical shape, trained by great coaches who follow strict regimes, are defeated by weak outsiders, like in 2004, when the Greek national soccer team won the European Cup.

The activation and interaction of man's genetic material may also be triggered accidentally. Random gene mutations lead to permanent, even hereditary changes. Darwin pointed out that chance—probability—is a key factor in the mechanical processes governing complex forms.[90] According to biologists, evolutionary processes exhibit the most complex dynamics.

Even among a crowd of incompetent or stupid people, some lucky ones will stand out. Taleb used computer simulation to create a cohort of incompetent portfolio managers, denoting as incompetent those who have negative expected returns—specifically, a 55 percent probability of losing money and a 45 percent probability of turning a profit. In a pool of 10,000 managers, 4,500 would be expected to turn a profit at the end of the first year. At the end of the second year, 2,025 of these managers, or 45 percent, would show a profit (the others would presumably change profession). In the third year, 911 managers would turn a profit; 410 in the fourth; and 184 in the fifth. These 184 would get all the attention, while the other 9,816 (98 percent of the original cohort) would not be mentioned by anyone. Thus, a "population entirely composed of bad managers will produce a small amount of great track records."[91] These are the managers who make the headlines and are treated as persons of high intelligence and exceptional skill. Some will even have books written about them.

THE STRANGE PATHWAYS OF SUCCESS

For want of a nail, the shoe was lost;
For want of a shoe, the horse was lost;
For want of a horse, the rider was lost;
For want of a rider, the battle was lost;
For want of a battle, the kingdom was lost![92]

How is the end result of a calculation affected by rounding the decimals of a number used in a weather forecasting model? In other words, what would happen if, instead of entering 14.54693 (degrees Celsius) we entered the number 14.547?

In the 1960s, MIT mathematician and meteorologist Edward Lorenz experimented with various methods of developing a weather forecasting model with a horizon of a few days. One day, Lorenz tried to use the data he had accumulated to repeat a forecast and check certain details of the model. He entered the data on the temperature, the air pressure, and the direction of the wind in his computer, rounding the numbers to three decimal places instead of the six he had used the last time he made the calculations. The results were shocking. The new forecast was not even an approximation of the previous one but a radically different prediction. This trivial difference of three decimal points led to entirely different results. Lorenz immediately realized that small, seemingly insignificant shifts from initial conditions may lead to dramatically different, nonlinear results.

With his findings, Lorenz paved the way for the development of a new scientific field, chaos theory. He showed that complex, nonlinear dynamic systems, such as the weather, are extremely sensitive and can be affected by the most inconsequential things. Thus, the flapping of a butterfly's wings in Hong Kong and the imperceptible shift it causes in local weather conditions can trigger a long chain of small changes that add up to huge effects, such as a rainstorm in New York.[93] This made Lorenz realize that it was impossible to make long-term predictions regarding the weather.

But if the flapping of a butterfly's wings can cause a rainstorm, how chaotic, unpredictable, and nonlinear must the interactions among humans and the results of their actions be? Human societies are dynamic systems, and dynamic systems are prone to chaos. Even in the extreme case that we know all initial conditions, this knowledge would be approximate, and therefore it would be impossible to make accurate predictions. As with weather conditions, slight changes can gradually lead to huge deviations from the starting point, leading to completely unpredictable end results.

In the world of action, in everyday life, chaos rules. In real life, not only are we unable to see the things to come, but, quite often, even if the innovation that will change our lives appears clearly in front of our eyes, we are incapable of perceiving it because we are anchored to yesterday's knowledge and beliefs.

Until the end of the 1990s, Google was not in demand, and no one was interested in buying its stock. Its founders were asking a mere $1.6 million for the company, but the best offer they got was $750,000.[94] Back then, nobody saw anything special in a company that possessed a different web-searching technology. Today, Google is admired by all and has really revolutionized our lives, providing each of us with unthinkable access to information and knowledge. Whether you are in San Francisco or a Nigerian village, if you have Internet access you can draw information about everything. To set the historical record straight, in June 2014 the price of Google stock was above $560 and its market capitalization stood at $380 billion (more than 500,000 times higher than the bid made to Google's founders at the end of the 1990s). The progress of Google and the adoption of its technology by society followed an unpredictable, nonlinear path.

Many scientific discoveries were made in a manner that verifies the adage "Better to be lucky than good." Some, such as the discovery of X-rays or radiation, were made completely by chance; others followed a peculiar course, the original intentions of the scientists-inventors having nothing to do with the actual outcome. When Alexander Graham Bell (1847–1922) invented the telephone, the first thought was that it could be used for broadcasting opera shows. It took years for people to realize the usefulness of the new invention. Similarly, when text messages were created by mobile operators, nobody thought that they could be as a new means of communication. Only when this technology came into the hands of society did the usefulness of text messages become apparent.

When the laser was invented, there was not the slightest suspicion (let alone intention) that this novelty could be put to uses as diverse as CD players and medicine. Viagra, which changed the lives of men (especially pensioners), was intended to be a drug for hypertension.

Many people believe that money makes the world go round and that powerful economic interests control governments and guide people's fortunes. Consider this: Of the 500 largest U.S. companies in 1957, only 74, or 14.8 percent, are still included on that list of the strong.[95] The remaining 85 percent have been swept away by the hurricane of creative destruction. All these giant corporations, with their unlimited resources and smart managements, not only failed to dominate the planet but could not even save themselves.

UNINTENTIONAL RESULTS

Adam Smith used the invisible hand metaphor to point to the difference between individuals' original intentions and the results that occur when these individuals act in accordance with these intentions. In other words, the metaphor helps us understand unintentional results.

Life is dominated by unintentional results, the discrepancy between what we seek and what actually happens. A classic example of an unintentional result can be found on the soccer field. Thousands of seated people are watching a soccer match. Suddenly one of the spectators stands up to have a better view, forcing the person behind him to rise as well, and so on. Soon a large part of the audience is standing. Everyone is still watching the match, only now they are on their feet.

Quite often, the relationship between causes and effects remains inexplicable. You raise taxes to enhance public revenues, but the impact on economic activity is such that, in the end, revenues fall. Or even worse: By imposing a tax on tea in 1773, the British caused the American colonists to react *en masse*. In Boston, not only did they stop buying the British companies' tea, but they destroyed large loads of it, dumping it into the sea. The British reacted by sending 4,000 troops to punish Boston, and this was more or less the beginning of the American Revolution, which led to the establishment of the United States (1783).

In the nineteenth century, the British settlers of Australia decided to bring along to their new home foxes and rabbits (to remind them of the English countryside). The introduction of these two species was not random but intended, and after many efforts the animals managed to adapt to, and start reproducing in, Australia's environment. An unspeakable disaster ensued. Foxes exterminated many species of native Australian mammals (which had no evolutionary experience of foxes), "while rabbits consume[d] much of the plant fodder intended for sheep and cattle, outcompete[d] native herbivorous mammals, and undermine[d] the ground by their burrows." Foxes and rabbits multiplied uncontrollably, and even today Australians spend billions of dollars to keep their populations under control, although with limited success.[96]

In 1985, Mikhail Gorbachev decided to deal with the scourge of alcoholism in Russia, and in general in the USSR. In order to reduce consumption, he tripled vodka prices overnight. A few months later, not only had he managed to create a large black market, but alcohol-related deaths had increased dramatically, as many people tried to replace expensive vodka with various home-distilled alcoholic drinks that were no better than poisons.[97]

In Haifa, Israel, certain day care centers faced a problem with some parents who were late in picking up their children. So they decided to impose a fine of $3 per child if a parent arrived more than 10 minutes late. To the great surprise of the day care management, "after the fine was enacted the number of late pickups promptly went...up [to]...more than double the original average." What happened? Parents simply did not feel any more compelled to pick up their kids on time, since "just a few dollars each day...could buy off their guilt."[98]

Two great European statesmen, Winston Churchill and Eleftherios Venizelos, met with electoral defeat while at the apogee of their political careers. The victor of World War II and the creator of the Greece of "five seas and two continents"* were, quite unexpectedly, scorned by the citizens at what should have been a moment of absolute triumph. As a matter of fact, Venizelos—who only a few months earlier had been named "worthy benefactor of Greece and savior of the country" by the Parliament—did not even manage to get reelected as an MP.[99] The farsighted Cretan statesman had instigated the elections himself, certain of his victory.

The unintentional result, i.e., the unanticipated, nonlinear path from an action to an effect, is the natural ending of a situation determined by human weaknesses and limitations and a chaotic, complex evolutionary reality—a reality that we humans fail to understand.

---

* After the signing of the Treaty of Sèvres (1920), Greece acquired large territories, such as Eastern Thrace, Smyrna, and the Dodecanese. Thus, the Great Idea of a big Greece, stretching over two continents (Europe and Asia) and five seas (the Aegean, Ionian, Libyan, and Black Seas and the Sea of Marmara), was realized.

PART FOUR

THE FALL OF HOMO ECONOMICUS

The magnitude, breadth, and severity of the financial crisis that broke out in 2007 took policymakers, regulators, and the scientific community by complete surprise. According to economic models and theory, such a crisis should never have occurred. It was a totally baffling anomaly. But it did occur.

As it turned out, the standard economic model was wrong, a mortified Alan Greenspan had to admit. As he wrote, "In the run-up to the crisis, the Federal Reserve Board's sophisticated forecasting system did not foresee the major risks to the global economy."[1]

The tough reality, which swept away the entire intellectual work of the neoclassical economists, marked the end of certainties for economics. The convenient disregard of the complex human psyche, of social interactions, and of the chaotic evolutionary reality had disastrous effects.

The intensity and extent of disagreement among economists had, for quite some time, been sending out a strong warning signal regarding the discipline's intellectual state. Despite the widespread effort made in the early 20th century to root out any political-ideological elements and to rephrase economic theories with mathematical strictness and elegance, economists failed to come up with a single theoretical platform. They disagreed, and continued to disagree, in their analyses, at the same time holding completely different views regarding both the nature of economic problems and the policies required for dealing with them.

Of course, such disagreements and differences of approach are commonplace in social sciences. Nonetheless, the existential problem of economics lies in the economists' obsession with presenting and establishing their field as hard science—a science that has, according to academic economists, developed methodologies and scientific processes that record economic phenomena with physics-like accuracy and objectivity, thanks to the incontestable authority of differential calculus and other mathematical techniques.

"Economists," says Andrew Lo, a professor of finance at the Massachusetts Institute of Technology "suffer from a deep psychological disorder that I call 'physics envy.' We wish that 99 percent of economic behavior could be captured by three simple laws of nature. In fact, economists have ninety-nine laws that capture 3 percent of behavior."[2]

As we saw in Part One, the structure, mathematical simplifications, assumptions, and axioms of neoclassical economics became from very early on the target of severe criticism. Logic rebelled against the single-minded view of humans as models of rationality.

Neoclassical economists responded to this criticism with even more complex mathematics, ignoring developments in other scientific fields and shutting down all channels of communication and debate. While admitting that many assumptions were oversimplified, they stressed that theory and models should be judged on their effectiveness.

Apart from any reasonable criticism regarding the structure and effectiveness of economic science, the 2007 crisis brought economists up against a new, tough question: whether economics, by giving assurances regarding the efficiency of markets, the reduction of macroeconomic instability, the supremacy of mathematical tools and financial innovations, and the ability to control risks, was the factor that led to the outbreak of the great financial crisis of 2007—a crisis that soon became a global pandemic, bringing economies face to face with the specter of a disaster similar to that of 1929.

1

THE TOWER OF BABEL

Winston Churchill used to say, "If you put two economists in a room, you get two opinions, unless one of them is Lord Keynes, in which case you get three opinions."

Economists disagree on almost everything: the role of the state in the economy, the efficiency of markets, monetary policy, the advisability of running budget deficits or surpluses, tax policy, the risks of inflation, and many, many more issues. They even disagree on the exact definition of economic science!

The Greek crisis is a case in point. In early 2012, while concern and uncertainty regarding the outcome of the fiscal crisis loomed large, the citizens of the country were incessantly bombarded with the absolute certainties of economists about what the problems were and how they should be dealt with. Some claimed that salvation lay in exiting the euro zone. Others said that such a "Grexit" would be disastrous. Still others insisted that the solution was a default, at the same time assuring the public that the country would not leave the euro zone. And many, many more.

Similar "certainties" are expressed from time to time regarding the sustainability of the euro zone, the situation in the United States, the course of emerging markets, and so on.

The failure of economics to formulate uniform, or at least converging, proposals for dealing with economic problems confuses public opinion and weakens trust, which is key to the smooth operation of an economy.

Not only do economists disagree about today and tomorrow; they even disagree about yesterday. Consider the 1929 Crash and the Great Depression that followed, events that have been deeply etched into our collective memory and have been thoroughly studied by all schools of economic thought. The intervening period has now been long enough to let us see these events with calm, sober, and, to the extent possible, objective eyes.

What were the causes of the Great Depression? Why wasn't the crisis effectively dealt with? What should have been done?

More than eighty years later, economic science has neither managed to bring forth a uniform interpretation of the causes of the Great Depression, nor reached any consensus on how it should have been dealt with. Economists disagree on the causes of the crisis, on the effect of the policies that were implemented, and on the measures that should have been taken to minimize the impact of, and ensure the quickest possible exit from, the crisis.

The orthodoxy of that time, the classical view, abhorred state intervention and recommended patience and balanced budgets, anticipating an automatic restoration of equilibrium. "Economic depression can not be cured by legislative action or executive pronouncement," U.S. President Herbert Hoover declared in 1930. "Economic wounds must be healed by the action of the cells of the economic body—the producers and consumers themselves."[3]

In contrast, Keynesians believed that the antidote to the crisis was government expenditure. They argued that there was no automatic equilibrium-restoring mechanism and prescribed government expenditure for rekindling demand. According to their rationale, the government should make up for the private sector's unwillingness to take action in periods of crisis and use public funds to help the economy regain its footing.

Monetarists believed that the Great Depression had not been caused by a collapse of demand (as Keynesians argued), but was the result of the sudden drop in banking deposits—the quantity of money circulating in the economy. They believed that the crisis would have been dealt with had the Federal Reserve System aggressively reduced interest rates and had injected the banking system with the requisite quantities of money, assuming the crucial role of lender of last resort and restoring trust within the economy.

For the economists of the Austrian school, the development of capitalism is characterized by waves of innovation and growth in good times, alternating with violent storms of creative destruction during recessions. The economists of this school believed that the fiscal intervention of the U.S. government intensified the recession, as the policies that were pursued prevented weak, over-indebted banks and businesses from being ruined in a blaze of creative destruction. Saving both solvent and insolvent organizations, the U.S. government created an economy of the living dead, infecting all healthy cells of economic activity and causing a multiyear recession.

Finally, Marxists believed that the 1929 crisis provided one more proof of capitalism's inherent instability. It was an episode in a process that would inescapably lead, sooner or later, to the self-destruction of the capitalist system.

Feel free to choose among the above views. Whatever you choose, you will have guaranteed theoretical support.

In *Principles of Economics*, one of today's influential textbooks on economics, authors Gregory N. Mankiw and Mark P. Taylor warn that the amount of disagreement among economists should not be overstated. Indeed, they present a table containing ten propositions about economic policy that were endorsed by an "overwhelming majority of respondents" in a survey. Each proposition was accepted by 78 percent to 93 percent of those surveyed.[4] This is a curious argument, since it easily could be used the other way round: to demonstrate the limited degree of consensus among economists.

Does hard science—what economics aspires to be—include any discipline where scientists disagree so strongly on almost everything?

A WEIRD CONSTRUCTION

The easiest way to criticize economics is simply to present its structure, its basic axioms, and the assumptions that underlie its theory.

As we saw in Part One, some pioneering economists, fascinated by the huge intellectual influence of Newtonian physics, embarked in the late nineteenth century on a colossal effort to reformulate economics, in order to establish it as a proper science on a par with physics. However, in order to fit chaotic reality into mathematical models, the economists restructured it, creating a parallel universe. The complex psyche of humankind was arbitrarily defined as totally rational, and its social dimension was written off. Any nuance of social relations was rooted out. Economists like Paul Samuelson and Frank Knight argued that, for the sake of scientific generalization, we should not use the term "factors of production" because, they believed, it could add social content to economic inputs.

Neoclassical economists arbitrarily tailored reality to suit their models. The complexity of markets was drastically reduced through the intellectual invention of perfect competition and unrealistic assumptions.

Thus, having rational-selfish human behavior and market efficiency as a springboard, and using sophisticated mathematics that were barely comprehensible to most economists besides a small elite, the high priests of neoclassical economics managed to demonstrate the total superiority of unadulterated capitalism, free from any intervention, regulation, or control.

Gradually, economics became trapped in complacency: Economists were writing only for other economists, developing theories for the sake of theory. Reality became an outcast. Thus economics came to be "the most insular of fields," "the one that quotes least from outside itself."[5]

Academic economists locked themselves up in this parallel universe, constructing complex and abstruse models to explain economic phenomena; these models, though, have nothing at all to do with reality, with the world of action. According to the economist William Lazonick, the twentieth century was marked by a disregard of both the history of economic science and the history of capitalist economies. "It was by combining a methodological obsession with equilibrium and an ideological obsession with market coordination that mainstream economic theory lost touch with the realities of successful capitalist development and its practitioners became ideologically bound by the myth of the market economy," Lazonick wrote.[6]

BANKS? WHAT BANKS?

The neoclassical economics' divorce from reality is illustrated by the case of the financial sector. As we have seen, economists disagree on a wide range of issues; nowadays, though, there is no one who doesn't acknowledge the banking system's key role in the way economies operate.

The banks are the heart and the nervous system of the economy, and even small bouts of arrhythmia in the financial system are more than enough to shake the real economy.

Today, banks are doing almost everything. They pool the savings of households and businesses and channel them, through lending, to individuals, businesses, and states in order to cover investment or consumer needs. This intermediary role is the core of banking operations.[7]

Banks play a key role in the diffusion and implementation of the central banks' monetary policy because they are directly involved in enhancing or reducing liquidity in the economy.[8] Moreover, banking subsidiaries offer investment products, invest in all kinds of markets, manage the capital and savings of individuals and pension funds, discount future claims, provide insurance services, and so on. Apart from mere financing, banks also facilitate business activity. Commercial, construction, industrial, importing, and exporting companies cannot operate in international markets, or even in local ones, unless they present bank letters of guarantee, which provide financial assurances to counterparties in case of failure. At the same time, banks develop payments systems for the secure processing of transactions, both commercial and private, throughout the world. Wherever money goes round, there is a bank.

Banking is not, nor is it considered to be, just one more out of the dozens of business sectors that compose the financial circuit. The banking system is much more than a run-of-the-mill industry. Thus, following the shock of 2008, governments all over the world, from the United States to Europe, rushed to offer generous state aid in order to stabilize the banking system and restore confidence.

Banking is the most strictly regulated industry in the economy. Even if a bank fails as a result of mismanagement, it is almost certain that the authorities will intervene, and even uninsured deposits are almost never threatened.

The credibility of the banking system is crucial, and without a stable and robust financial sector, no economy could remain standing in today's world for even a single minute. The economics literature is full of stories regarding bank-centered financial crises: From 1974 to 1995, almost twenty crises—of which five can be characterized as almost systemic—hit the banking systems of developed countries such as the United Kingdom, the United States, France, Finland, Sweden, Japan, and others.[9]

Nowadays, trouble spreads instantly across banks and, by extension, across economies, as a result of the great degree of interconnection through the interbank market (where banks lends to one another) and many other transactions. As the 2007 financial crisis taught us, banks not only play a key role in the economy but are also too big to fail. The fall of a big bank may disrupt the functioning not only of a single economy but of the global economy as well, because of the large degree of interconnection among credit institutions and the rapid spread of problems.

No one questions the importance of banks.

But what does the mainstream neoclassical model have to say about the banking system? How does mainstream economic theory approach the role of financial organizations in economic activity?

The answer is astonishing. Economic theory has nothing, or almost nothing, to say about banks. Its elaborate models and mathematical equations ignore both the banking system and its role in the economy. The architects of neoclassical economics never took the banking system seriously, despite its increasing importance to the economy, especially following the end of World War II.

In the neoclassical universe, banks are superfluous. Normally, they shouldn't exist. They have no role to play. As we have seen, the philosopher's stone of neoclassical theory, the Arrow-Debreu theorem, showed that markets are not only efficient, but also perfect. In other words, every future transaction can be executed today. Thus, in a system where businesses and households have access to perfect financial markets, there is absolutely no role for intermediaries, i.e., banks. In such a perfect situation, banks have no reason to exist and cannot generate profits. So theory left the banking sector aside.

Neoclassical economists remained firm in their original views despite the fact that the financial system played a decisive role in every, or almost every, financial crisis since the early 20th century. For these theorists, the gap between reality and theory was a mere detail.

THE ALMIGHTY MARKET

Driven by their unswerving belief that the market—the coordination of economic activities through the mechanism of the free market—is the only way to maximize outcomes, academic economists promoted the concept of perfectly competing markets as the ultimate ideal.

The market was attributed superpowers. It became a sentient superorganism that always leads to the optimum result, provided that it is unfettered.

Every other dimension is dwarfed by the glory of free markets. According to the neoclassical view, businesses are nothing but passive walk-ons in a play, since markets create businesses and not vice-versa. Who cares if the real world is rife with examples of companies that create new markets through innovation?

Apart from innovation, neoclassical economists also chose to ignore the importance of organizational change and the role of the entrepreneur. They believed that companies are driven by market forces and that neither organizational change nor business talent has any considerable, systematic effect.

Everything is determined by the ideology of self-interest. Individuals, consumers, *Homo economicus*, make all the crucial decisions that guide economic activity—not businesses. Individuals decide and businesses follow. Academics, totally certain that the ideology of self-interest was universally applicable, generalized the analysis of consumer choice in order to describe business behavior. Assuming that the behavior of a business is similar to that of an individual, they formulated the laws of a business's market behavior in a similar manner.

2

THE WALL OF REALITY

Many people could, legitimately, contradict the academic economists' view, saying that a theoretical system based on such an extensive distortion of human nature and on an artificial, ideal world that is a far cry from the dynamically evolving world we live in can in no way produce results that are compatible with reality.

If we consider the labyrinth that the mind is, the complexity of human behavior (senses, beliefs, expectations, etc.), the maze of social relations, the role of chance and all the things discussed in detail in Part Three, then the economists' assumptions, axioms, hypotheses, and tools seem frustratingly naive.

How seriously can we take the single-minded view of humans as rational, self-interested beings? Or the concept of perfect competition? Or price theory? Or the general equilibrium approach? That said, such easy criticism would also be unfair. Economists are not trying to persuade us that humans are rational or that markets are perfect. They acknowledge that many axioms are extreme and many assumptions are oversimplified. However, they also insist that the effectiveness of the hypotheses and models should be tested not by the realism of their assumptions, but by their ability to predict future economic phenomena.[10] In other words, economics should be judged on the basis of its effectiveness in the arena of reality.

Surprisingly, despite the importance attached by academic economists to the predictive power of models, there are no studies that monitor, record, and compare predictions with the actual evolution of economic phenomena and fundamentals. Scientific research abstains from checking economic predictions in a systematic manner that would render them useful to society.

This abstention should not come as a surprise, for the simple reason that, more often than not, the predictions are not borne out. The models may seem to work fairly well for two or three years, but in the fourth year the unexpected, the impossible, occurs, consigning both predictions and economies to the abyss.

The systematic occurrence of crises and the systematic failure of economics to predict or even to diagnose the signs of an impeding economic disruption raise a huge wall that separates theory from reality.

In theory, economists have answers to every problem; in reality, though, problems abound. And it is not only the large-scale unexpected crises. The inability of economics to offer meaningful solutions is illustrated by chronic problems—unemployment, widening inequality, poverty, and so on—that plague even the most advanced economies, even in periods of strong growth and prosperity.

Confined, like all of us, by the bonds of human weaknesses and limitation, economists and policymakers not only are unable to predict the future, as they claim, but quite often fail to perceive and manage the very reality that unfolds in front of their eyes. They see what they want to see.

In December 1928, a few months before the Great Crash, U.S. President Calvin Coolidge (1872–1933) said with certainty: "No Congress of the United States ever assembled…has met with a more pleasing prospect than that which appears at the present time…The country can regard the present with satisfaction and anticipate the future with optimism."[11]

In the autumn of 1929, just weeks before the collapse, the great economist Irving Fisher, a professor at Yale University, pointed out that "stock prices have reached what looks like a permanently high plateau."[12] Even after the crash, when the economy was sinking into recession, most experts, "anchored" to what they knew, failed to face reality. On November 10, 1929, the Harvard Economic Society said that "a severe depression like that of 1920–21 is outside the range of probability."[13]

Any attempts to predict the future are lost in the intricate cogs of a chaotic reality. In theory, chaotic phenomena can be predicted. In practice, though, this is impossible because of the overabundance of information that has to be input in the model and the supercomputing powers that are required to ensure an accurate prediction. Most times, predictions fail simply because no model can factor in the infinite number of micro-elements of everyday life that interact to form a sensitive, dynamically evolving system in which the slightest disruptions can lead to dramatically different outcomes. In addition, as we saw in Part Three, no prediction can incorporate technological progress or chance.

As Herbert Simon, holder of a Nobel Prize in Economic Sciences, writes, economic theory "is widely taught in both senses in business schools and universities, just as if it described what goes on, or could go on, in the real world. Alas, the picture is far too simple to fit reality."[14]

THE ECONOMISTS' PREDICTIONS

Each year, economics produces a huge volume of predictions, and the media are incessantly publishing them. Predictions are made about the GDP, inflation, fiscal data, investment, savings, interest rates, consumption, stock markets, stocks, commodities, currencies, the course of individual sectors and companies, and many, many more topics.

Forecasts are issued by organizations such as the World Bank, the International Monetary Fund (IMF), and the Organization for Economic Cooperation and Development (OECD), as well as governments, credit rating agencies, banks, professors of economics, analysts, market pundits, journalists, and other experts.

In response to criticism regarding the gap between their predictions and reality, economists say that when they make a forecast and warn about a danger, such as an increase in inflation, then it is possible that the central bank will intervene and take the appropriate measures to deal with incipient problems. They claim that their suggestions mobilize policymakers, making them take prompt action and remedy the initial symptoms that could lead to serious and dangerous complications. So, they say, it would be unfair to judge the effectiveness of a prediction based on the end result.

This is a valid comment, but it nonetheless escapes the essence of the criticism. No one denies that an early warning that prompts a quick response from the authorities is important and socially useful. Also, no one criticizes economists when, for example, inflation reaches 2.1 percent instead of the predicted 2 percent.

The problem with these predictions is that economists attribute to them powers and capacities that are simply nonexistent. Encouraged by the predictive success of their models within a limited range of economic phenomena (e.g., inflation, the effect of investment or consumption on business activity), economists extend the use of these forecasting models to other, totally inappropriate fields, such as risk management.

There are two intellectual tricks that economists employ in order to claim that they possess strong predictive powers (and here I will stress, once again, that the economy is decisively affected by technology, which is humanly impossible to predict). The first trick is to dodge uncertainty, focusing only on the concept of risk. As we saw, the economist Frank Knight made a distinction between uncertainty, which cannot be measured, and risk, which can be quantified and measured with the help of statistics. The gap between uncertainty (the possibility of an earthquake, a great terrorist strike, a deadly flu epidemic, and so on) and risk (e.g., the probability of hitting boxcars at craps) is chaotic.

Mainstream utility theory allows the analysis of individual behavior only under conditions of certainty. Chance is not susceptible to analysis and, as a result, no theoretical attention could be paid to it. Neoclassical economics, unable to deal with wild and intractable uncertainty, assumes—arbitrarily—that there is only quantifiable risk in life. This improves the models' functionality to a great extent, as the ability to measure risk with the use of statistical tools, combined with the neoclassical hypothesis regarding the rationality of individuals, leads to a predictable and controlled view of the economic world. Risk is quantified on the basis of our (limited) experience of the past and is priced with the help of statistics.

This illusion of control paved the way for incredible excesses. On the basis of super-models that were supposed to accurately estimate risks, bank managements assumed huge risks and pursued policies during the 2000s that turned out to be disastrous, and as a result in 2008 the financial system was brought to the brink of total collapse.

On the basis of past knowledge regarding the political stability of Egypt since 1980, economists and analysts in the mid-2000s recommended this country as an excellent investment destination. Many businesses and banks rushed to invest in the safe and dynamic market of Egypt until, quite unexpectedly, the impossible happened in early 2011: The mighty Mubarak regime, seemingly unshakable for many decades, crumbled within a few weeks. Today, more than three years after Mubarak's fall, Egypt still hasn't regained its footing, and political instability persists.

In the same manner that, a few years ago, everyone predicted that China would replace the United States as the world's leading economy before 2020, economists and other analysts use their elaborate models to project impressive economic growth rates to the unknown tomorrow and make ponderous predictions. Thus, the Nobel Prize–winning economist Robert Fogel has predicted that China will grow at an average annual rate of 8 percent until 2040.* If his prediction is borne out, China will account for 40 percent of global GDP, as compared with 14 percent for the United States and 5 percent for Europe.[15] However, reality is infinitely more complex, and economic models fail to incorporate the dynamic factors that determine developments. The great environmental problems and huge inequalities China faces, combined with issues of favoritism, the sustainability of the existing political system, social stability and so on, are difficulties that economists simply choose to ignore and sweep under the rug. And since the experts' linear predictions are very rarely verified, it is highly possible that in the forthcoming years China will draw our attention with some totally unexpected developments that derail its expected carefree ascent to the top of the global economy.† Remember the case of Japan, discussed in Part Three.

The second trick employed by economists is to make extensive use of mathematics. The economists' ability to speak in the "pure" language of mathematics lends them an aura of intellectual superiority and scientific status. Using the incontestable authority of differential calculus, mathematical analysis, linear algebra, and the power of sophisticated algorithms, economics extracts credibility, objectivity and substantiation it does not deserve. Phrasing their theories in the language of mathematics, economists manage to sound more weighty and important than reality would warrant. Who would dare question the "unreasonable effectiveness of mathematics"?[16]

---

* From 1990 to 2010 the Chinese economy grew at an average annual rate of 9.6 percent.

† The enthusiasm regarding the potential of the Chinese economy has already started to subside, and many analysts express concern regarding the country's future.

Even the greatest platitudes, when translated into equations and presented through the power of numbers, are turned into ponderous and highly prestigious scientific analyses. If someone were to write zero (0), they would make no impression. If, though, they wrote $\sin(\pi)$—as zero can be expressed in mathematical form—they *would* make an impression. Similarly, the number 1 can be expressed as $\cos(-\pi)$ or, even more impressively, as $-e^{\wedge}(i\pi)$!

Remember the gibberish we referred to in Part Three and the insidious power of scientific terminology. Remember professor Alan Sokal, who managed to have a jumble of scientific-looking nonsense published in a scientific journal.

Armed with the certainty and confidence generated by sophisticated techniques and models, economists march on. However, expert predictions are barely related to reality. Thus, in the 2000s, while economists smugly talked about a "great moderation," complex, imperceptible, and powerful forces were interacting below the surface—forces that, contrary to all prediction, led to the crisis of 2007 and the near collapse of 2008.

The excessive mathematization of economics has been the object of harsh criticism for many decades, albeit to no avail. Francis Edgeworth, as early as 1896, warned about the danger of overestimating the potential of the mathematical method.[17] Karl Popper pointed out that "pure mathematics and logic, which permit of proofs, give us no information about the world, but only develop the means of describing it."[18] Keynes noted that the widespread use of mathematics "allows the author to lose sight of the complexities and interdependencies of the real world."[19] And the criticism goes on: The use of advanced mathematics hinders communication between economists from different specializations and trends.[20] Mathematical economists use assumptions that are convenient mathematically but are poor economics, running the risk of distorting reality.[21] Mathematics cannot express certain economic generalizations, human activities, and goals that have qualitative characteristics.[22] The use of mathematics does not ensure against the development of irrelevant and simplistic models and the distorting conclusions that emanate from them.[23] However, this criticism was disregarded. In the worlds of Paul Samuelson, "Those who can, do science; those who can't prattle about its methodology."

It is comical (as well as typical of human arrogance) that in 2007, in his autobiographical book *The Age of Turbulence*, Alan Greenspan made predictions about how the U.S. economy and the world would look in 2030. While Greenspan, the great sage, snugly predicted the future, he failed to sense the strong vibrations of pre-seismic activity that had been brewing since 2006 in the United States, right under his feet.

FINANCIAL ENGINEERING

By combining rational expectations, faith in the efficiency of markets, risk-gauging techniques, and the supremacy bestowed by the language of mathematics, economics created a huge and extremely profitable industry: financial engineering. Although Myron Scholes, Robert Merton, and Fischer Black are considered to be the founders of modern financial engineering, the roots of this peculiar type of engineering can be traced to the work of the great French mathematician Louis Bachelier (1870–1946), who in 1900 published his book *The Theory of Speculation*. Arrow, Debreu, Lucas, Fama, and other great economists were important precursors as well, dealing with the issue of risk and incorporating it into neoclassical economics.

Financial engineering develops tools and techniques for managing liquidity and financial risks. Using mathematical analysis, linear algebra, differential equations, and probability theory as its main tools, financial engineering creates innovative investment products (e.g., securitization), assigns prices to financial products (stocks, futures, options, swaps, and so on), assists investment decision making and investor portfolio optimization, and also measures and manages risk by employing complex hedging strategies. At the core of financial engineering is the Gaussian distribution, named after the great German mathematician Carl Friedrich Gauss (1777–1855).

The Gaussian distribution is also called the bell curve, owing to its shape. It is used to describe random variables of real values, which tend to concentrate around a mean. Mathematicians named this distribution "normal" because the great majority of deviates are near the mean, near to normality, and the farther we get from the mean, the rarer they become. Consider average height. In Greece, the average height of men is approximately 1.76 meters. This is where the vast majority of the male population lies. As we move away from the mean, either up or down, the number of people decreases. Thus, one in seven men is ten centimeters taller than the average man, or 1.86 meters tall. One in fifty men is twenty centimeters taller than average, one in 750 is thirty centimeters taller, and so forth. It is very rare to see a 2.15-meter-tall man walking down the street.

Financial engineering is founded on the logic of the Gaussian distribution—that is, on normal deviates. It assumes that large deviations from the mean are so rare that we can ignore them for practical purposes. In finance, both the Black-Scholes model and the risk management model that is based on the work of Merton, Scholes, and Harry Markowitz are founded on the assumption that the logarithm of various variables tends to be normally distributed.

Assisted by this peculiar type of engineering, banks, hedge funds, investment organizations, pension funds, private investors, and others are daily investing many hundreds of billions of dollars and assuming risks. In principle, all these entities are aware of the risk they have assumed, and, since they can measure this risk accurately, they are able to actively manage it. Risk is treated like something that can be measured and controlled. All this is in theory.

Let's see, now, what happens in the real world. On August 31, 1998, as a result of the Russian crisis, the main index of the U.S. stock market, the Dow Jones Industrial Average, fell by 6.8 percent. According to the Gaussian distribution and the risk management models, the odds of such a drop were estimated at one in twenty million.[24] On Monday, October 19, 1987, the Dow Jones fell by an unprecedented 29 percent (the causes of this so-called Black Monday remain unclear); according to the models, the possibility of such a thing happening was one in 10^{50}, a number so small that is outside the scale of nature.[25]

According to theory, the Dow Jones should have shown unusual changes of more than 3.4 percent on only about 58 days from 1916 to 2003. In fact, though, there were 1,001 such unusual days.[26] The Gaussian distribution may not be at fault, but it is absolutely wrong to apply it to the jungle of the economy and the markets, where "rare" deviations and fluctuations are actually not so rare at all.

In the real world, just one exception, one "anomaly," is enough to wipe out the normality of many consecutive years. This is the so-called "tail risk," i.e., the risk referring to the type of investment outcomes that, theoretically, have very low probabilities, albeit when occurring, cause huge losses.

In markets and economies, though, experience has shown that the "exceptions" are not exceptions, but phenomena that occur rather frequently. According to the mainstream models, things such as the violent turbulence of 2008 and the damning synchronization of markets throughout the world are impossible.

Focusing on what is normal, on what is usual, and rejecting all unusual movements, financial engineering claims to be able to measure and manage risks with great effectiveness. This is what led to the creation of all those sophisticated, innovative, and "safe" exotic investment products that led the banking industry to the brink of collapse.

The financial system was, and to a great extent still is, flying blind, guided only by its blind faith in the efficiency of markets and the illusion that, thanks to advanced mathematical tools, everything—even risk—can be kept under control.

It is no coincidence that two of the founders of financial engineering, Myron Scholes and Robert Merton, went bankrupt (with the collapse of Long-Term Capital Management) when they tried to implement their models in the real world.

As the Nobel laureate economist Wassily Leontief (1906–1999) said regarding the use of the Gaussian distribution in the maze of the economy: "In no field of empirical inquiry has so massive and sophisticated a statistical machinery been used with such indifferent results."[27]

WHAT SMOKE? WHAT FIRE?

Today, everyone speaks with awe about the great crisis, but until the middle of 2008, the armies of the IMF, World Bank, OECD, and various bank economists, as well as many others, did not have an inkling of the breadth and depth of this phenomenon. There is no use even considering whether there was any relevant prediction or even warning in 2006 or 2007. The smug optimism that prevailed is evident in the fact that on September 12, 2008, just three days before the collapse of Lehman Brothers, JP Morgan, one of the leading financial institutions in the United States, "projected that the U.S. GDP growth rate would accelerate during the first half of 2009."[28]

A similar situation existed on the other side of the Atlantic. Until the end of 2008, the political elite of the euro zone did not believe that Europe faced a possible banking and financial collapse. They considered the crisis to be an essentially American problem.[29]

Experts and policymakers alike not only failed to predict the crisis, but even failed to notice, after the first half of 2006, the strong and intensifying symptoms of the brewing crisis in order to act accordingly.

In Part Two we discussed the unfolding of the 2007 crisis in detail. Let me recapitulate: In early 2006, the ratio of nonperforming mortgage loans started to rise at an accelerating pace, and in mid-2006 housing prices in the U.S. stopped increasing, for the first time in many years. By the end of 2006, almost ten firms and small banks operating mainly in the subprime lending market had gone belly-up. By March 2007, more than fifty organizations had become insolvent, followed by New Century Financial, the second-largest subprime loan provider, in early April. In the summer of 2007 the problems multiplied, and one year later the crisis was almost out of control. In a nutshell, there were clear signs that something was awry from as early as the beginning of 2006.

All this happened in the real world. In the economists' parallel universe, with its sophisticated models, the situation was totally different. In 2006, 2007, and even a large part of 2008, economists were absolutely confident about the robustness and the positive prospects of global economies.

The projections of the experts for 2007 and 2008 were rather sanguine. At the end of 2006, the World Bank predicted that the global economy would grow 3.2 percent in 2007 and 3.5 percent in 2008.[30] The OECD projected growth rates of 2.5 percent in 2007 and 2.7 percent in 2008 for its thirty member states. The IMF, in September 2006, estimated that in 2007 the global economy would grow at 4.9 percent, projecting 2.7 percent growth for developed economies and 2.9 percent for the United States in particular.[31] The IMF's projections had been revised upward from those in its April 2006 report. As a matter of fact, IMF economists reached the conclusion that "the balance of risks to the global outlook is slanted to the downside."[32]

A few months later, in April 2007, while the U.S. economy was being shaken by the problems in the housing market and their transmission to the banking system, the IMF kept its forecast for 4.9 percent growth in 2007 unchanged, and it predicted a similar growth rate for 2008. No worry! According to the IMF report, "Notwithstanding the recent bout of financial volatility, the world economy still looks well set for continued robust growth in 2007 and 2008."[33] IMF economists were not worried, and in fact they perceived, after analyzing data and developments, that the risks were subsiding. "The risks to the growth outlook are less threatening than at the time of the September 2006 World Economic Outlook," the IMF report stated.[34] In regard to the U.S. economy, the IMF predicted 2.2 percent growth in 2007 and 2.8 percent growth in 2008.[35]

In its annual report for the year 2008, the World Bank warned about the worsening of conditions in the financial sector, stressing the risks generated by the tightening of credit conditions. Still, it projected that in 2008 the global economy would grow at 3.3 percent, a rate that would pick up to 3.6 percent in 2009 as, according to the predictions of World Bank economists, the U.S. economy regained momentum.[36]

One year later, in April, just a few months before September's near-collapse, the IMF underlined the challenges for the banking sector as a result of those problems; overall, though, the report was reassuring. The IMF predicted that global growth would stand at 3.7 percent in 2008 and 3.8 percent in 2009. It anticipated that the U.S. economy would "tip into a mild recession in 2008 as the result of mutually reinforcing cycles in the housing and financial markets, before starting a modest recovery in 2009."[37]

These projections were made only a few weeks before the U.S. financial system found itself on the brink of total collapse.

At last, in April 2009, following the unimaginable failure of Lehman Brothers and after the entire financial system of the U.S. had come face to face with the specter of collapse, IMF economists realized what they were up against: the deepest post–World War II recession by far.[38]

However, by then, one didn't have to be an economist of any kind, let alone one as highly qualified as required by the IMF, to reach such a conclusion. In hindsight, everything seemed obvious and expected.

THE BEST OF THE BEST

The banking sector was the spearhead of Greece's European dream and the epitome of success in the 2000s. The early 1980s saw the launch of the restructuring and opening of the Greek banking system, which gained momentum in the 1990s. The opening of the market was completed in June 2000 with the transposition of European legislation into Greek law and the preparation of Greek banks for the large operational changes required by the adoption of the euro.[39]

Then came a decade of unprecedented growth and profitability for the Greek banking industry. Lending to the private sector—businesses and households—rose, as a percentage of the country's GDP, from 37.4 percent in 2000 to 72.6 percent in 2005.[40] By the end of 2007, the assets of Greek banks stood at $520 billion, compared with $210 billion in 2000.[41] In 2010, Greece's gross domestic product stood at $222 billion, while outstanding loans reached $354 billion, accounting for 117 percent of GDP. In other words, lending to the private sector more than tripled as a percentage of GDP in just a decade. Bank profits followed a similar frenetic course, and in 2007—a record year for Greek banks—they broke the $5.4 billion barrier.[42]

A substantial part of the excess profits generated by the banks during the bull run of the Greek market was invested abroad. In the early 1990s, Greek banks had made the first steps of expansion into the neighboring countries of southeastern Europe; from 2000 to 2007, not a single Greek bank failed to acquire a foreign one. By the end of 2007, Greek banks were operating in 15 countries (all the nations of the Balkan peninsula, plus Egypt, Turkey, and Ukraine). They controlled 48 subsidiary banks with a network of 3,500 branches, total loans of $83 billion, and total assets of $122 billion.[43]

The banks' performance was unprecedented, and there was no questioning the superior abilities of their managements. The combination of great success and high profitability enabled the banks to attract top executives, the best of the best, both from Greece and from the pool of Greeks living abroad, establishing the most advanced managerial structures in the country. It was an executive crème de la crème, rewarded with extremely generous salaries, bonuses, and stock options.

In 2006, this select group of banking executives started making plans for the years to come, with the aim—as stated in the banks' press releases—of becoming leaders in the region of southeastern Europe.

In February 2007, the management of the National Bank of Greece presented its business plan for 2007 through 2009; among other things, it projected average profit growth of 22 percent annually. According to the forecasts of NBG's executives, profits would increase to $2.5 billion in 2009 (from $1.4 billion at the end of 2006). On January 31, 2007, Piraeus Bank presented its new, revised business plan for the 2007 through 2010, which projected average annual profit growth of 24 percent. According to this business plan, the bank's profits would exceed $1.4 billion by the end of 2010 (from $592 million at the end of 2006).

One year later, in the beginning of 2008, and despite the turbulence in the global economy as a result of the financial crisis, Greece's banks remained unwaveringly optimistic. On January 16, 2008, the management of Alpha Bank presented its revised business plan, according to which profits would rise above $1.9 billion at the end of 2010 (from $1.2 billion at the end of 2007). On February 11, 2008, Eurobank EFG predicted that by the end of 2010, its profits would rise to at least $1.6 billion (from $1.2 billion in 2007).

These projections were made by the most expert, experienced, and academically qualified bankers. However, reality took an entirely different course. As early as the end of 2008, the dramatic deterioration of economic conditions worldwide had turned these business plans—and the sanguine forecasts that accompanied them—into dead letters. Since the middle of 2010, Greek banks have been dependent on the public sector both for capital and for liquidity. At the end of 2010, the profits of all four big Greek banks stood at $736 million, as compared with a projection of profits amounting to at least $7.8 billion!

Still, the banks, with their top-quality staffs and vast resources, failed to grasp the course of events and the severity of the crisis that had stricken Greece. In May 2009, the heads of the largest commercial banks estimated that the worse was behind them and anticipated stabilization in both the United States and Europe.[44] As a matter of fact, at the end of 2010 the management of the National Bank decided that it was the right time to repurchase the preferential shares the government had bought and exit the government's financial system support program.[45]

The best of the best still failed to see anything. In 2011, the country, and its banking system, faced the perfect storm. The four big banks closed the fiscal year 2011 with losses amounting to $38.5 billion, and in 2012 their losses stood at $7.5 billion. This is an unprecedented negative record. In those two years alone, total losses exceeded $45 billion, almost double the profits ($24.5 billion) made during the "golden" decade of 2001–2010. Prior to the fiscal derailment, at the end of 2010, the bank shareholders' equity stood at $34 billion. By the end of 2012, the big Greek banks not only had lost all their capital, but faced negative equity, on the consolidated level, of $5.6 billion![46]

The situation had been violently and radically reversed, crushing the banks' projections. In the end, what actually happened was the "haircut," the impairment of the value of Greek government bonds, something that, until the end of 2010, was considered by Greek bankers to be outside the range of probability.

Of course, no one can blame economists (and other experts) for failing to predict the future. This is not humanly possible. However, we can easily challenge the contention of experts and academics that the theories and the elegant economic analysis models they have developed are indeed effective and have systematic predictive powers.

DANGEROUS PROJECTIONS

The frequent occurrence of crises (and the genuine surprise of economists), the failure to grasp the tangible realities (as happened in the 2007 crisis), the chaotic nature of reality, and plain common sense (which rebels when uncertainty is ignored) leave no room for illusion. Reality is erecting a huge wall against which the economists' certainties and predictions are, consistently and systematically, crushed.

That said, the problem does not lie only in the economists' failure, but also in the potential for their predictions to inadvertently boost instability and stir the economy's animal instincts. German economist Klaus Zimmermann expressed the view that no predictions should be published during periods of crisis because they have an adverse effect on human behavior.[47]

Greece learned firsthand how the estimates made by credit rating agencies can fuel a downward spiral. Spurred by the country's fiscal problems, the rating agencies downgraded its credit score. This downgrade caused the cost of money to increase, leading to the further deterioration of the fiscal situation. As a result of this new deterioration, the agencies downgraded the credit rating again. Thus, a downward spiral was set in motion, leading to an impasse: Without any dramatic change in the real fundamentals of the economy from one year to the next, the rating agencies' assessments cut off from all sources of financing a country that, until recently, had been borrowing on the same terms as Germany. In exactly the same way, in the mid-2000s, their favorable assessments had led many billions of dollars to be invested in dangerous, toxic products that wreaked havoc.

Expert opinions have a direct effect on individual behavior. In 2011 and in early 2012, whenever there was a surge in the number of predictions or estimates regarding a possible "Grexit," banks suffered large outflows of deposits. As a matter of fact, certain economists attribute the intensity of the recession in Greece during the fourth quarter of 2011 to the continuous demands of the country's lenders (the European Union and the IMF) regarding the imposition of painful new measures, as well as to their extremely negative estimates concerning the possibility of an exit from the crisis.[48] These unfavorable predictions acted as a self-fulfilling prophecy.

The certainty regarding Greece's inability to exit the crisis originated, to a great extent, from the same agencies and individuals (rating agencies, investors, banks, politicians, and so on) that, from 2003 to 2006, had been generously lending money to Greece on the same terms—that is, at the same interest rate—that they used in lending money to Germany. When optimism was at its peak, the yield spread between the Greek bonds and the German bonds stood at 6 basis points.* 49 In those carefree days, the possibility of a euro zone member-state's defaulting was unimaginable to most people. In 2011 and 2012, and even in 2013, many of these people and agencies were equally certain that Greece would be unable to recover.†

Expert predictions and estimates do not only cause bear runs, but also fuel bull runs. When an economist as prestigious as Irving Fisher confidently proclaims his certainty that stock prices have reached a permanently high plateau (believing that prices cannot fall below that level), why shouldn't the less expert believe him? Let's assume that you are a freelance car mechanic. You have bought a house on mortgage, and business is brisk. One morning you get a call from your banker asking for an appointment. At the meeting you are presented with economic data saying that your house, which you bought five years ago for $300,000, is now worth $450,000, thanks to the rise of the market. Therefore, you are eligible for an additional loan of $150,000. Why not take it? If experts are willing to lend you money, they definitely know something you don't. This is your chance to buy the new car you've been dreaming of. Remember the Mexican strawberry picker we saw in Part Two, who was deemed eligible by the bank for a $724,000 loan, when his annual income was $14,000!

---

* 100 basis points equals 1 percent. The yield spread (the difference in the interest rates) between Greek and German 10-year government bonds reached its historical low in June 2003, when it fell to 6 basis points. In other words, if Germany borrowed at 3 percent, Greece borrowed at 3.06 percent. In the summer of 2010, when Greece's fiscal crisis was in full swing, the yield spread rose to 1,091 basis points. A little later, it rose to almost 3,000 basis points!

† In April 2014, Greece announced that the 2013 budget had closed with a primary surplus of $2 billion.

3

THE GREAT EMBARRASSMENT

The question is pressing: To what extent did the mainstream economic model, as developed by the neoclassical economists, contribute to the brewing of the 2007–2008 crisis, whose magnitude, breadth, and impact can only be compared to those of the Great Depression?

Modern economics is strongly suspected of being intellectually dishonest. Instead of dealing with the real economic problems of society, neoclassical economists created an ideal model-world and used it as the basis for a series of theories and policy proposals that they subsequently tried to transpose to the real world.

By extensively using mathematics, they assumed a feigned intellectual superiority and embarked on a systematic effort to idealize market mechanisms and economic freedom. They weren't interested in reality; they were interested only in what had to be done to fit the real world into the ideal "reality" they had laid out in their theoretical structure. Armed with the prestige of scientific authority, economics assured us that we could control things that are impossible to control. The models were presented as if referring to reality, with no mention whatsoever that a model examines only one version of reality, under very specific assumptions, and nothing more. As certain economists say, paraphrasing Einstein, the models that refer to reality do not offer any certainty, and the models that offer certainty do not refer to reality!

It would be exaggerated, unfair, and wrong to blame economics for all the hardship caused by the crisis. That said, there is no doubt that economics provided the intellectual cloak and the scientific legitimization for the implementation of hard-core and, as it turned out, disastrous policies. The 2008 collapse belied neoclassical certainties for the first time.

THE MINSKY MOMENT

Having offered methodological proof of the hard core of their theory, in the early 1980s neoclassical economists started transferring their theories to the real world. This effort culminated in the 2000s.

The irony is that the neoclassicals started to implement their teachings (deregulation, liberalization, etc.) in a sector of the economy they had cast out of their field of scientific research as irrelevant: the financial system.

In 1986, American economist Hyman Minsky (1919–1996), a professor of economics at Washington University in St. Louis, wrote an excellent book, *Stabilizing an Unstable Economy*, in which he stressed the importance of the financial sector in modern economies. According to Minsky, instability is inherent in capitalism and originates in the financial system, which is essential for the development of a free market. Minsky, who based his work on the ideas of Keynes, said that the latter makes a point regarding the imperfection of capitalist free economies. This "flaw exists because the financial system necessary for capitalist vitality and vigor…contains the potential for runaway expansion, powered by an investment boom… This runaway expansion can readily grind to a halt because 'accumulated financial changes render the financial system fragile.'"[50]

Minsky argued that banks and other financial organizations become increasingly large, complex, and interdependent, and this can bring the entire system crashing down. His analysis focused on the creation of debt, its distribution among various types of borrowers, and the way pyramids of debt are created. He pointed out that lending drives the prices of assets (real estate, stocks, etc.) to higher levels, and these increased prices, in turn, encourage borrowers to take on more debt. When the economy reaches a saturation point, the rise in asset prices ends, and the number of loans that cannot be repaid gradually increases. At some point, said Minsky, a trigger (the failure of a firm or a bank, or simply the fact that some prudent players leave the market) causes the market to crash, leading to financial panic. The collapse of prices and the ensuing panic cause banks to stop providing the economy with credit; as a result, borrowers rush to sell off their assets in order to pay their debts and reduce their exposure to borrowing. This sets off a disastrous downward spiral. Minsky described the recurring pattern of crisis with great precision.

Neoclassical economists hurriedly rejected Minsky's analysis, on the basis of their belief that each crisis is different and we cannot study all crises as a whole.

At the apex of neoclassical reasoning, theorists such as Milton Friedman argued that, since economic agents are rational, there can be no speculation in the market, and what we call speculation is nothing more than the desperate effort of rational individuals to protect themselves from the irrational policies of their governments.

AN INTELLECTUAL TRAGEDY

In 1975, Robert Gordon, then president of the American Economic Association, pointed out, "We economists pay too little attention to the changing institutional environment that conditions economic behavior... [T]he mainstream of economic theory sacrifices far too much relevance in its insistent pursuit of ever increasing rigor."[51]

The magnitude and breadth of the 2007 crisis took the scientific community by total surprise. A guilty silence spread in economist cycles, while the credibility and prestige of the sophisticated and supposedly infallible models vanished overnight.

The intellectual tragedy of economics began with the rather ill-conceived decision to base it on the model of natural sciences. Economic science aims very high, and does not hide it: "The art in scientific thinking," wrote Mankiw and Taylor, "—whether in physics, biology, or economics— is deciding which assumptions to make."[52] It was physics envy, as MIT professor A.W. Lo quipped.

In previous sections we discussed the logical leaps, the unrealistic simplifications, and the extreme assumptions and axioms on which the theoretical structure of modern economics has been based. The entire intellectual effort of academic neoclassical economists involved—and still involves—a parallel ideal world, reminiscent of those who believe their dreams to be reality.

This is not unheard of. Before finding their way, many sciences have taken weird paths. The roots of chemistry, for example, can be traced to alchemy and the alchemists' quixotic effort to turn base metals into gold. However, the irresistible force of the scientific method, through the process of trial and error, enables scientists to identify pitfalls and make the necessary adjustments.

Economics did not allow the scientific progress to flourish. The dogmatic advocacy of its original unrealistic positions constituted the second intellectual tragedy of economics. Economists shut their eyes and ears to the barrage of developments in other scientific fields (biology, neuroscience, psychology, sociology, and so on) that overturned many of the certainties of the nineteenth century and revolutionized the way we understand human beings and social relations. These findings shook modern economics from the ground up, and should have brought about a new start. But such a thing never happened. Neoclassical economists ignored everything. They didn't deign to respond to challenges, considered them irrelevant, and did not move an inch from their positions. They turned their backs on all attempts to debate and burned down all bridges of communication with other disciplines.

They obsessively defended their scientific structure and responded to criticism with even more complex mathematics and intricate equations, denying access to "all those ignorant of geometry." Consciously or unconsciously, economists erected thick and tall walls around themselves, essentially cutting off all access to their domain for scientists from other fields. Anthropologists, sociologists, psychologists, and biologists simply weren't mathematically competent enough to understand (let alone challenge) economic theories expressed in advanced mathematics.

To cut a long story short, economists were not updated on developments in other disciplines, while scientists from other fields stopped to take economic theory into consideration, unable to follow the sophisticated mathematical-economic equations.

THE ACADEMIC ESTABLISHMENT

The academic establishment is very powerful. It is not easy for outsiders to become aware of its operations and unwritten laws, or of the way in which ideology and relationship networks determine a scientist's progress and elevation to success.

The prevalence of a model, such as the neoclassical one, means that re-search funds are channeled mainly to those who abide by it. Therefore, if a new scientist wishes to become a professor and make a name as an academic, he or she has to follow the mainstream model; otherwise there is no hope.

There is a complex relationship network in academia that has very little to do with the quality of scientific work. It is simply impossible to go against the grain. As Lazonick advises economics students: "A belief in the market economy, not empirical verification, is the key to publication in major eco-nomics journals."[53] The control of publications in key scientific journals is so powerful that heretics are cast away and marginalized.[54]

The academic establishment has invested so much intellectual effort in, and has devoted so much time to, the construction of the neoclassical model that it would be extremely painful to admit the existence of flaws and shortcomings in the theory. The experience of professor Spyros Makridakis is characteristic and instructive. In the 1970s, Makridakis worked as a statistician at a business school that was attended mainly by managers and business executives. There, he found out that the executives preferred the simpler statistical techniques because, as they said, these made it easier for them to explain their forecasts to senior management. Makridakis, certain about the superior predictive power of more sophis-ticated statistical methods, decided to teach them a good lesson. His aim was to demonstrate to the executives the superiority of more advanced (that is, complex) techniques. So he gathered more than 100 different time series.* He divided each time series into two parts, initial data and end data. Then he modeled the initial data, first with the simple and then with the advanced methods, in order to find which method yielded results that were closer to reality (that is, to the end data). To his great surprise, the

---

* A time series is a sequence of real numbers that represent values of a real variable at regular time intervals, such as stock prices, the monthly sales of a book, or daily temperatures.

predictions made with the simpler statistical techniques proved to be more precise that those of the sophisticated ones. Stunned by this unexpected finding, Makridakis submitted a paper for publication in a prestigious scientific journal. However, to his even greater surprise, a few months later his paper was rejected by the journal's editors, "on the grounds that the results did not square with statistical theory."[55]

The great mathematician Benoit Mandelbrot, founder of fractal geometry, was branded as a controversial person when, in 1966, he developed a mathematical model that explained how even the rational mechanisms of the market can produce bubble prices. His work refuted the largest part of econometrics and steamrolled financial engineering. So it was cast aside. Nowadays, Mandelbrot's work is considered, beyond any doubt, to be groundbreaking and important, although it remains unknown to the vast majority of economists.

A study by John Ioannidis, an epidemiologist at Ioannina School of Medicine in Greece, showed that a large fraction of the research findings published in prestigious scientific journals are refuted by subsequent evidence. Examining a sample of forty-nine papers published in leading journals—papers that had been cited by more than a thousand other scientists—he found that only a few years after publication, almost one-third of them had been refuted by other studies.[56] However, for a substantial time period these papers prevailed and were propagated, building careers and relationships of power.

SCIENCE AND POWER

Why didn't economics adapt to developments? Why did it kept on defending extreme views with such persistence? Why did it stubbornly ignore reality and get trapped on a lonely path?

The deviation of economics is not only an intellectual tragedy. Moreover, it does not just have to do with a bunch of very intelligent people who were unlucky enough to follow, and make an intellectual investment in, some very flawed ideas.

Sincere longing for knowledge and scientific progress has been accompanied by a powerful link to political and business interests. Modern economic theory provided the scientific seal and the ideological cover for the implementation of policies that consolidated and served some very powerful interests. Neoclassical economics and its firm belief in the superiority of total economic freedom, which had been "proved" through the infallible language of mathematics, were adopted by political and business forces that used them as a scientific alibi for expanding their influence within society.

Under the presidency of George W. Bush, the United States saw an unprecedented tipping of the scales against the public and in favor of the private sector. Public schools were shut down, to be replaced by the more efficient private ones, while free market fundamentalism even led to the assignment of military and national security operations to private companies. All this was combined with an unheard-of deregulation of the markets, which left the financial system almost unfettered. Taxes were reduced, public investment was cut, markets were liberalized, regulations were abolished, the role of the state in the economy was diminished. And all this came under the cover and the scientific seal of economics.

This policy not only resulted in a major economic crisis, but almost vindicated Karl Marx's prophecies regarding the collapse of capitalism. The general public has not yet realized that in 2008 capitalism faced extinction.

That said, the dynamic reality unfolded in a uniquely unpredictable manner. In the end, the obsession with complete freedom inadvertently led to an unparalleled enhancement of the public sector in the United States. The

U.S. economy was saved only through the complete abandonment of neo-classical certainties: Banks, insurance companies, and manufacturers were nationalized (temporarily), something that was unheard of and unthinkable in U.S. history. At the same time, the crisis overturned the absolute political power of the neoliberals, allowing president Barack Obama to pursue revolutionary (by U.S. standards) policies in health, education, and public investment.

4

IT'S THE HUMANS, STUPID

Every time, though, something comes to upset this apparent progress. How come? Why do we keep repeating the same mistakes, again and again?

The problem does not lie in economics, nor in economic theories. The real problem is us humans, and our refusal to acknowledge our weaknesses and limitations.

I will repeat just a few of the things we discussed in detail in Part Three. The process that determines our behavior is a complex one, and we can understand it only to a limited degree. Intuition, and not thought, plays the greater role in everyday decision making. Our senses systematically deceive us and make us believe that our cognitive ability is greater than it actually is. Our expectations and beliefs dictate how we perceive and understand the world. In addition, social relations and social interaction are crucial parts of our life.

Everything, even the way the mind works, creates the illusion that we understand the world better than we actually do. We are certain that we know more than we actually know, and we rush to apply our special knowledge to totally inappropriate fields.

We have a (false) sense of control, and with the power of our (unwarranted) faith in our abilities we plan and foretell the future, marching straight ahead toward an uncertain tomorrow. The omniscient brain we possess has an inexhaustible talent to interpret the world and discover "logical" connections in everything that happens. Justifying the unjustifiable, we overlook the embarrassing disparity between our original intentions and the final outcomes that emerge when we act on those intentions.

We feel the urge to believe that every positive development (which may be coincidental and random) can be attributed to our knowledge, superior skills, and talents, blaming all bad outcomes on mischance, bad luck, and external factors. As a rule, we credit ourselves for any success and charge all failures to third parties. Moreover, we overlook the importance of the omnipresent factor of chance.

The great foe of economic science is no one else but us humans and the chaotic, evolving world we live in. Neither humans nor reality can fit into models and be understood as the product of a perfectly designed world that passively obeys invisible laws.

How can we expect that a science based on such an extensive distortion of human nature and on an artificial, ideal world would be able to produce results that are compatible with reality? The irrationality of this seems more than obvious. No matter how we see it, the theoretical "versions of rational choice are hard to accept as credible portraits of actual individual...actors."[57]

A man of action, the prominent financier George Soros, has developed the concept of reflexivity. The starting point of his thinking is the idea that our understanding of the world "is inherently imperfect because we are part of the world we seek to understand." According to Soros, people (with their imperfect understanding) interact with reality in two ways. On one hand, we seek to understand the world in which we live. On the other hand, we seek to make an impact on the world and change it to our advantage. The interplay between what we think we understand and what we seek to do (on the basis of that understanding) adds uncertainty, as it reflects and affects our thinking. This inherent flaw does not allow us to base our decisions on knowledge. Our lack of knowledge must be made up for with "guesswork based on experience, instinct, emotion, ritual, or other misconceptions." As Soros points out, "People base their decisions not on the actual situation that confronts them but on their perception or interpretation of that situation." However, their decisions have an impact on the situation, "and changes in the situation are liable to change their perceptions."[58]

ECONOMICS: THE DAY AFTER

If economists hadn't burned all bridges of contact with other sciences, they would have realized that the model on which their theories were based—that is, physics—did not remain fixed on Newtonian achievements. As we have already seen, Poincaré warned about the weaknesses of mainstream physics as early as the end of the nineteenth century. Moreover, quantum theory overturned Newtonian certainties of absolute causality, introducing those "damn quantum jumps."[59]

Marie Curie (1867–1934), had noted, at the end of the nineteenth century, the spontaneity (unpredictability) of radiation.[60] Soon after that, Werner Heisenberg (1901–1976) presented his famous uncertainty principle, and experiments that were later conducted (on subatomic systems) showed that the observation itself determines the outcome of an event.

From very early on, physicists recognized the fact that instability necessitated the restatement of the classical laws, since the conventional laws of nature were not enough to describe the phenomenon. So physics made spectacular progress in describing far-from-equilibrium situations, as well as the dynamics of unstable systems that are connected to the concept of chaos. Physicists saw that reality is infinitely more complex and dynamic than Newtonian stability and harmony. They found out that at equilibrium and near equilibrium the laws of nature apply to all systems, but in far-from-equilibrium conditions everything changes. Matter acquires new properties, becomes more active, and fluctuations and instabilities become the norm.[61]

According to physicists, the farther we get from equilibrium, the more likely it is that new bifurcations typical of chaotic behavior will arise. While near-equilibrium fluctuations are harmless, in conditions far from equilibrium they play a central role. Nobel laureate and physical chemist Ilya Prigogine wrote: "Even if we know the initial values and boundary constraints, there are still many states available to the system among which it 'chooses' as a result of fluctuations. Such conclusions are of interest beyond the realms of physics and chemistry. Indeed, bifurcations can be considered the source of diversification and innovation. These concepts are now applied to a wide group of problems in biology, sociology and economics."[62]

Economists (barring a few heretics) resisted the temptation to apply these concepts to their own field. With sheer ignorance, they shut their eyes and ears, shut themselves up in their own world and devoted themselves to it.

Today, many years after the outbreak of the great crisis of 2007, economic science still remains in a state of bewilderment. The first reaction to the new reality was the dynamic return of Keynesian economists to the scene, while a guilty silence spread across the neoclassical camp. Now, though, as economies get stabilized and both the United States and Europe regain their footing, the neoclassical model, assisted by the mighty academic establishment, is gradually making up for lost ground. Commercial banks, investment banks, and hedge funds continue to measure risks with the sophisticated models that led to the 2008 debacle.

This is indeed weird. If economic science wishes to play a useful role in society, it will have to gallantly admit its errors and shortcomings, even if this means forsaking a large part of the research done by economists in the 20th century. This is not some kind of ideological retreat, but an inescapable adaptation to reality.

Economics has to tear down the walls that keep it apart from other sciences. Disciplines such as neuroscience, biology, physics, psychology, anthropology, and sociology have accumulated a huge volume of knowledge. Chaos theory opened new intellectual vistas on how we perceive the world and life. Economics can't afford to disregard all these things.

Physics, biologists, chemists, evolutionary scientists, and mathematicians emphasize that linear approaches cannot describe the complexity of nature and life. Our world is inexplicably strange. Prigogine pointed out the paradox of the brain's structure, noting that the human heart has to be largely regular or we die, while the brain has to be largely irregular to function properly; otherwise we have epilepsy.[63] Too much regularity is bad for us!

Irregularity—chaos—gives rise to complex systems. But this does not mean disorder. Quite the contrary. The brain was developed to be so unstable that even the smallest influence produces order. According to John Briggs and David Peat, the brain is the nonlinear product of a nonlinear evolution on a nonlinear planet.[64] For Prigogine, nonlinearity is the essence of creation and evolution.

In physics there is a distinction between stable and unstable systems, and the difference between them is huge. Take, for example, the movement of a pendulum. After each small disturbance, the pendulum returns to its equilibrium position. The pendulum's equilibrium status is stable. On the other hand, if we manage to balance a pencil on its point, this equilibrium will be extremely unstable. Even the slightest, most minuscule disturbance will be enough to tip it over.

According to neoclassical theory, the economy is a stable equilibrium system resembling a pendulum. However, experience has shown, beyond any doubt, that things are not like that. The evolution of the world resembles not a calm, stable state, the product of a perfect design, but a sensitive, complex system in which even small changes of the initial conditions can, with time, lead to completely different outcomes.

Economics cannot keep on the same path, merely aping the laws of physics in their most traditional form and focusing on an idealized and stable economic world that has very little to do with the unstable, evolving world we live in.

Economics must overcome its obsession with mathematical methodology, which fails to incorporate the dynamic-chaotic aspects of human beings and social life. It must, instead, promote alternative tools for research and analysis. Pursuing a degree of accuracy that cannot be achieved in the real world is meaningless.

Economists have to deal with the real economic problems that concern real people, and do away with their theoretical wanderings in ideal worlds. They must realize that they are dealing with a world of willful, living beings and that they are studying the most elusive creatures of all: humans.[65]

In life, there are no certainties; uncertainty is inherent in every realistic description of the world. Economists must sincerely recognize their limitations and boundaries instead of being fixated on nonexistent abilities of divination.

However, this does not mean that the absence of predictive certainty renders all relevant efforts futile. We may well make predictions and plan for the future, but on the basis of probability. In other words, we should be prepared for contingencies instead of nonchalantly walking on supposedly certain paths.

Economists should reread physics, which stresses that when studying unstable systems we have to formulate the laws of dynamics at the statistical level, through probabilities.[66] Physicists, mathematicians, biologists, and others have identified and described simple systems that give rise to complex behavior and complex systems that give rise to simple behavior.[67] In real life, there are no certainties.

5

BEHAVIORAL ECONOMICS

Behavioral economics was developed in the past few decades with the aim of analyzing mankind's real economic behavior. In a nutshell, behavioral economics acknowledges that people are not the best decision makers, a fact that affects their economic decisions.[68] Behavioral economics overturns the effective market hypothesis, which is the cornerstone of neoclassical theory, and uses cognitive, social, emotional, and other factors to understand how individuals reach decisions. To achieve this, behavioral economics utilizes the findings of sciences such as neurology, biology, history, psychology, and sociology. Although interest in behavioral economics has been growing in recent years, it remains an overlooked and heretical field of economics; this was more or less expected, given that it undermines the largest part of mainstream economic theory.

It is criticized for opening a can of worms, since many more economic phenomena can be explained by adopting psychological factors than by an interpretative system based on economic theory.[69] If that is the case, does economics have any reason to exist? Mainstream economists claim that behavioral economics is not so much a theory or a discipline as it is a collection of anomalies and individual histories. So they reject it.

In 1979, psychologists Kahneman and Tversky emphasized the need to create an alternative theory that would explain the violations of the theory of expected utility. On the basis of a series of experiments, they argued that we humans perceive gains in a manner that is different from the way we perceive losses (in short, the pain from the loss of 1 euro is much greater than the joy from a gain of 1 euro). There are also differences in our perceptions according to the magnitude of a change. (In other words, we evaluate a change from 5 to 10 differently from the way we evaluate a change from 30 to 35.) Kahneman and Tversky also showed that individuals attach greater weight to outcomes that are considered certain than to outcomes that are considered simply possible. So they created prospect theory, which is centered on the assumption that individuals do not always behave rationally.

According to behavioral economics, when making decisions, people are decisively influenced by a series of heuristics that includes the way a problem is expressed, what others do, emotional factors, even random facts—all the things we discussed in Part Three. Professor George Akerlof argues that if there is any economic subject that should be behavioral, this subject is macroeconomics.

BEHAVIORAL ECONOMICS AND POLITICS

The demise of neoclassical certainties makes it necessary to revise the way economic policy is made and implemented. We have seen that, driven by faith in the rationality of economic actors and the efficiency of free markets, the financial system, and by extension the global economy, were transformed in just a few years into a huge lottery that brought Western economies to the brink of collapse.

Reality cannot stand fixations. The shock of 2008 shook mainstream theoretical views from the ground up, overturning everything that was considered certain and given. Economies do not suffer only from the painful boom-bust cycle, but also from the significant pro-cyclicality of the financial system. Nowadays, instability has substantially increased, owing to a greatly inflated banking system and high leverage: Boom stages see an irrational exuberance and inordinate expansion with excessive risk-taking, while bust stages are characterized by panic and a disorderly decline.

However, theory saw things differently: By prevailing over the economists' views, the theory of rational expectations constrained all practical research on the issue of the pro-cyclicality of the banking sector.[70] This dogmatic attitude is not sustainable anymore. Policymakers and implementers should confront reality instead of trying to reshape it through the distorting lens of mainstream theories and ideologies.

We should never forget that economics is not some abstract theory, and that economic decisions affect the lives of people. They concern real people, and no one, no matter how sure he or she may be about theories, has the right to play with other people's lives. No theory should ever turn society and the lives of people into a huge social experiment.

The economy requires moderation, not certainties. In the complex, evolutionary world that we live in there are no risk-free paths and assurances, and every theory that promises such things is doomed to failure. Economics should accept volatility, the capriciousness of human nature, and the limits of our knowledge and should design policies aimed at making societies more resistant to the inescapable instability.

An economic crisis is not just an unpleasant parenthesis that briefly upsets our comfort before everything goes back to normal. History has shown that an economic crisis—with 1929 standing out—can help bring out the worst in humans and society. The huge economic problems of the 1930s led to the absolute triumph of the extremes. Populism, fascism, racism, and war were among the hallmarks of the 20th century. European policymakers, as well as all those who bemoan the economic inefficiency of the euro zone, at least in comparison with the United States, should remember that, before the European Union was formed, successive generations had seen large-scale bloodshed: the Napoleonic Wars, the Franco-Prussian War, World War I, World War II, and so on. Just for this, just for putting an end to a bloody and violent tradition, the "European project" deserves our respect and attention.

Problems, which in our time are big and complex, cannot be magically solved, nor can reality be adapted to the politico-economic agenda or the mainstream theories of each time. Quite the opposite: Policymakers must rise above any ideologies and theoretical biases and be flexible, utilizing all the weapons available in their arsenal in order to deal with and solve problems.

6

A NECESSARY CLARIFICATION

The dramatic collapse of the neoliberal ideology that followed the 2007 crisis has given rise to a threat similar to that of 1989. That was the year when the fall of the Soviet empire led many people to the spurious conclusion that pure capitalism and the free market had finally prevailed. Something similar seems to be happening now: Many people have rushed to condemn market economies and hype the advantages of a strong state presence.

We have seen that the neoclassical-neoliberal edifice was built on shaky theoretical foundations. However, the 2007 crisis did not disprove the superiority of the free market. Rather, it crushed the doctrine of market fundamentalism, i.e., the blind, dogmatic faith in the economy's amazing capability for self-regulation in a state of absolute freedom.

The neoclassical failure in no way negates the tested advantages of the free market. Nor does it in any way vindicate socialism and central planning. As dogmatically preposterous as it might be to assert that total economic freedom leads to the optimum social outcome, it would be equally dogmatic and absurd to contend that one group of people (even the smartest of the smart) are capable of grasping our needs, making plans, and directing both the economy and society along the desired path. Although we humans are not even capable of foretelling with any degree of accuracy what will happen on just a single day in our lives, central planning professes to be in possession of a superior wisdom, capable of planning and steering the future.

It is not only naive but also dangerous that some people consider themselves so capable, and their theory so superior, that they can guide the economy and society through five-year growth plans!

Even the mildest suggestion that we can and must intervene in the economy through central planning and guide it in this or that direction has to be taken with many grains of salt, given the chaotic path of reality.

The great socioeconomic experiment of the Soviet Union, which, sadly, had a tragic impact on the lives of many millions of real people, provides us with an abundance of examples concerning the inefficiency of a planned economy. From trivial things like women's hairclips or cocoa to basics like clothing and shoes and even food, production was either limited or nonexistent, as the (infallible) Plan directed resources to certain fields only. It left no room for covering any deficits. Everything had to go according to the Plan.

Even when reality took a completely different direction from that prescribed by the Plan, the communists pretended that all was going well, since it was unthinkable to dispute the Plan's correctness. If, in the end, it failed, the blame was never laid on the omniscient planners of the Party but on some external or internal enemy. All those who expressed different views were branded as saboteurs, enemies of the people, agents of capitalism. Detached from reality, the communists marched straight ahead, certain that the collapse of capitalism was inevitable and that the currents of history were moving in their favor.

In contrast, the free market never claimed to be able to foretell or control the future, and never professed that everything was perfect. The great advantage of the free market is that it allows trial and error. No sage determines, for example, how many restaurants should be open—the market simply gives individuals a free hand to judge and decide by themselves. The invisible hand of Adam Smith works perfectly. Individuals, freely participating in the economic and social process, make up a superorganism possessing a combined collective wisdom that not even a pool of the thousand smartest people on the planet can ever comprehend.

It is no coincidence that the heart of innovativeness (the Internet, the iPad, iPod, Google, Facebook, and so on) is located in the United States, the country that encourages trial and error more than any other and does not put much of a stigma on those who fail. Innovation and progress do not originate so much in the research and development laboratories of large multinationals and multibillionaires, but mainly stem from "nerdy" kids—such as Bill Gates (Microsoft), Larry Page and Sergey Brin (Google), and Mark Zuckerberg (Facebook)—or from "losers" like Steve Jobs, who in 1985 was ousted in humiliation from Apple, only to return triumphantly a few years later.

But even if freedom introduces an even greater degree of instability into society, this, in my opinion, is far preferable to an ostensible stability dictated by a ruling elite. The superiority of the market is demonstrated every day, every moment, through living reality, and capitalism's resilience over time is not accidental. This does not mean, however, that the market is perfect or infallible and that it should be left unchecked, free from any control or intervention. Even if we accept that the mechanism of the market works perfectly, we, the human beings that form the market, are in no way perfect or infallible.

It is perfectly clear, as experience has shown, that key functional elements of the economy and society, such as the banking system, should operate on the basis of rules and under strong institutional supervision, the main aim not being maximizing results but mitigating the risk of accidents.

Every aspect of organized society has to be subject to rules and obligations. Yes, anyone can open, let's say, a restaurant; however, this restaurant will have to fulfill certain conditions (space, hygiene, and so on) and be subject to potential inspections to verify compliance with the rules.

A free market is one thing; an uncontrolled market is another. Figuratively speaking, consider a sage who claims with certainty that the stoplights that regulate road traffic should be abolished because they limit drivers' freedom and prevent the maximization of results (cars are moving at speeds slower than those they could achieve). Or imagine a science that, armed with an irrefutable theoretical base and powerful mathematical tools, "proves" that stoplights are redundant and prevent us from maximizing the efficiency of our cars.

The crisis of 2007 is not a failure of the free market; it is a failure of the dogmatic view regarding the unlimited potential of totally unfettered economic activity. The year 2007 saw the collapse of market fundamentalism and, once again, of unfaltering human certainties.

7

THE THIRD WAY TO KNOWLEDGE

Ancient Greeks used the word *hubris* to describe any breach of moderation, arrogant behavior, or insolence stemming from excessive passion or the feeling of absolute power. The gods' response to hubris was *nemesis*, well-deserved divine punishment and revenge.

Unpredictable reality always comes to remind us all of our limitations, to shatter our illusions and underline our flaws and weaknesses.

Nonetheless, as soon as the crisis is over, the gods are forgotten again. The lessons of the past are lost in the oblivion of prosperity. We keep repeating the same mistakes, showing excessive trust in our abilities, feeling unwarranted confidence in our knowledge, even believing that we have the ability to predict and shape the future.

We perceive of the world in a linear manner, and we predict the future linearly too. The evolution of economic thought reflects the shortcomings, limitations, and finite boundaries of the cognitive powers of even the smartest and most talented among us.

Adam Smith, looking at the capitalism of his era, the eighteenth century, saw a beautiful, self-regulated system that could lead to steady and long-term growth. But he failed to see the business cycle, the Industrial Revolution, the social tensions; he failed to see the importance of technology.

Karl Marx saw the harsh face of capitalist England in the nineteenth century and predicted, in a "scientifically" irrefutable manner, the inescapable social clash and the collapse of capitalism. He could not think that capitalism could possibly change, offer better pay and working conditions and adopt a widespread web of social protection. He failed to see the contribution of technology and the spectacular growth of productivity, nor did he see the dramatic improvement of the workers' lives and the emergence of the middle class, which was finally brought on by capitalism.

Of course, I do not say that we should be passive, that we should not prepare for tomorrow, never make predictions or construct theories aiming for the better. Many men and women of action do a great job predicting situations and events and successfully adapting their choices and plans to changing conditions. However, this is a rough process that develops through action and experience; it is not based on dogmatic certainties and cure-all models. Seasoned businessmen, bankers, investors, and many other people made good decisions and managed to reduce their exposure in the years before the 2007 crisis, mitigating its consequences after it started unfolding. This was not the product of chance (although chance can play a major role) but of undisputed personal skills. That said, most of those who managed, to a greater or lesser degree, to stand out did not rely on the infallibility of their judgment, dogmatic certainties, or fail-safe models. Their skills were developed through a daily process of trial and error.

The trouble for society begins when some people become unwaveringly certain that their ideas, theories, and projections are absolutely correct and, if implemented, will improve the lives of people and societies. The danger continues when they manage to persuade parts of society that they possess abilities they do not actually possess and offer certain paths and guaranteed results. Even worse, some people, believing that their theories are superior, and in the name of the "general good" and "democracy," do not hesitate to resort even to lies, deception, and violence in order to ensure the implementation of their views.

AWAY FROM CERTAINTIES

The effects of the certainty of some people who considered themselves gifted and select have been felt by humanity in the past, are being felt by humanity today, and will very possibly be felt by future generations.

A practical way of enhancing society's durability and its ability to avoid unnecessary and meaningless mishaps is to adopt an automatic response to whatever presents itself as certainty. Given that life is uncertain and the future is unpredictable, whoever provides assurances for tomorrow must somehow be "cheating."

We shouldn't easily accept certainties, even when they are based on rational foundations. We must put all ideas, all theories to continual scrutiny and testing. Paraphrasing the words of astrophysicist Sir Arthur Eddington (1882–1944), we can say that reality is not only stranger than we imagine, but stranger than we *can* imagine.[71]

The philosopher Karl Popper disagreed with the total prevalence of rationality. "When I speak of rationalism," he wrote, "I am not thinking of…the highly unreasonable belief that man is a purely rational creature.[72] According to Popper, "a rationalist is simply someone for whom it is more important to learn than to be proved right."[73] He argued that logic is not enough to establish final or complete knowledge or truth, but is a tool that helps us learn from our mistakes. Popper underlined the importance of falsifiability: All scientific statements must be formulated in a way that allows continuous testing and contestation. If these efforts do not lead to a refutation of the statement, then it can be incorporated into scientific knowledge. However, Popper stressed that the laws of science must be treated as hypotheses that are provisionally valid, until they are (if they are) refuted. "In so far as scientific statements refer to the world of experience, they must be refutable; and, in so far as they are irrefutable, they do not refer to the world of experience."[74] The scientific method lies in trying to find the facts that can be used to disprove theory.[75]

Popper made an appeal for moderation, stressing that, instead of seeking things that are very difficult, if not impossible, to achieve (for example, finding a new economic system that leads to optimality or this "something" that leads people to happiness), we should focus on solving the tangible problems that beset people. It is not easy to find the thing that brings happiness, but it is evident that, for example, unemployment brings misery.

This is where the new starting point for economics probably lies: in abandoning the lofty targets of maximization, optimality, and equilibrium, and instead developing an "economic engineering" designed to solve problems such as unemployment, instability, inequality, resource allocation, poverty, development, productivity growth, and so on, which are testing and plaguing the lives of real people.

As Adam Smith wrote, "No society can surely be flourishing and happy, of which the far greater part of the members are poor and miserable."[76] Similarly, in our own era, we can say that global prosperity and growth cannot be sustained and increased in a world where the majority of people live in hunger and misery. Rich countries must recognize that there are no fixed states and accept that their current prosperity not only is the product of hard work, efficiency, and superior skill, but is also based on less flattering factors (war, colonial exploitation, violent extraction of resources, slavery, and so on). A part of these controversial gains, which laid the foundations for the consequent strong economic growth of the Western world, will have to be returned in the form of investment, assistance, and so on, to the weakest members of the international community.

If the advantages and the benefits of globalization and free trade are not diffused to all countries and to more social groups, there is a great risk that this course may be reversed. The risk does not come only from the poorer countries and the weakest members of the international community. The rise of poverty and the great widening of inequalities observed in many economically advanced countries generate risks and may possibly lead to political outcomes that will not be to anyone's benefit. In other words, we could have a regression to extremes through the ascendancy of populism, nationalism, xenophobia, and protectionism. This must not happen. We cannot avoid mistakes, but we can avoid repeating the same mistakes. Or, even better, as a famous psychologist said, to replace our mistakes with other, smaller ones.

REFERENCES

PART ONE

1. Michael Mann, *The Sources of Social Power, Volume 1: A History of Power from the Beginning to AD 1760*, Cambridge University Press, 1986, p. 384.

2. Robert L. Heilbroner, *The Worldly Philosophers—The Lives, Times and Ideas of the Great Economic Thinkers*, Revised Seventh Edition, Simon & Schuster, 1999, p. 22.

3. Carlo M. Cipolla, *Before the Industrial Revolution—European Society and Economy, 1000–1700*, Third Edition, Routledge, 1993, pp. 122-123.

4. Robert L. Heilbroner, *The Worldly Philosophers—The Lives, Times and Ideas of the Great Economic Thinkers*, Revised Seventh Edition, Simon & Schuster, 1999, p. 30.

5. Ibid.

6. Yanis Varoufakis, *Political Economy—Economic Theory Under Criticism* (in Greek), Gutenberg Publications, 2007, p. 27.

7. Karl Polanyi, *The Great Transformation—the Political and Economic Origins of Our Time*, Beacon Press, 2001, p. 48.

8. Ibid., p. 66.

9. Douglass C. North, *Structure and Change in Economic History*, W.W. Norton, 1981, p. 158.

10. Eric John Hobsbawm, *The Age of Revolution 1789-1848*, Vintage Books, August 1996, p. 38.

11. Ibid., p. 27.

12. Ibid., p. 52.

13. Ibid., p. 27.

14. Eric John Hobsbawm, *The Age of Capital 1848-1875*, Abacus, 1995, p. 13.

15. Ibid., p. 29.

16. Henri Pirenne, *Medieval Cities—Their Origins and the Revival of Trade*, Princeton University Press, 1952, p. 114.

17. Ibid., p. 122.

18. Ibid., p. 126.

19. Carlo M. Cipolla, *Before the Industrial Revolution—European Society and Economy, 1000-1700*, Third Edition, Routledge, 1993, p. 93.

20. Ibid., p. 92.

21. Ibid., p. 93.

22. Ibid., p. 36.

23. Niall Ferguson, *Civilization—The West and the Rest*, Allen Lane, 2011, p. 36.

24. Robert L. Heilbroner and William Milberg, *The Making of Economic Society*, Thirteenth Edition, Pearson, 1998, p. 36.

25. Isaak Ilych Rubin, *A History of Economic Thought*, translated and edited by Donald Filtzer, Ink Links Ltd., 1979, p. 91.

26. Robert L. Heilbroner and William Milberg, *The Making of Economic Society*, Thirteenth Edition, Pearson, 1998, p. 40.

27. Ibid., p. 35.

28. Christopher Minster, *The Ransom of Atahualpa*, About.com, Latin American History, available at http://latinamericanhistory.about.com/od/theconquestofperu/p/The-Ransom-Of-Atahualpa.htm.

29. For a brief history of the *Golden Hind*, see Wikipedia.com, *Golden Hind*: http://en.wikipedia.org/wiki/Golden_Hind.

30. Niall Ferguson, *Civilization—The West and the Rest*, Allen Lane, 2011, p. 102.

31. Robert L. Heilbroner and William Milberg, *The Making of Economic Society*, Thirteenth Edition, Pearson, 1998, p. 55.

32. Isaak Ilych Rubin, *A History of Economic Thought*, translated and edited by Donald Filtzer, Ink Links Ltd., 1979, p. 81.

33. Ibid., p. 101.

34. Ibid., p. 106.

35. Robert L. Heilbroner, *The Worldly Philosophers—The Lives, Times and Ideas of the Great Economic Thinkers*, Revised Seventh Edition, Simon & Schuster, 1999, p. 45.

36. Ibid.

37. Isaak Ilych Rubin, *A History of Economic Thought*, translated and edited by Donald Filtzer, Ink Links Ltd., 1979, p. 171.

38. Adam Smith, *The Wealth of Nations*, Books I–III, Penguin, 1979, p. 119.

39. Ibid., p. 109.

40. Ibid., p. 110.

41. Ibid., p. 176.

42. Terence Ball and Richard Dagger, *Political Ideologies and the Democratic Ideal*, Canadian Edition, Pearson, 2010, p. 58.

43. Robert L. Heilbroner, *The Worldly Philosophers—The Lives, Times and Ideas of the Great Economic Thinkers*, Revised Seventh Edition, Simon & Schuster, 1999, p. 78.

44. Isaak Ilych Rubin, *A History of Economic Thought*, translated and edited by Donald Filtzer, Ink Links Ltd., 1979, p. 231.

45. Robert L. Heilbroner, *The Worldly Philosophers—The Lives, Times and Ideas of the Great Economic Thinkers*, Revised Seventh Edition, Simon & Schuster, 1999, p. 82.

46. David Ricardo, *On the Principles of Political Economy and Taxation*, Chapter 2, paragraph 2.28, available at http://www.econlib.org/library/Ricardo/ricP1a.html.

47. Ibid., Chapter 7, paragraph 7.11, available at http://www.econlib.org/library/Ricardo/ricP2a.html.

48. Isaak Ilych Rubin, *A History of Economic Thought*, translated and edited by Donald Filtzer, Ink Links Ltd., 1979, p. 351.

49. Robert L. Heilbroner, *The Worldly Philosophers: The Lives, Times and Ideas of the Great Economic Thinkers*, Revised Seventh Edition, Simon & Schuster, 1999, p. 127.

50. John Stuart Mill, *Principles of Political Economy*, Hackett Publishing Company, 2004, p. 189.

51. Isaak Ilych Rubin, *A History of Economic Thought*, translated and edited by Donald Filtzer, Ink Links Ltd., 1979, p. 353.

52. Terence Ball and Richard Dagger, *Political Ideologies and the Democratic Ideal*, Canadian Edition, 2010, Pearson, p. 62.

53. Andrew Heywood, *Political Ideologies—An Introduction*, Third Edition, Palgrave McMillan, 2003, p. 330.

54. Terence Ball and Richard Dagger, *Political Ideologies and the Democratic Ideal*, Canadian Edition, Pearson, 2010, p. 137.

55. Ibid., p. 130.

56. Robert L. Heilbroner, *The Worldly Philosophers—The Lives, Times and Ideas of the Great Economic Thinkers*, Revised Seventh Edition, Simon & Schuster, 1999, pp. 144-145.

57. Terence Ball and Richard Dagger, *Political Ideologies and the Democratic Ideal*, Canadian Edition, Pearson, 2010, p. 131.

58. Karl Marx, *The Poverty of Philosophy*, p. 49, available at http://www.marxists.org/archive/marx/works/download/pdf/Poverty-Philosophy.pdf.

59. Robert L. Heilbroner, *The Worldly Philosophers—The Lives, Times and Ideas of the Great Economic Thinkers*, Revised Seventh Edition, Simon & Schuster, 1999, pp. 144-146.

60. Karl Marx, *Manifesto of the Communist Party*, Chapter I, available at http://www.marxists.org/archive/marx/works/1848/communist-manifesto/ch01.htm.

61. Terence Ball and Richard Dagger, *Political Ideologies and the Democratic Ideal*, Canadian Edition, Pearson, 2010, p. 131.

62. Robert L. Heilbroner, *The Worldly Philosophers: The Lives, Times and Ideas of the Great Economic Thinkers*, Revised Seventh Edition, Simon & Schuster, 1999, p. 147.

63. Ibid.

64. Ibid., p. 155.

65. Karl Marx, *Capital*, Volume One, Chapter 32, available at http://www.marxists.org/archive/marx/works/1867-c1/ch32.htm.

66. John Briggs and David Peat, *Turbulent Mirror: An Illustrated Guide to Chaos Theory and the Science of Wholeness*, Harper and Row, 1990, p. 21.

67. David Lindley, *Uncertainty: Einstein, Heisenberg, Bohr, and the Struggle for the Soul of Science*, Doubleday, 2007, p. 22.

68. John Briggs and David Peat, *Turbulent Mirror: An Illustrated Guide to Chaos Theory and the Science of Wholeness*, Harper and Row, 1990, frontmatter.

69. Ernst Mayr, *One Long Argument: Charles Darwin and the Genesis of Modern Evolutionary Thought*, Harvard University Press, 1991, p. 48.

70. Ilya Prigogine, *The End of Certainty—Time, Chaos and the New Laws of Nature*, The Free Press, 1997, p. 12.

71. Gregory N. Mankiw, *Principles of Economics*, Cengage Learning, 2008, p. 21.

72. Jeremy Bentham, *An Introduction to the Principles of Morals and Legislation*, Chapter 1, paragraph 1.1, available at http://www.econlib.org/library/Bentham/bnthPML1.html.

73. Robert L. Heilbroner, *The Worldly Philosophers: The Lives, Times and Ideas of the Great Economic Thinkers*, Revised Seventh Edition, Simon & Schuster, 1999, p. 233.

74. Ibid., p.232.

75. Ibid.

76. Ibid., pp. 246-247.

77. Nicholas Shaxson, *Treasure Islands—Tax Havens and the Men Who Stole the World*, The Bodley Head, 2011, p. 71.

78. Panayiotis Korliras, *The Philosophy of Political Economy* (in Greek), Gnosi, 1991, p. 146.

79. Robert L. Heilbroner, *The Worldly Philosophers: The Lives, Times and Ideas of the Great Economic Thinkers*, Revised Seventh Edition, Simon & Schuster, 1999, p. 275.

80. John Maynard Keynes, *The General Theory of Employment, Interest and Money*, Atlantic, 2008, p.140.

81. Amos Tversky and Daniel Kahneman, "Judgment Under Uncertainty: Heuristics and Biases." *Science*, Vol. 185, No. 4157, September 27, 1974,

available at http://www.math.mcgill.ca/vetta/CS764.dir/judgement.
pdf.

82. Nikos Theocharakis, *The Neoclassical Theory of Labor* (in Greek), Tipothito, 2005, p. 33.

83. Ibid., p. 46.

84. Theodoros Gamaletsos, *Theoretical Economics* (in Greek), Stamoulis SA, 1991, Part A, p. 35.

85. Kenneth Arrow, "Methodological Individualism and Social Knowledge." *American Economic Review*, Vol. 84, No. 2, p. 3.

86. William Lazonick, *Business Organization and the Myth of the Market Economy*, Cambridge University Press, 1993, p. 63.

87. Robert A. Gordon, "Rigor and Relevance in a Changing Institutional Setting." *American Economic Review*, Vol. 66, March 1976, p. 1.

88. Panayiotis Korliras, *The Philosophy of Political Economy* (in Greek), Gnosi, 1991, p. 47.

89. Nikos Theocharakis, *The Neoclassical Theory of Labor* (in Greek), Tipothito, 2005, p. 58.

90. Panayiotis Korliras, *The Philosophy of Political Economy* (in Greek), Gnosi, 1991, p. 48.

91. Nikos Theocharakis, *The Neoclassical Theory of Labor* (in Greek), Tipothito, 2005, p. 54.

92. Frédéric Lemaître, "La crise remet en cause le savoir et le statut des économistes." *Le Monde*, April 9, 2009, available at http://www.lemonde. fr/idees/article/2009/09/04/la-crise-remet-en-cause-le-savoir-et-le-statut-des-economistes-par-frederic-lemaitre_1235793_3232.html.

93. Wassily Leontief, "Theoretical Assumptions and Nonobserved Facts." *American Economic Review*, March 1971, p. 3.

94. Panayiotis Korliras, *The Philosophy of Political Economy* (in Greek), Gnosi, 1991, p. 89.

95. Paul Samuelson, *Economics: An Introductory Analysis*, Third Edition, New York, McGraw—Hill, p. 212.

96. Milton Friedman, *Capitalism and Freedom*, Phoenix Books, 1982, p. 15.

PART TWO

1. Carmen M. Reinhart and Kenneth S. Rogoff, *This Time Is Different: Eight Centuries of Financial Folly*, Princeton University Press, 2011, p. 1.

2. Christos Alexakis and Manolis Xanthakis, *Behavioural Finance* (in Greek), Stamoulis Publications, 2008, p. 110.

3. Lodewijk Petram, *The World's First Stock Exchange*, (Greek Edition), Eora, 2013.

4. Charles P. Kindleberger, *Manias, Panics, and Crashes: A History of Financial Crises*, Revised Sixth Edition, Palgrave Macmillan, 2011, p. 111.

5. Christos Alexakis and Manolis Xanthakis, *Behavioural Finance* (in Greek), Stamoulis Publications, 2008, p. 111.

6. Charles P. Kindleberger, *Manias, Panics, and Crashes: A History of Financial Crises*, Revised Sixth Edition, Palgrave Macmillan,2011, p. 273.

7. Nouriel Roubini and Stephen Mihm, *Crisis Economics: A Crash Course in the Future of Finance*, Penguin Books Ltd., 2010, i 3, section 2.

8. Eric John Hobsbawm, *The Age of Revolution 1789-1848*, Vintage Books, August 1996, p. 44.

9. John Micklethwait and Adrian Wooldridge, *The Company: A Short History of a Revolutionary Idea*, Modern Library Chronicles, 2005, p. 49.

10. Nouriel Roubini and Stephen Mihm, *Crisis Economics: A crash Course in the Future of Finance*, Penguin Books Ltd., 2010, chapter 1, section 3.

11. Eric John Hobsbawm, *The Age of Capital 1848-1875*, Abacus, 1995, p. 62.

12. Ibid.

13. John Kenneth Galbraith, *The Great Crash 1929*, Houghton Mifflin Harcourt, 2009, p. 99.

14. Robert L. Heilbroner and William Milberg, *The Making of Economic Society,* Thirteenth Edition, Pearson, 1998, p. 91.

15. Carmen M. Reinhart and Kenneth S. Rogoff, *This Time Is Different: Eight Centuries of Financial Folly*, Princeton University Press, 2011, p. 1.

16. Paul Krugman, *The Return of Depression Economics and the Crisis of 2008*, W.W. Norton, 2009, p. 34.

17. Ibid., p. 61.

18. Ibid., p. 80.

19. Tali Sharot, "The Optimism Bias by Tali Sharot: Extract." *The Observer*, January 1, 2012, available at http://www.theguardian.com/science/2012/jan/01/tali-sharot-the-optimism-bias-extract.

20. Adam Smith, *The Wealth of Nations*, Books I-III, Penguin, 1979, p. 211.

21. Nouriel Roubini and Stephen Mihm, *Crisis Economics: A Crash Course in the Future of Finance*, Penguin Books Ltd., 2010, chapter 3, section 4.

22. Michael Lewis, *The Big Short: Inside the Doomsday Machine*, W.W. Norton & Company, 2010, p. 93.

23. Jérôme Kerviel, *L' engrenage* (Greek translation), translated by Ioanna Syrigou, Papadopoulos Editions, 2010 p. 34.

24. Michael Lewis, *The Big Short: Inside the Doomsday Machine*, W.W. Norton & Company, 2010, p. 97.

25. John Kenneth Galbraith, *The Great Crash 1929*, Houghton Mifflin Harcourt, 2009, p. 72.

26. Alan Greenspan, *The Age of Turbulence: Adventures in a New World*, Penguin Press, 2007, p. 175.

27. Theodoros Karatzas, "A Large Part of the ASE Is Sick" (in Greek). *Kathimerini* newspaper, September 1, 1999, p. 23.

28. Nicolaos Karamouzis and Gikas Hardouvelis (eds.), *From Global Crisis to the Crisis in the Euro Zone and Greece: What Does the Future Have in Store?* (in Greek), AA Livanis Publications, 2011, p. 35.

29. Harry Markopolos, No One Would Listen: A True Financial Thriller, John Wiley & Sons, 2010, p. 3.

30. Gordon Brown, *Beyond the Crash: Overcoming the First Crisis of Globalization*, Free Press, 2010, part 3, chapter 7.

31. Dimitris Spartiotis and Yannis Stournaras, *The Fundamental Reasons of the Banking Collapse* (in Greek), Gutenberg, 2010, p. 168.

32. Ibid..

33. Ibid., p. 172.

34. Ibid., p. 171.

35. Paul Krugman, *The Return of Depression Economics and the Crisis of 2008*, W.W. Norton, 2009, p. 9.

36. Alan Greenspan, *The Age of Turbulence: Adventures in a New World*, Penguin Press, 2007, p. 161.

37. Ibid., pp. 162-163.

38. Ibid., pp. 257, 370-371, 407, 489, 490.

39. Nouriel Roubini and Stephen Mihm, *Crisis Economics: A Crash Course in the Future of Finance*, Penguin Books Ltd., 2010, chapter 3, section 4.

40. Ibid., chapter 3, section 5.

41. Minos A. Zombanakis, "The Financial Crisis: How Did We Get There?" *Lectures in International Banking and Finance*, Hellenic Bank Association, September 2008, p. 7.

42. Gordon Brown, *Beyond the Crash: Overcoming the First Crisis of Globalization*, Free Press, 2010, part 2, chapter 3.

43. Gikas Hardouvelis, "The Pro-cyclicality of the International Financial System," in *From Global Crisis to the Crisis in the Euro Zone and Greece: What Does the Future Have in Store?* (in Greek), Nicolaos Karamouzis and Gikas Hardouvelis (eds.), AA Livanis Publications, 2011, p. 343.

44. Michael Lewis, *The Big Short: Inside the Doomsday Machine*, W.W. Norton & Company, 2010, pp. 97-98.

45. Nouriel Roubini and Stephen Mihm, *Crisis Economics: A Crash Course in the Future of Finance*, Penguin Books Ltd., 2010, chapter 4, section 2.

46. Ibid., chapter 3, section 6.

47. Ibid., chapter 3, section 3.

48. Gordon Brown, *Beyond the Crash: Overcoming the First Crisis of Globalization*, Free Press, 2010, [art 2, chapter 3, section 5 ("Justice and Bankers' Pay").

49. Jim O'Neil, "Crisis and the Business Cycle: The View of the Market," in *From Global Crisis to the Crisis in the Euro Zone and Greece: What Does the Future Have in Store?* (in Greek), Nicolaos Karamouzis and Gikas Hardouvelis (eds.), AA Livanis Publications, 2011, p. 157.

50. Gikas Hardouvelis, "The Chronicle of the International and the Subsequent Greek and European Crisis," in *From Global Crisis to the Crisis in the Euro Zone and Greece: What Does the Future Have in Store?* (in Greek), Nicolaos Karamouzis and Gikas Hardouvelis (eds.), AA Livanis Publications, 2011, p. 36.

51. Vicky Ward, *The Devil's Casino: Friendship, Betrayal, and the High-Stakes Games Played Inside Lehman Brothers*, John Wiley & Sons, Inc., 2010, p. 165.

PART THREE

1. Colin Blakemore, *The Mind Machine*, Penguin Books,1994, p. 16.

2. Sandra Aamodt and Sam Wang, *Welcome to Your Brain*, Bloomsbury USA, p. xix.

3. Michael S. Gazzaniga, *Human: The Science Behind What Makes Us Unique*, Harper Collins, 2008, p. 9.

4. Nicky Hayes, *The Foundations of Psychology*, Third Edition, Thomson Learning, 2000, p. 64.

5. Ibid., p. 95.

6. Christopher F. Chabris and Daniel J. Simons, *The Invisible Gorilla: And Other Ways Our Intuitions Deceive Us*, Crown Publishing, 2010, pp. 46-48.

7. Ibid., p. 48.

8. Ibid., pp. 48-49.

9. Colin Blakemore, *The Mind Machine*, Penguin Books,1994, p. 240.

10. Amos Tversky and Daniel Kahneman, "Availability: A Heuristic for Judging Frequency and Probability." *Cognitive Psychology*, Vol. 5, 207-232 (1973), pp. 220-221.

11. Joyce W. Lacy and Graig E.L. Stark. "The Neuroscience of Memory Implications for the Courtroom." *Nature Reviews Neuroscience*, Vol. 14, September 2013.

12. Christopher F. Chabris and Daniel J. Simons, *Invisible Gorilla: And Other Ways Our Intuitions Deceive Us*, Crown Publishing, 2010, pp. 5-6.

13. Michael S. Gazzaniga, *Human: The Science Behind What Makes Us Unique*, Harper Collins, 2008, p. 121.

14. Christopher F. Chabris and Daniel J. Simons, *The Invisible Gorilla: And Other Ways Our Intuitions Deceive Us*, Crown Publishing, New York, pp. 19-20.

15. Ibid., p. 60.

16. Colin Blakemore, *The Mind Machine*, Penguin Books,1994, p. 172.

17. Gene Weingarten, "Pearls Before Breakfast." *Washington Post*, April 8, 2007, available at http://www.washingtonpost.com/wp-dyn/content/article/2007/04/04/AR2007040401721.html.

18. Mimis Androulakis, *Hey, President!* (in Greek), Kastaniotis Publications, 2009, pp. 23-24.

19. Nicky Hayes, *The Foundations of Psychology*, Third Edition, Thomson Learning, 2000, p. 67.

20. Daniel Kahneman, *Thinking, Fast and Slow*, Farrar, Straus and Giroux, 2011, pp. 153-155.

21. Michael S. Gazzaniga, *Human: The Science Behind What Makes Us Unique*, Harper Collins, 2008, p. 95.

22. Frans de Waal, *Our Inner Ape: A Leading Primatologist Explains Why We Are Who We Are*, Riverhead Books, 2005, p. 13.

23. Ibid.

24. Nicholas A. Christakis and James H. Fowler, *Connected: The Surprising Power of Our Social Networks and How They Shape Our Lives*, *Little, Brown and Company, 2009*, p. 232.

25. Alan Greenspan, "Never Saw It Coming: Why the Financial Crisis Took Economists by Surprise." *Foreign Affairs*, November/December 2013, available at http://www.foreignaffairs.com/articles/140161/alan-greenspan/never-saw-it-coming.

26. Nicholas Humphrey, "The Social Function Intellect," in P.P.G. Bateson and R.A. Hinde (eds.), *Ethology*, Cambridge University Press, 1976, pp. 303-317.

27. Michael S. Gazzaniga, *Human: The Science Behind What Makes Us Unique*, Harper Collins, 2008, p. 160.

28. For a quick look at how mirror neurons function, see "The Neurons That Shaped Civilization," a TED lecture given in November 2009 by neurologist V.S. Ramachandran, available at http://www.ted.com/talks/

vs_ramachandran_the_neurons_that_shaped_civilization.html.   Also
see M. Iacoboni and M. Dapretto, "The Mirror Neuron System and the
Consequences of Its Dysfunction." *Nature Reviews Neuroscience*, December
2006.

29. Richard Dawkins, *The Selfish Gene*, 30th Anniversary Edition, Oxford
University Press, 2006, pp. 31-32.

30. Nicholas A. Christakis and James H. Fowler, *Connected: The Surprising
Power of Our Social Networks and How They Shape Our Lives*, Little, Brown and
Company, 2009, p. 113.

31. Nicholas Christakis, "The Hidden Influence of Social Networks."
TED lecture, February 2010, available at http://www.ted.com/talks/
nicholas_christakis_the_hidden_influence_of_social_networks.
html.

32. Ibid.

33. Robert J. Shiller, *Irrational Exuberance*, Princeton University Press, 2000,
p. 149.

34. Nicholas A. Christakis and James H. Fowler, *Connected: The Surprising
Power of Our Social Networks and How They Shape Our Lives*, Little, Brown and
Company, 2009, p. 140.

35. Ibid.

36. Nicky Hayes, *The Foundations of Psychology*, Third Edition, Thomson
Learning, 2000, p. 174.

37. Steven D. Levitt and Stephen J. Dubner, *Freakonomics: A Rogue Economist
Explores the Hidden Side of Everything*, Perfectbound, 2005, p. 8.

38. Spyros Makridakis, Robin Hogart, and Anil Gaba, *Dance with Chance: Making Luck Work for You*, OneWorld Publications, 2009, p. 41.

39. Steven D. Levitt and Stephen J. Dubner, *Freakonomics: A Rogue Economist Explores the Hidden Side of Everything*, Perfectbound, 2005, pp. 26-27.

40. Ibid., p. 25.

41. Sun Tzu, *The Art of War*, translated by Lionel Giles, D.E. Tarver.

42. Michael S. Gazzaniga, *Human: The Science Behind What Makes Us Unique*, Harper Collins, 2008, pp. 101-102.

43. Richard Dawkins, *The Selfish Gene*, 30th Anniversary Edition, Oxford University Press, 2006, p. 5.

44. James Gleick, *The Information: A History, a Theory, a Flood*, Pantheon Books, 2011, p. 31.

45. Ibid., p. 33.

46. Nassim Nicholas Taleb, *The Black Swan: The Impact of the Highly Improbable*, Random House, 2007, p. xxv.

47. For some great insights on this issue, see "How Schools Kill Creativity," delightful TED lecture given in February 2006 by Ken Robinson, available at http://www.ted.com/talks/ken_robinson_says_schools_kill_creativity.html.

48. Adam Smith, *The Wealth of Nations*, Books I-III, Penguin, 1979, p. 209.

49. Rebecca Rupp, *Four Elements: Water, Air, Fire, Earth*, Profile Books, 2005, p. 70.

50. Naomi Klein, *The Shock Doctrine: The Rise of Disaster Capitalism*, Metropolitan Books, 2007, pp. 23, 26.

51. Colin Blakemore, *The Mind Machine*, Penguin Books,1994, pp. 106-107.

52. Nassim Nicholas Taleb, *The Black Swan: The Impact of the Highly Improbable*, Random House, 2007, p. 55.

53. CNN Money, "JPMorgan Suffers Big Loss," November 5, 2012, available at http://money.cnn.com/2012/05/10/news/companies/jp-morgan-losses/

54. Nicky Hayes, *The Foundations of Psychology*, Third Edition, Thomson Learning, 2000, p. 70.

55. Umberto Eco, *I limiti dell'interpretazione* (Greek translation), translated by Marianna Kondyli, Gnosi Publications, 1994, p. 73.

56. James Gleick, *The Information: A History, a Theory, a Flood*, Pantheon Books, 2011, p. 29.

57. "Narrative: E.M. Forster's King and Queen and Narrative Across the Disciplines." available at http://science.jrank.org/pages/10374/Narrative-E-M-FORSTER-S-KING-QUEEN-NARRATIVE-ACROSS-DISCIPLINES.html

58. Nassim Nicholas Taleb, *The Black Swan: The Impact of the Highly Improbable*, Random House, 2007 p. 76.

59. Karl R. Popper, *The Open Society and Its Enemies*, Princeton University Press, 2013, p. 475.

60. Christos Alexakis and Manolis Xanthakis, *Behavioural Finance* (in Greek), Stamoulis Publications, 2008, p. 174.

61. Robert Wright, *The Moral Animal*, First Vintage Books, 1995, p. 193.

62. Michael S. Gazzaniga, *Human: The Science Behind What Makes Us Unique*, Harper Collins, 2008, p. 294.

63. Colin Blakemore, *The Mind Machine*, Penguin Books,1994, pp. 165-166.

64. For a detailed presentation of Stanley Milgram's experiments, see his book *Obedience to Authority: An Experimental View*, Harper & Row, 1974.

65. Georg Wilhelm Friedrich Hegel, "Philosophy of Nature," translated by Karl Popper in Karl R. Popper, *The Open Society and Its Enemies*, Princeton University Press, 2013, p. 243.

66. Christopher F. Chabris and Daniel J. Simons, *The Invisible Gorilla: And Other Ways Our Intuitions Deceive Us*, Crown Publishing, 2010, pp. 141-142.

67. Frank H. Knight, *Risk, Uncertainty and Profit*, Hart, Schaffner & Marx and Houghton Mifflin Co., 1921, part III, chapter. VII, pp. 197-232.

68. Daniel Kahneman, *Thinking, Fast and Slow*, Farrar, Straus and Giroux, 2011, p. 22.

69. Ibid., p. 23.

70. Deanna Kuhn, "How Do People Know?" *Psychological Science*, Vol. 12, No. 1, January 2001.

71. Michael S. Gazzaniga, *Human: The Science Behind What Makes Us Unique*, Harper Collins, 2008, p. 73.

72. Ibid., p. 157.

73. Nicky Hayes, *The Foundations of Psychology*, Third Edition, Thomson Learning, 2000, p. 148.

74. Amos Tversky, Daniel Kahneman, "Judgment Under Uncertainty: Heuristics and Biases." *Science, New Series*, Vol. 185, No. 4157, September 27, 1974, pp. 1124-1131.

75. Daniel Kahneman, *Thinking, Fast and Slow*, Farrar, Straus and Giroux, 2011, p. 118.

76. Nicky Hayes, *The Foundations of Psychology*, Third Edition, Thomson Learning, 2000, p. 151.

77. Nassim Nicholas Taleb, *The Black Swan: The Impact of the Highly Improbable*, Random House, 2007, pp. 53-54.

78. Nicky Hayes, *The Foundations of Psychology*, Third Edition, Thomson Learning, 2000, p. 152.

79. Henry Kissinger, *Diplomacy*, Simon & Schuster, 1994, p. 783.

80. John Briggs and David Peat, *Turbulent Mirror: An Illustrated Guide to Chaos Theory and the Science of Wholeness*, Harper and Row, 1990, pp. 27-29.

81. Ernst Mayr, *One Long Argument: Charles Darwin and the Genesis of Modern Evolutionary Thought*, Harvard University Press, 1991, pp. 1-2.

82. James D. Stein, *How Math Explains the World*, Harper Collins, 2008, p. 195.

83. Eric John Hobsbawm, *The Age of Capital 1848-1875*, Abacus, 1995, p. 60.

84. Paul Krugman, *The Return of Depression Economics and the Crisis of 2008*, W.W. Norton, 2009, p. 58.

85. Christopher F. Chabris and Daniel J. Simons, *The Invisible Gorilla: And Other Ways Our Intuitions Deceive Us*, Crown Publishing, 2010, p. 118.

86. "Arctic Summers Ice-Free 'by 2013,'" BBC News, December 12, 2007, available at http://news.bbc.co.uk/2/hi/7139797.stm.

87. "And Now It's Global COOLING! Return of Arctic Ice Cap as It Grows by 29% in a Year." Mail Online, July 9, 2013, available at http://www.dailymail.co.uk/news/article-2415191/And-global-COOLING-Return-Arctic-ice-cap-grows-29-year.html.

88. "Deadly Crossroads," *Mayday (Air Crash Investigations)*, season 2, 2004

89. *Road Police Statistical Data, 2011* (in Greek), Hellenic Police, Ministry of Public Order and Citizen Protection, available at http://www.astynomia.gr/index.php?option=ozo_content&perform=view&id=5005&Itemid=86&lang=.

90. John Briggs and David Peat, *Turbulent Mirror: An Illustrated Guide to Chaos Theory and the Science of Wholeness*, Harper and Row, 1990, p. 22.

91. Nassim Nicholas Taleb, *Fooled by Randomness: The Hidden Role of Chance in Life and in the Markets*, Penguin Books, 2004, pp. 153-154.

92. James Gleick, *Chaos: Making a New Science*, Open Road, 2011, p. 24.

93. John Briggs and David Peat, *Turbulent Mirror: An Illustrated Guide to Chaos Theory and the Science of Wholeness*, Harper and Row, pp. 68-71.

94. Spyros Makridakis, Robin Hogart, and Anil Gaba, *Dance with Chance: Making Luck Work for You*, OneWorld Publications, 2009, p 115.

95. Nassim Nicholas Taleb, *The Back Swan: The Impact of the Highly Improbable*, Random House, 2007, p. 221.

96. Jared Diamond, *Collapse: How Societies Choose to Fail or Succeed*, Viking, 2005, p. 431.

97. Victor Sebestyen, *Revolution 1989: The Fall of the Soviet Empire*, Phoenix, 2009, pp. 134-135.

98. Steven D. Levitt and Stephen J. Dubner, *Freakonomics: A Rogue Economist Explores the Hidden Side of Everything*, Perfectbound, 2005, pp. 19-20, 23.

99. "Greek Legislative Election, 1920," Wikipedia, available at el.wikipedia. org/wiki/Greek_legislative_election,_1920.

PART FOUR

1. Alan Greenspan, "Never Saw It Coming: Why the Financial Crisis Took Economists by Surprise." *Foreign Affairs*, November/December 2013, available at http://www.foreignaffairs.com/articles/140161/alan-greenspan/never-saw-it-coming.

2. Andrew Lo, as quoted by Gary Stix in "The Science of Economic Bubbles and Busts." *Scientific American*, No. 301, July 2009, pp. 78-85.

3. Nouriel Roubini and Stephen Mihm, *Crisis Economics: A Crash Course in the Future of Finance*, Penguin Books Ltd., 2010, p. 109.

4. Gregory N. Mankiw, *Principles of Economics*, Cengage Learning, 2008, pp. 32-33.

5. Nassim Nicholas Taleb, *The Black Swan: The Impact of the Highly Improbable*, Random House, 2007, p. 155.

6. William Lazonick, *Business Organization and the Myth of the Market Economy*, Cambridge University Press, 1993, p. 11.

7. Dimitris Spartiotis and Yannis Stournaras, *The Fundamental Reasons of the Banking Collapse* (in Greek), Gutenberg, 2010, p. 45-47.

8. Ibid.

9. Carmen M. Reinhart and Kenneth S. Rogoff, *This Time Is Different: Eight Centuries of Financial Folly*, Princeton University Press, 2011, p. 216.

10. Milton Friedman, "The Methodology of Positive Economics," in *The Philosophy of Economics*, Daniel M. Hausman (ed.), Second Edition, Cambridge University Press, 1984, pp. 180-213.

11. John Kenneth Galbraith, *The Great Crash 1929*, Houghton Mifflin Harcourt, 2009, p. 1.

12. Ibid., p. 70.

13. Ibid., p. 71.

14. Herbert A. Simon, *The Sciences of the Artificial*, Third Edition, MIT Press, 1996, p. 26.

15. Salvatore Babones, "The Middling Kingdom: The Hype and the Reality of China's Rise." *Foreign Affairs*, September/October 2011, available at http://www.foreignaffairs.com/articles/68207/salvatore-babones/the-middling-kingdom.

16. Eugene Wigner, "The Unreasonable Effectiveness of Mathematics in the Natural Sciences." *Communications in Pure and Applied Mathematics*, Vol. 13, No. 1, February 1960.

17. Anastassios Karagianis, *General Economic Equilibrium: A Critical Analysis of the Modern Model* (in Greek), Stamoulis Publications, 1988, p. 104.

18. Karl R. Popper, *The Open Society and Its Enemies*, Princeton University Press, 2013, p. 230.

19. John Maynard Keynes, *The General Theory of Employment, Interest and Money*, Atlantic, 2008, p. 272.

20. Frederik Zeuthen, *Economic Theory and Method*, Longmans, Green & Co., 1955, p. 19. J.M. Clark, "Some Current Cleavages Among Economists." *American Economic Review*, May 1947, p. 6.

21. Diran Bodenhorn, "The Problem of Economic Assumptions in Mathematical Economics." *Journal of Political Economy*, Vol. 64, No. 1, 1956, p. 25. Eugene Rotwein, "Mathematical Economics: The Empirical View and an Appeal to Pluralism," in *The Structure of Economic Science: Essays on Methodology*, S.R. Krupp (ed.), Prentice Hall, 1966, p. 105.

22. Anastassios Karagianis, *General Economic Equilibrium: A Critical Analysis of the Modern Model* (In Greek), Stamoulis Publications, 1988, p. 104.

23. William Baumol, "Economic Models and Mathematics." in *The Structure of Economic Science: Essays on Methodology*, S.R. Krupp (ed.), Prentice Hall, 1966, p. 94.

24. Benoit Mandelbrot and Richard Hudson, *The (Mis)behavior of Markets: A Fractal View of Risk, Ruin and Reward*, Basic Books, 2006, p. 20.

25. Ibid.

26. Ibid., p. 25.

27. James Gleick, *Chaos: Making a New Science*, Open Road, 2011, p. 68.

28. Alan Greenspan, "Never Saw It Coming: Why the Financial Crisis Took Economists by Surprise." *Foreign Affairs*, November/December 2013, available at http://www.foreignaffairs.com/articles/140161/alan-greenspan/never-saw-it-coming.

29. Gordon Brown, *Beyond the Crash: Overcoming the First Crisis of Globalization*, Free Press, 2010, p. 37.

30. World Bank, *Global Economic Prospects 2007: Managing the Next Wave of Globalization*, 2007, p. 3, table 1.1, "The Global Outlook in Summary."

31. IMF, *World Economic Outlook*, September 2006, chapter 1, "Global Prospects and Policy Issues," table 1.1, p. 2, "Overview of the World Economic Outlook Projections."

32. IMF, *World Economic Outlook*, September 2006, Executive Summary, "Outlook and Risks," p. xiv.

33. IMF, *World Economic Outlook*, April 2007, "Spillovers and Cycles in the Global Economy," Executive Summary, p. xv.

34. Ibid., Executive Summary, "Outlook and Risks," p. 2.

35. Ibid., table 1.1, p. 2, "Overview of the World Economic Outlook Projections."

36. World Bank, *Global Economic Prospects: Technology Diffusion in the Developing World*, 2008, Overview, p. 1.

37. IMF, *World Economic Outlook: Housing and the Business Cycle*, April 2008, Executive Summary, "Outlook and Risks," p. xv.

38. IMF, World Economic Outlook Crisis and Recovery, April 2009. Prospects xii.

39. Georgios Provopoulos and Panagiotis Kapopoulos, *The Dynamics of the Financial System* (In Greek), Kritiki Publications, 2001, p. 88.

40. Yannis Papadogiannis, *The Inglorious End: The Precarious Fight, Crash-landing and Rebirth of Greek Banks* (in Greek), Papadopoulos Publications, 2013, p. 72-73.

41. Ibid., p. 95.

42. Ibid., p. 87.

43. Ibid., p. 70.

44. Yannis Papadogiannis, "Greek Bankers See Light at the End of the Crisis Tunnel" (in Greek). *Kathimerini* newspaper, May 28, 2009.

45. "NBG Asks to Repurchase Preferred Shares." *Kathimerini* newspaper, November 27, 2010.

46. Yannis Papadogiannis, *The Inglorious End: The Precarious Flight, Crash-landing and Rebirth of Greek Banks* (in Greek), Papadopoulos Publications, 2013, p. 190-191.

47. Klaus Zimmerman, "Prognosekrise: Warum weniger manchmal mehr ist" (in German), *Wirtschaftsdienst*, April 2009, available at http://ftp.iza.org/sp4.pdf.

48. *Weekly Economic Report* (in Greek), Economic Analysis Division, Alpha Bank, March 2, 2012, available at http://www.alpha.gr/files/infoanalyses/weekly20120302.pdf.

49. Yannis Papadogiannis, *The Inglorious End: The Precarious Flight, Crash-landing and Rebirth of Greek Banks* (in Greek), Papadopoulos Publications, 2013, p. 80.

50. Nouriel Roubini and Stephen Mihm, *Crisis Economics: A Crash Course in the Future of Finance*, Penguin Books Ltd., 2010, pp. 39-40.

51. Robert A. Gordon, "Rigor and Relevance in a Changing Institutional Setting." *American Economic Review*, Vol. 66, March 1976, p.1.

52. Gregory N. Mankiw, *Principles of Economics*, Cengage Learning, 2008, p. 22.

53. William Lazonick, *Business Organization and the Myth of the Market Economy*, Cambridge University Press, 1993, pp. 185-186.

54. Nikos Theocharakis, *The Neoclassical Theory of Labor* (in Greek), Tipothito, 2005, p. 21.

55. Spyros Makridakis, Robin Hogart and Anil Gaba, *Dance with Chance: Making Luck Work for You*, OneWorld Publications, 2009, pp. 155-156.

56. John P.A. Ioannidis, "Why Most Published Research Findings Are False," *PLoS Medicine*, Vol. 2, No. 8, August 2005, available at http://www.plosmedicine.org/article/fetchObject.action?uri=info%

3Adoi%2F10.1371%2Fjournal.pmed.0020124&representation=PDF. For a brief presentation of this study, see "Publish and Be Wrong," *The Economist,* October 2008, available at http://www.economist.com/node/12376658.

57. James G. March, *A Primer on Decision Making: How Decisions Happen,* The Free Press, 1994, p. 9.

58. George Soros, *The New Paradigm for Financial Markets: The Credit Crash of 2008 and What It Means,* Public Affairs, 2008, pp. 3-5, 8, and 10.

59. David Lindley, *Uncertainty: Einstein, Heisenberg, Bohr, and the Struggle for the Soul of Science,* Doubleday, 2007, p. 138.

60. Ibid., p. 38.

61. Ilya Prigogine, *The End of Certainty: Time, Chaos and the New Laws of Nature,* The Free Press, 1997, p. 65.

62. Ibid., p. 70.

63. John Briggs and David Peat, *Turbulent Mirror: An Illustrated Guide to Chaos Theory and the Science of Wholeness,* Harper and Row, 1990, p. 136.

64. Ibid.

65. James Gleick, *Chaos: Making a New Science,* Open Road, 2011, p. 69.

66. Ilya Prigogine, *The End of Certainty: Time, Chaos and the New Laws of Nature,* The Free Press, 1997, p. 73.

67. James Gleick, *Chaos: Making a New Science,* Open Road, 2011, p. 237.

68. Christos Alexakis and Manolis Xanthakis, *Behavioural Finance* (in Greek), Stamoulis Publications, 2008, p. 147.

69. Ibid.

70. Gikas Hardouvelis, "The Pro-cyclicality of the International Financial System," in *From Global Crisis to the Crisis in the Euro Zone and Greece: What Does the Future Have in Store?* (in Greek), Nicolaos Karamouzis-Gikas Hardouvelis (eds.), AA Livanis Publications, 2011, p. 326.

71. James D. Stein, *How Math Explains the World*, Harper Collins, 2008, p. 63.

72. Karl R. Popper, *All Life Is Problem Solving*, Psychology Press, 1999, p. 84.

73. Ibid.

74. Karl R. Popper, *The Open Society and Its Enemies*, Princeton University Press, 2013, p. 230.

75. Karl R. Popper, *All Life Is Problem Solving*, Psychology Press, 1999, p.40.

76. Adam Smith, *The Wealth of Nations*, Books I-III, Penguin, 1979, p. 181.

www.ingramcontent.com/pod-product-compliance
Lightning Source LLC
Chambersburg PA
CBHW051631170526
45167CB00001B/147